Judaism in Modern Times

Judaism in Modern Times

An Introduction and Reader

Jacob Neusner

First published 1995

Blackwell Publishers, the publishing imprint of
Basil Blackwell Inc.
238 Main Street
Cambridge, Massachusetts 02142, USA

Basil Blackwell Ltd
108 Cowley Road
Oxford OX4 1JF
UK

Library of Congress Cataloging-in-Publication Data
Neusner, Jacob, 1932–
Judaism in modern times: an introduction and reader/Jacob Neusner.
p.   cm.
Includes bibliographical references and index.
ISBN 1-55786-683-X. – ISBN
1-55786-684-8 (pbk.)
1. Judaism – History – Modern period, 1750 – Sources.
2. Jews – Politics and government – Sources.   I. Title.
BM195.N49 1995
296'.09'034 – dc20
94-29537
CIP

British Library Cataloguing in Publication Data
A CIP catalogue record for this book is available from the British Library.

Typeset in 10½ on 12 pt Plantin
by Best-set Typesetter Ltd., Hong Kong
Printed in the USA
This book is printed on acid-free paper.

Contents

Letter to the Student

This is a book about what it means to be a human being in the conditions of modern times, defined as the nineteenth and twentieth centuries. The book portrays a religious answer to the modern and contemporary framing of the question of the worth and purpose of life, an appeal to God's will in account for the enduring religious community formed by the faithful. The people whom we shall consider in these pages addressed questions they had never before had to consider, not for fifteen hundred years or more. Their received religion explained who they are, viewed from the perspective of eternity. It told them little about who others, outsiders, are and how to understand the worth of those who differ. So the people who thought the thoughts and did the deeds recorded here had to find out for themselves how to live not only among, but with, strangers.

While in the nineteenth century the other was perceived as benign, in the twentieth the outsider turned out to be malign, so from asking how to live with the world, the people we meet here had to ask yet another question. It was, and is, how to survive at all in a world that denies the right to life and wishes to destroy them. They framed a set of coherent answers to these questions, which tell us how, in terms of ideas, attitudes, sentiments – the raw material of intellect – people worked out as best they could unprecedented problems of life and death that could not be avoided and had to be addressed.

The unprecedented character of the issues – how to deal with the other, formerly ignored; how to find a final solution to the problem of the hatred of the other, formerly treated as a triviality – is what makes the age "modern." Before the advent of the age in which people compared themselves with the outsider, they regarded the other as alien, themselves as autonomous. Afterward they wanted to know about the other and enter into dialogue with the stranger. Before the modern time people endured the hostility of the other, sometimes even dying by reason of it, without seriously contemplating the possibility of doing something to change the other or to escape the hostility of the stranger. Afterward, they proposed to take an active role in finding a final solution to the hostility of the outsider, either changing the outsider, or forming a world beyond the reach of the other.

So what defines modern times is captured in the term integration as against the segregation – by serene faith and affirming will, not by hostile law – characteristic of the long prior centuries. In the long centuries that closed with the advent of the nineteenth century, the people who meet here lived a life of segregation – by choice. They maintained good relations with the world beyond, but took for granted that the things God cared about happened in their midst. But now, some of the same people wished to be not only what they had been for so long, but also other things altogether. They cared for more than the things God cared for – many more.

The religious responses to issues of integration take diverse forms, one set for the first of the two centuries that make up modern times, the other for the second, as I shall explain. Some of the responses to these two urgent questions continued the received, religious ways of living and thinking; others struck out in new and secular directions, taking as their point of departure that same received tradition. The former qualify by conventional definitions as religious, the latter do not, except by extension of those definitions beyond their natural limits. So here we take up a well-defined case of the condition of religion in the circumstance of modernity.

The urgency of informing ourselves about religion in modern times hardly requires explanation. We simply cannot understand the world we have known for the past two hundred years unless we consider the public facts of religious life. Not only so, but given the decisive role of religion in framing the world today, we must form for ourselves a coherent theory of what religion is and does if we are to make sense of the coming century. The reason is simple. Viewed from the perspective of the faithful, religion defines the condition of humanity under the aspect of eternity: how (from the perspective of the faithful) God sees us. Seen from the more secular angle of vision, religion forms a way of projecting onto Heaven the shadows of the human condition, and when we study about religion, we enter into the consciousness and character of humanity contemplating its own, deepest concerns.

What we learn when we study religion, believed or merely observed, in this-worldly terms is the same thing: the way in which people, working together in community, proposed to sort out the issues of acutely contemporary crisis: who are we? what are we supposed to do? why does it make a difference? Secular systems of thinking about the social order provide their responses to these same questions. Here we focus upon what we learn about humanity, and about religion, from the way in which a particular set of the faithful framed their accounts of themselves.

That definition maintains, then, that religion responds to critical questions people ask themselves, questions of purpose and meaning. It further takes as a matter of fact to be studied, not solely faith to be reported upon and admired, the reality of religion in this world: the answers people give to urgent questions, the sources for the urgency of the questions, and the self-evident relevance and pertinence of the answers. Religion viewed as something people do together then forms what is public and subject to description, analysis, and interpretation – not what is private and available only for display. Religion, then, is a mode of negotiating existence. Wanting to know why they live, on the one side, and how the community of which they are part means to serve God, on the other, they pursue those concerns. The pursuit leads to the conduct of life in response to that goal, the formulation of answers to critical questions in accord with that purpose which the community of the faithful formulates. So religion described in this-worldly terms forms a statement of how and why people share their lives together, providing answers to questions of ultimate concern. These questions find their answers in the details of the way of life, the world-view, and the explanation of the purpose of the social group of the believers.

Viewed in this way – as something people do together in this world, responding, at least in the perspective of their faith, to God's presence – religion may be studied as a set of facts that we may understand in a this-worldly framework. That is so, even though those allegations concerning facts speak of the world to come and the transcendent God. We do not have to share a religious tradition to want to understand it, since every religious tradition (or "faith," or "religion") teaches us important facts and insights concerning the way the world now is and why it is one way and not another. Religion, after all, may speak of Heaven, but it does its work on earth. As soon as we list some of the main religions – Christianity, Islam, Buddhism, Judaism, for example – we realize that, when we study religion, we take up formative forces in the politics and social order of the entire world of humanity. We cannot understand this morning's headlines if we do not know what religion is and how it shapes the world, whether the world of Asia or Europe or Africa or Latin America or North America, or, especially, the USA.

This book tells the story of how people turned their attention from their own affairs to the world beyond, moving from a position on the margins of human affairs to a place in the very center of matters. For more than fifteen hundred years that people through their religion asked questions concerning their inner life with God: what does it mean to be a saint? how shall I know God? what does God think of me? how shall I enter the world to come and what will happen to me after I die? That people knew perfectly well that they shared the world, even near at hand, with others; but they also took for granted – and rightly so – that the others, however different, shared the same fundamental convictions about the purpose of humanity's life and the presence of God in the world. They lived separate from the others, who lived in their own distinctive worlds as well. No one thought that strange, since each group bore its distinctive message from God and entertained no doubts concerning God's will and purpose for humanity.

But, in the period treated in this book, which we call "modern times," that is, the past two hundred years, from the late eighteenth century to the late twentieth century, the people studied here asked themselves questions formerly not contemplated. These concerned not only the world to come but this world, not only the life of the faithful but the rest of the people round about. Now people wanted to know not only what it means to be a saint or how to know God, but also what is to be known about the world beyond the lessons of the faith, and how to live not only with God but with people unlike oneself.

In modern times the people we consider in these pages, the Jews of Europe and the USA, pursued as urgent a range of questions that formerly were not addressed or produced answers of slight consequence. For fifteen centuries viewing themselves always and only as "Israel" (meaning the living heirs of the holy people descended according to Scripture from Abraham, Isaac, and Jacob, Sarah, Rebecca, Leah and Rachel), this holy people, elect by God, formed a covenant at Sinai through the Torah – God's revelation to them in particular – and lived in accord with the promises of the covenant.

Gentiles – everyone in the world but this singular, holy community – were welcome to enter into the genealogy and its promise, the covenant and its law; this they did by an act of conversion (baptism for women and men, circumcision for men). So this "Israel" formed not a this-worldly ethnic group at all, but only a transcendent community, comparable with the Church, the mystical body of Christ. And, as is clear, the religion, Judaism, that in our category encompasses the world-view, way of life, and theory of the social entity "Israel," answered a single urgent question: who are we, what should we do, and how does God want us to live? To that question, the rest of the world contributed no answers at all; a presence, sometimes threatening and destructive, other times benign, the outsider played no role in the faith or in the holy lives of the faithful.

The inner-directed, transcendent life of the faith answered every question but the one that became urgent in Western European countries from the US Constitution and Bill of Rights (1789, 1791) and the French Declaration of the Rights of Man (1791). That question was, how shall we be both "Israel" and something else? That something else may be defined in politics, as citizens of not only a supernatural community of the faith but also a this-worldly nation, France, the USA, Britain, or Germany. It may also find its formulation in intellectual life: may we devote our best energy to studying not only the Torah of Sinai but also the philosophy and science that now presents (equally) compelling truths? And, finally, it may come to expression in matters of clothing, food, residence, occupation, marriage – all of those humble things that really dictate the character of a human life. Do we now dress like Jews or do we dress like other people? Eat only Jewish (kosher) food and only with other Jews, or eat with others? Live in Jewish towns or neighborhoods not by law but by choice, or live not only among, but with, the gentiles? Pursue a livelihood particular to our group or work alongside others? So, in a word, Jews who had wanted to live, and who did live, in segregation by choice now contemplated the questions of integration. Formerly looking inward, they now turned outward.

That did not mean they wished to take the paths that led away from the community of Jewry (in secular terms) or "Israel" (in theological ones). Those who wished simply to leave that "Israel" into which they were born, either to join some other holy community as circumstances dictated, or to find a place in a contemplated (but rarely real) undifferentiated secular mass, did what they wanted to do. Some became Christians – Lutherans in Germany, Catholics in Poland, Orthodox in Russia, Anglicans in Britain, Unitarians or Congregationalists or Evangelicals in the USA. A great many gave up the Torah as a supernatural identity and formulated a conception of a more limited Judaism, framed in this-worldly, ethnic terms, or

Jewishness, a wholly ethnic definition of the Jews as a completely secular community, defined not by God but by politics and sociology, sentiment and culture, history and this-worldly ideology of peoplehood. The ones who took their own way ceased to form part of holy "Israel" and tell us nothing about Judaism; the others, those who recast a supernatural community into secular and ethnic terms, attest to data for the study of sociology, economics, politics, and modern culture.

At issue in this book are two sets of Jews: first, the Jews who remained practitioners of Judaism, who formed out of the received tradition a response to the urgent questions of their own circumstance; second, the Jews who formed Judaic systems ("Judaisms") different from those that drew guidance from the received tradition that had served for so many centuries. The first of the two asked, how can we be both "Israel" and other things, living not only among, but with, gentiles? The second asked, how can we live at all among the gentiles? The first addressed the circumstances of the nineteenth century, hopeful and promising for all of humanity; the second, the conditions of the twentieth, the age of total war, the dominion of the Holocaust. The nineteenth-century Judaisms wanted to know how to live as Jews in the gentile world, the twentieth, how to live at all in that same world.

The first of the two sets of Jews defined their Judaisms in the interplay between their question, how to be both "Israel" and other things, and the received Judaism, the one that held the purpose of the Torah is to purify the heart of humanity, and focused upon the moral and intellectual sanctification of "Israel," the holy people. All of these Judaisms formed their systems in the nineteenth century, and each became influential in twentieth-century USA. These are Reform Judaism, the first of the Judaisms to answer the question of integration, Orthodox Judaism, a response to, and creation of, Reform Judaism, which held together both segregation and integration as guiding poles, and Conservative Judaism, a mediating position between Reform and Orthodoxy.

The second of the two sets of Jews – the ones who answered questions quite unrelated to those that preoccupied the continuators of the received Judaic system – framed their systems in an ethnic and political, not a religious, framework. Three twentieth-century Judaic systems asked the same question: how can we live in a world that denies our elementary right to life?

The first answer came from Zionism, the Judaic movement that saw the Jews not as "holy Israel," but as a political entity, which should (and ultimately did) constitute itself into "the State of Israel," in the Land of Israel. Zionism, with its language, Hebrew, reborn as a living language, was a Judaic system that answered the question how can we live among gentiles, by saying, we cannot; the gentiles will never accept us, because we are really a nation and should therefore build our own state. Zionism began as an organized movement in 1897 and achieved its goal in 1947, with the recognition by the world of the right of the Jewish people to form the State of Israel.

The second answer came from Jews who wished to form of all humanity a single community, overcoming lines of ethnic or religious division in the name of the unity of the workers of the world. This answer – formulated by Jewish Socialism, with its language, Yiddish, the vernacular of most of the Jews in the world – found its organization in the Jewish Workers Union, or Bund, formed also in 1897; it aimed at creating a world in which Jews, too, might survive on an equal basis with everyone else. Far more influential than Zionism among the great masses of Jews, located in the countries of Eastern Europe, the movement perished in the Holocaust, when those who aspired to form a community with all humanity were denied the right to life. But Jewish Socialism also formed an influential chapter in Zionism, with the framing of a Zionist Socialism, or a Socialist Zionism, one that defined the State of Israel in its formative decades.

The third answer – framing a secular Judaic system to answer the question of how and why Jews can endure in an open society – came from the USA. It reached its expression in 1967 and remains influential to this time. It is the Judaism of Holocaust and Redemption, which appeals for its system of belief and behavior in explanation of the life of the community of Jewry to the facts of the murder of many millions of European Jews in World War II and the creation of the State of Israel afterward.

Now that we know what is at stake in this book and the program that is followed, let me explain my procedure, which is simple. Each century, represented by a unit of the book, is treated in the same way: an introduction, offering generalizations on the Judaic systems that came to expression, then a systematic presentation by me of each of the three systems under study. My own representation of matters is followed by a reading, in which a different perspective on the same subject is set forth; sometimes the purpose of the reading is to amplify matters of fact, others, to underscore a different way of seeing and talking about the same topic, and still others, an effort to provide an introduction to a complementary system alongside the one at issue. In this way I mean to open up a conversation between my way of seeing things and the perspective of others seeing the same things; and once that conversation gets under way, you are invited to join in. The readings each commence with a statement of why I have chosen the passage before us and what I want readers to watch for therein.

My chapters all derive from, and set forth extensive revisions of my treatment of the same subjects in, my *Death and Birth of Judaism: The Impact of Christianity, Secularism, and the Holocaust on Jewish Faith.*[1] The sources of the readings are specified in context and listed in full in the acknowledgements.

NOTE

1 New York, 1987: Basic Books. Second printing: Atlanta, 1993: Scholars Press for South Florida Studies in the History of Judaism.

Acknowledgments

I edited this book during my stay as Gästforskarprofessor (Visiting Research Professor) at Stiftelsens för Åbo Akademi Forsknings-institut, the research institute of the Swedish-language university of Finland. I express thanks to Stiftelsens för Åbo Akademi Forsknin-gsinstitut for a very generous research stipend for April through August 1993, from the close of 1992–3 classes at the University of South Florida to the start of the 1993–4 school year, and for providing in addition comfortable living and working conditions. Among the research institutes at which I have worked, none exceeds in cordiality or hospitality the one at Finland's Swedish-language university.

During this same span of time, I was invited to lecture at the fifth congress of the Scandinavian Congress for Jewish Studies, at Lund, and also for the Theological Faculty, University of Lund. I express my thanks to my colleagues at Lund and also those in Judaic studies throughout Scandinavia, who received me very cordially and re-sponded to my lectures with penetrating and stimulating questions. During this same period I lectured for the Jewish communities of Stockholm, Uppsala, Helsinki, and Åbo, and express appreciation for the warm hospitality my wife and I received there. The lectures I gave in Finland and in Sweden are published in *Åbo Addresses, and Other Recent Essays on Judaism in Time and Eternity*. Atlanta, 1993: Scholars Press for South Florida Studies in the History of Judaism.

This book takes its place in a continuous research inquiry. I edited this book as part of my long-term labor of advancing higher educa-tion in the field of the study of Judaism within the academic study of religion. Most of this commitment is expressed through my teaching at the University of South Florida, which has afforded me an ideal situation in which to conduct a scholarly life. No work of mine can omit reference to the exceptionally favorable circumstances in which I conduct my research and teaching as Distinguished Research Professor in the Florida State University System at the University of South Florida.

I owe thanks also to the following copyright holders for permission to reprint the specified chapters:

Chaim Grade, "Reb Simkha Feinerman's Sermon," from Chaim Grade, *The Yeshiva*, vol. II. Translated from the Yiddish, with an Introduction, by Curt Leviant. Reprinted with the permission of Macmillan Publishing Company. Copyright © 1977 by Chaim Grade.

Chaim Grade, "The Yeshiva," from Chaim Grade, *The Yeshiva*, vol. II. Translated from the Yiddish, with an Introduction, by Curt Leviant. Reprinted with the permission of Macmillan Publishing Company. Copyright © 1977 by Chaim Grade.

Abraham Cronbach, "The Issues of Reform Judaism in the USA," from Abraham Cronbach, *Reform Movements in Judaism*. Preface by Jacob Rader Marcus. New York, 1963: Bookman Associates, pp. 116–21. © 1963 by Bookman Associates. Reprinted by permission.

Charles Liebman, "Religion and the Chaos of Modernity: The Case of Contemporary Judaism", in Jacob Neusner, ed., *Take Judaism, for Example: Studies toward the Comparison of Religions*. Chicago, 1983: University of Chicago Press. Second printing: Atlanta, 1992: Scholars Press for South Florida Studies in the History of Judaism, pp. 152–6. © 1992 by University of South Florida. Reprinted by permission of South Florida Studies in the History of Judaism.

Seymour Siegel, "The Meaning of Jewish Law in Conservative Judaism," in Seymour Siegel with Elliot Gertel, eds, *Conservative Judaism and Jewish Law* (New York, 1977: The Rabbinical Assembly), pp. xiii–xxvi. © 1977 by The Rabbinical Assembly. Reprinted by permission.

Richard L. Rubenstein, "Religion and History: Power, History, and the Covenant at Sinai", in Jacob Neusner, ed., *Take Judaism, for Example: Studies toward the Comparison of Religions*. Chicago, 1983: University of Chicago Press. Second printing: Atlanta, 1992: Scholars Press for South Florida Studies in the History of Judaism, pp. 147–64. © 1992 by University of South Florida. Reprinted by permission of South Florida Studies in the History of Judaism.

David Vital, "Herzl and *The Jews' State*," from David Vital, *The Origins of Zionism*. Oxford, 1975: Clarendon Press, pp. 260–6. © 1975 by Oxford University Press. Reprinted by permission.

Nora Levin, "Socialist Zionism," from Nora Levin, *While Messiah Tarried: Jewish Socialist Movements, 1917–1971*. New York, 1977: Schocken Books, pp. 400–4. © 1977: Schocken Books, Inc. Reprinted by permission of Schocken Books, published by Pantheon Books, a division of Random House, Inc.

Nathan Glazer, "The Year 1967 and its Meaning," from Nathan Glazer, *American Judaism*. Second edition, Chicago, 1972: University of Chicago Press, pp. 169–76. © 1972: The University of Chicago. Reprinted by permission.

Jacob Neusner

Gästforskarprofessor
Stiftelsens för Åbo Akademi Forskningsinstitut
Fin 20700 Turku/Åbo, Finland

and

Distinguished Research Professor of Religious Studies
University of South Florida
Tampa, Florida 33620-5550, USA

July 28, 1993, my sixty-first birthday

Introduction:
What Do We Mean by
"Judaism" and by
"Modern Times"?

Modern Times

By "modern times," in the study of religion, is meant the age in which religion lost its status of self-evident truth. For Judaism, Europe forms the center of modern life, and in modern times in Europe and its overseas diaspora in the Americas, North and South, in particular, the religion that lost its position as the dominant and acknowledged framer of civilization was Christianity. The story of Judaism in modern times takes place therefore in the setting of the encompassing tale of what happened to Christianity, and that is for particular and very specific reasons. When Christianity lost its status as the self-evident answer to the urgent question of humanity, Judaism framed in the setting of Christianity also changed.

From the eighteenth century onward the religious, biblical, and Christian world-view and way of life competed with secular ones; then Christianity lost its status as self-evident truth. And it was when Christianity had to explain itself to the world in confrontation with competing modes of thought and inquiry that Judaism too was forced to turn outward and address the world beyond its social limits. In the aftermath of the French Enlightenment and the advent of the nation-state, specifically, Christianity lost its paramount position in the politics and culture of Christian Europe, and as Christianity went in the world beyond, there went Judaism in the world within the setting of Israel, the holy people that formerly lived apart.[1] Competition for the complete loyalty of the faithful confronted both religions, and for the same reasons and in the same period, through the nineteenth century and onward to our own day.

Redefining the political civilization of the West, a vast process of secularization removed Christianity, first in the Protestant West, then in the Roman Catholic West, East, Center and South, and finally in the Christian Orthodox (Greek, Russian, Romanian, Ukrainian) East, of Europe, from its established position as the definitive force.[2] Through the nineteenth century important political movements, appealing to the nation-state and to "man"[3] as the measure of all things, rather than to the kingdom of God and to Heaven's will, set forth a new politics. That program of secularization raised a fresh set of questions also for holy Israel.

"Israel" had always meant "the holy people, the elect," to whom God gave the Torah, children of Abraham, Isaac, and Jacob, Sarah, Rebecca, Leah and Rachel. Now that same "Israel" was reframed in this-worldly terms, as a secular social entity: an ethnic group, a "minority." In the nature of things, these social categories had nothing whatever to do with Israel's supernatural standing in God's plan for creation and the history of humanity. Posed by political changes, the new set of urgent concerns engaged in a new set of inquiries the focused attention of many Jews, at first particularly in Western European countries, later on in the Eastern European ones and in their extension in America. These inquiries produced a fresh program of self-evident answers, and those answers in the nineteenth century constituted a new set of Judaisms, a term introduced in the Letter to the Student: Judaic systems that explained the social order formed by Jews with an account of a coherent world-view, way of life, and theory of the Jews' social entity or the "Israel" that they constituted.

Judaism in Modern Times

In this book we consider six Judaic systems or Judaisms, three of the nineteenth century, three of the twentieth. All of them take shape in the circumstance of modern times, and each addresses the paramount question of that age. Continuous with the received system of the dual Torah, these new Judaisms broke from that system because they took up a critical issue wholly outside of the imagination of the received Judaism. Indeed, all of them took as their principal concern the definition and justification of permissible change, on the one side, and the possibilities of living no longer segregated but integrated lives with gentiles, on the other. The two added up to the same thing, for change meant change in the fundamental traits of the Jews' social order. For two hundred years all new Judaisms began by defining the character and meaning of their departure from the old, received one.

The generative issue faced by each new Judaic system had to do with the secular standing and status of Jews, seen as individuals and (at least ideally) as citizens like all other citizens. In the age of the nation-state, everyone was supposed to be a citizen, with equal rights and responsibilities – even the Jews. But aforetimes, the Jews regarded themselves as special, a holy community; they were not undifferentiated on earth, because they saw themselves as selected by Heaven. Not only so, but they also regarded themselves as "Israel" both collectively and individually; the conception of an individual who framed identity separately from the community found no resonance in the Judaic system. Consequently, the advent of the nation-state, which recognized not communities (of the faithful) but only individuals, produced a category that the received religion did not comprehend: the individual Jew.

The Nineteenth Century

The formulation of matters that emerged from the French Revolution to be carried by the French armies across Europe, "To the Jews as citizens, everything, to the Jews as a nation, nothing," found in Israel the counterpart: "A Jew at home, a man outside."[4] That formulation violated the language rules of the received Judaism, for the appropriate subject of any verb was not *a* Jew but *Israel*, understood always to refer to the holy people. The received Judaism did not (and did not have to) deal with the possibility that Jews could ever be individual, let alone secular, that is to say, anything other than holy Israel, all together, all at once. It made no provision for Jews to be something else, unless they ceased, of course, to be Jews at all. The Judaism of the Torah surely could not imagine the Jews ever to be something in addition, over and above Israel. But all Judaisms of the nineteenth century explained that *something else* that Jews could and should become.

Taking that same political form that the received system had adopted, the new Judaisms explained where, how, and why Jews could find a place in a new classification, in addition to the category Israel, namely, the classification of citizens of diverse countries, not solely (or not mainly) members of a holy, supernatural nation of their own. In exploring the premise that Jews could be also German or

American or British or French, the Judaisms of the nineteenth
century, first Reform, then Orthodox, finally Conservative, provided
self-evidently valid answers to their communicants. Concurring that
Jews would continue to be Israel, all three Judaisms redefined the
category Israel that formed the centerpiece of any Judaism. All three,
moreover, reworked the world-view contained within the canon of
the Judaism of the dual Torah and reconsidered the way of life
required by it.

And, finally, addressing the condition of secularity in which, Jews
imagined, they would find for themselves a place within the nation-
state then coming into existence, the three Judaisms of continuation
of the Judaism of the dual Torah further adopted the premise of the
secular as distinct from the religious and – in answering the question
how to be both Israel and something in addition – posited that
Judaism is, therefore always had been, a religion. In Part I of this
book, comprising Chapters 2, 3, and 4, I describe and interpret the
self-evident answers produced by three Judaisms that presented, as
the ineluctable question, the issue of political change joined to the
secularization of the politics of the West.

The Twentieth Century

Unhappily for Israel, the Jewish people, the political changes that
framed the urgent question for nineteenth-century Judaisms in fact
generated quite different issues from those people had anticipated.
Jews (and not they alone) imagined that they had to find a way of
being both Jewish and something else. But their enemies wanted to
find a way for Jews to stop *being* altogether. And they very nearly
succeeded. They began their work in the late nineteenth century,
writing a chapter in the history of imperialism and racism that encompasses in a single history most of Europe, Africa, and Asia, as
well as the Western hemisphere.

Part of that long and dismal story, anti-Semitism, culminating in
the Holocaust (but, alas, still a powerful force in today's world),
forced upon the Jews a question they never before had had to answer.
The generally benign, but sometimes malign, settlement of
Christendom and Islam ordinarily promised the Jews (at least) their
lives, so the critical question facing them involved merely their dig-
nity and self-respect, of which they themselves could take charge.
The new issue, by contrast, changed the circumstances of Jews'

existence no less drastically than had the destruction of the Second Temple in Jerusalem, in the year 70, and far more decisively than had the rise of Christianity to political dominance in the fourth century CE.

The impact of the Holocaust on Judaism began long before the advent of Hitler. Anti-Semitism from the late nineteenth century identified the Jews as the source of all misfortune. Economic changes at the same time dislocated those long-term structures that for centuries had sustained the peoples of Eastern Europe, including the Jews. While Jews identified as the critical issue the question of change, political but also religious, the world as it happened changed in other ways. The stakes proved those of life or death, in both politics and economics. When large numbers of Jews faced a condition of underemployment and near-starvation, as they did in Eastern Europe in the general changes accompanying the modernization of the economy of the region, political and even religious change seemed trivial. For the Judaisms of the twentieth century, the new age began in 1897, the year in which were founded the two great systems which came to dominate – Zionism, a less popular Judaism until the Holocaust and the creation of the State of Israel, and Jewish Socialism (in the form of the Jewish union, the Bund), the most powerful Judaism of the first half of the twentieth century.

While both fell into the classification of secular and political movements, concentrating on organizing powerful institutions of political and economic change, each in its way framed a Judaic system. For the requirements of such a system, a world-view that answered the critical question, a way of life that expressed in concrete terms the elements of the world-view, the two components coherently and explicitly addressed to a clearly defined Israel, were met by both. Zionism answered the political question with the (to its devotees) self-evidently true answer that the Jews constituted a people, one people, and should found the Jews' state. Jewish Socialism answered the economic question (which also was a political one) with the (to its adherents) obviously true answer that the Jews had to form their own union and to undertake economic action as the Jewish sector of the working class of the entire world, united effectively to reform the economic foundations of the West. Jewish Socialism further identified itself with the Yiddish language, and the ideology of Yiddishism joined Jewish Socialism, so that Yiddishism formed the cultural and ideological statement – the world-view, in terms of the analytical categories used here – for that Judaism for which Jewish Socialism dictated the way of life.

Chapters 6 and 7 describe and analyze the Judaisms that maintained, as self-evident truths, the positions that the Jews form a political entity like other polities (Zionism) or constitute part of the international working class and must organize themselves as a distinct ethnic entity with its own language (Yiddishism) into effective unions for class interest (Jewish Socialism).

The twentieth century produced one further Judaism of note, like the others stressing political questions, but framing its own set of urgent questions and producing its distinctive, self-evident answers. It is what I call here *American* Judaism, that is, a Judaic system particular to the American setting (though with counterparts in other parts of the Judaic world, including the State of Israel).[5] American Judaism is the Judaism of Holocaust and Redemption, which takes as its ineluctable question the meaning of Jewish existence after the systematic murder of most of the Jews of Europe, and offers as its self-evident reply the proposition that the redemption constituted by the creation of the State of Israel serves as the other half of the whole story of the meaning of what has happened. The way of life of that distinctive Judaic system – flourishing side by side with the way of life of the continuator-Judaisms of the nineteenth century – lays emphasis upon activities in support of the State of Israel and other political causes closely related to Israeli concerns, for example, the liberation of Soviet Jewry. Its world-view, a set of self-evidently valid truths identified or discovered (not merely formed) in response to this essentially political agenda, sees the Jews as beleaguered, without choices or alliances, facing a world of unremitting hostility, which, however, Jews can through political action change to their own taste.

That distinctively *American* Judaism, separate in all important ways from the Judaism of the dual Torah, should not be confused with the nineteenth-century Judaisms of continuation, which had carried forward the system of the dual Torah. Reform, Orthodoxy, and Conservative Judaisms formed Judaisms *in America*, adapting to the American circumstance Judaisms that had taken shape elsewhere and answering a set of questions essentially distinct from the concerns that would prove particular to the American context. *American* Judaism, by contrast, in no important way carried forward the received Judaism of the dual Torah, but created institutions distinct from the institutions that gave social and concrete form to that received Judaism in its American version, and drew not at all from the inherited canon, except for proof-texts. These proof-texts – quotations of Scripture, for instance – were assembled after the fact, to prove propositions already adopted for reasons unrelated to the proof-texts' canonical authority. In Chapter 8 I describe the single, native-born mass movement in Judaism which I call *American* Judaism, a Judaic system of Holocaust and Redemption.

In modern times that Judaic system for many Jews, particularly in the West and in contexts of political change and modernization, ceased to function as a Judaism of self-evident truth. For those Jews who determined both that they would remain Jews and that they would do so in ways not dictated by the received system, the received system lost not credibility but relevance (and, therefore, of course, credibility too). Those Jews responded to the questions they found inescapable and answered them with truths they regarded as unavoidable and self-evident. In doing so, they worked out new meanings to what it meant in the conditions of modernization to be human within their particular idiom. The Judaisms of continuity, in the nineteenth century, and the Judaisms of renewed self-evidence, in the twentieth, show us how inventive and brave people faced up to what was – we now know – change beyond measure, danger beyond endurance.

Judaism

Through the history of the Jewish people, diverse Judaisms have won the allegiance of groups of Jews here and there, each system specifying the things it regards as urgent both in belief and in behavior. All systems in common allege that they represent the true and authentic Judaism, or Torah, or will of God for Israel, and that their devotees are Israel. Each ordinarily situates itself in a single historical line – hence, a linear history – from the entirety of the past. Commonly a Judaism sees itself as the natural outgrowth, the increment of time and change. These traits of historical or even supernatural origin characterize nearly all Judaisms. In our examination of the six systems treated here, we shall see very clearly the claims of continuity and linearity.

But each system stands on its own. How, then, do we know one Judaism from another? When we can identify the principal symbol to which a given system on its own appeals, we realize that we have a wholly distinct and distinctive system in prospect. Each Judaism begins in its own time and place and then goes in search of a useful past. Every system serves to suit a purpose, to solve a problem, in our context, to answer through a self-evidently right doctrine a question that none can escape or ignore. Orthodoxy, no less than Reform, takes up fresh positions and presents stunningly original and relevant innovations.

The Beginning of the Judaism Deemed Self-Evident until Modern Times

What I have said to this point clearly takes for granted that a single Judaic system or Judaism flourished throughout Christendom (as well as in Islam) until the nineteenth century. That now requires definition in its context, which begins in the fourth century of the Christian Era, when Christianity became the official religion of the Roman Empire, and when the Judaic writing that set forth the counterpart to Judaism took shape. Judaism as it flourished when Europe was Christian was born in the age of Constantine, the first Christian emperor of Rome, at the end of the fourth quarter of the fourth century, and that Judaism died in the beginning of the American experiment, when, in 1789, an other-than-Christian politics began with the American Constitution and the French Revolution. Constantine inaugurated the politics in which Christianity defined the civilization of the West; the American Constitution and the French Revolution brought to a conclusion the age in which a politically paramount Christianity set the norm for the West.

What challenge emerged because the emperor of Rome adopted Christianity? To begin with, Jews had not anticipated that the new religion, Christianity, would amount to much. They paid slight attention to it, so far as the surviving documents indicate. But with their political triumph Christians maintained that their faith in Jesus as Christ, Messiah and God incarnate, found full vindication. They pointed to passages in the Hebrew Scriptures that, in their view, had now come to fulfillment. They declared themselves heirs of ancient Israel and denied to the Jews the long-standing position of God's first and chosen love. So at issue in the Christians' success in imperial politics we find profoundly theological questions critical to Judaism too: (1) does history now vindicate Christianity? (2) was and is Jesus the Messiah? (3) who, in light of events, is "Israel" and who is not? The foundations of the Judaic system and structure were laid down in explicit responses to these questions; the responses drew upon Scripture and traditions of interpretation of Scripture deriving from prior centuries but given new urgency at just this time.

At that time through the fourth and into the fifth century, important Judaic documents, particularly the Talmud of the Land of Israel, brought to a conclusion around ca. 400 CE, Genesis Rabbah, a systematic expansion of the story of Creation in line with Israel's later history, and Leviticus Rabbah, a search for the secret of salvation in the laws of the sanctification of society undertaken in passages of the book of Leviticus, were completed. These writings undertook to deal with agenda defined by the political triumph of Christianity. These questions for Jews? First, the meaning of history, second, the coming of the Messiah, third, the definition of who is Israel. The triumph of Christianity called all three, for Israel, into question.

The Judaism set forth in the documents of this period maintained that Israel's history governs world history, aiming at the coming of the Messiah at the end of days to, and through, that Israel after the flesh and after the promise constituted by the Jews of the day and of all times. These three propositions furthermore rested on the conviction that the sages who taught the Torah possessed an oral tradition, going back to Sinai. The Torah reached Israel in two parts – the written part or the Written Torah, which the Christians too possessed, as "the Old Testament," and the oral part, or the Oral Torah, which Israel possessed through the learning of "our sages of blessed memory." These doctrines formed together "the Judaism of the dual Torah," oral and written, known from then to now also as Orthodox Judaism, Normative Judaism, or just plain Judaism.

Why, specifically, did the advent of Christian rule in the Roman Empire make so profound an impact as to produce a Judaism? A move of the empire from reverence for Zeus to adoration of Mithra meant nothing. To Jews paganism was what it was, lacking all differentiation. Christianity was something else. Why? *Because it was like Judaism.* Christians claimed that theirs was a Judaism – in fact, *the* Judaism – now fulfilled in Christ. Christians read the Torah and claimed to declare its meaning. They furthermore alleged, like Israel, that they alone worshipped the one true God. And they challenged Israel's claim to know that God – and even to be Israel, continuator of the Israel of the promises and grace of ancient Scripture.

Accordingly, for their part, Israel's sages cannot have avoided the issue of the place, within the Torah's messianic pattern, of the remarkable turn in world history represented by the triumph of Christianity. Since the Christians celebrated confirmation of their faith in Christ's messiahship and Jews were hardly prepared to concur, it falls surely within known patterns for us to suppose that Constantine's conversion would have been identified with some dark

moment to prefigure the dawning of the messianic age. The importance of the age of Constantine in the history of Judaism therefore
derives from a simple fact.

Why the Judaism of the Dual Torah Flourished

A Judaic system enjoys the standing of self-evidence when it answers
in a self-evidently compelling way the questions people find urgent.
When other questions arise, to which a given system does not respond, then other Judaic systems will compete with the original one.
The Judaism of the dual Torah, shaped in the confrontation with
triumphant Christianity in the aftermath of Constantine's legitimation of the formerly persecuted faith, flourished so long as Christianity defined the critical issues confronting humanity in Europe and its
diaspora. Then that same Judaism met competition when other issues proved urgent.

What exactly was the specific challenge of triumphant Christianity
to Judaism? The political success represented by the Christianization
of the Roman Empire was taken to validate the claim that Christ is
King, Judaism superseded. The sages of the Talmud provided a
reply. At those very specific points at which the Christian challenge
met head-on old Israel's world-view, sages' doctrines responded.
What did Israel's sages have to present as the Torah's answer to the
cross? It was the Torah. This took three forms. The Torah was
defined in the doctrine, first, of the status, as oral and memorized
revelation, of the Mishnah, and, by implication, of other rabbinical
writings. The Torah, moreover, was presented as the encompassing
symbol of Israel's salvation. The Torah, finally, was embodied in the
person of the Messiah who, of course, would be a rabbi. The Torah
in all three modes confronted the cross, with its doctrine of the
triumphant Christ, Messiah and king, ruler now of earth as of
Heaven.

So how exactly did the Judaic system exposed in the later fourth-
century writings deal with the Christian challenge? The symbolic
system of Christianity, with Christ triumphant, with the cross as the
now-regnant symbol, with the canon of Christianity now defined and
recognized as authoritative, called forth from the sages of the Land of
Israel a symbolic system strikingly responsive to the crisis. The Messiah served, for example, to explain the purpose of the Judaic way of
life: keep the rules of the Torah as sages teach them, and the Messiah

will come. So the coming of the Messiah was set as the teleology of the system of Judaism as sages defined that system. The symbol of the Torah expanded to encompass the whole of human existence as the system laid forth the outer boundaries of that existence. So the distinctive Judaic way of life derived, the system taught, from God's will.

What about the importance of the doctrine that when God revealed the Torah to Moses at Sinai, it was in two media, written (the Hebrew Scriptures) and oral (the teaching of the sages, beginning with the Mishnah)? The canon of Sinai is thereby broadened to take account of the entirety of the sages' teachings, as much as of the written Torah everyone acknowledged as authoritative. So the doctrine of the dual Torah told the Jews that their sages understood God's will, and the others did not. The challenge was met. How so? Jesus, now King-Messiah, is not what the Christians say. God will yet send Israel's Messiah – when Israel does what has to be done to hasten the day. And what Israel must do is keep the faith with the holy way of life taught as Torah – God's revelation – by the sages at hand. The Torah stood as the principal symbol – that and not the cross.

And with what outcome? A stunning success for that society for which, to begin with, sages, and, in sages' view, God, cared so deeply: eternal Israel after the flesh. For Israel did endure in the Christian West, enjoying the secure conviction of constituting that Israel after the flesh to which the Torah continued to speak. How do we know sages' Judaism won? Because when, in turn, Islam gained its victory, Christianity throughout the Middle East and North Africa gave way. But sages' Judaism in those same vast territories retained the loyalty and conviction of the people of the Torah. The cross would rule only where the crescent and its sword did not. But the Torah of Sinai everywhere and always sanctified Israel in time and promised secure salvation for eternity. When Christianity met the competition of secularism in various forms, then too Judaism confronted a new set of questions, and the ones that found their answers in the dual Torah lost their urgency. Then, and only then, other Judaic systems, taking up different questions altogether, competed with the paramount one that had come down from ancient times.

Why did the Judaic system shaped at that time persist with such power in Israel, the Jewish people? Because for fifteen hundred years Jews continued to resort to address the same perennially urgent questions and respond with the same arguments about who they were and where they were headed and why they should do what God wanted of them, which was to be who they were and to travel on the road of life on which they journeyed. The same symbols, the same myth (in the sense of truth told in the form of a tale), the same books enjoyed consistent attention for so long as (to continue the metaphor) the Judaic road passed through Christendom. Christianity, in its diverse forms, preserved the power of the Judaic system at hand, because the questions the system answered retained their force and immediacy: Christians kept asking them. When the Judaic road crossed frontiers into other territory entirely, then, as we shall see, people turned to new maps – or groped their way with none but their own sensibility. For the questions the received system satisfactorily answered no longer pressed on people's minds, and new questions demanded attention. So the system lost its centrality, and new Judaic systems competed for attention.

The Historical Context

Let us now place into the entire historical context of the history of Judaism the events of modern times. We may divide the history of Judaism into four principal periods, as follows:

The first age of diversity	ca. 500 BCE to 70 CE
The age of definition	ca. 70 CE to 640 CE
The age of cogency	ca. 640 CE to ca. 1800
The second age of diversity	ca. 1800 to the present

The first age of diversity begins with the writing down, in more or less their present form, of the Scriptures of ancient Israel, beginning with the Five Books of Moses. Drawing upon writings and oral traditions of the period before the destruction of the first Temple of Jerusalem, in 586 BCE, the authorship of the surviving leadership of that Temple and court, the priests, produced most of the books we now know as the Hebrew Bible ("Old Testament," or "Tanakh"), specifically the Pentateuch or Five Books of Moses, the prophetic writings from Joshua and Judges through Samuel and Kings and Isaiah, Jeremiah, Ezekiel, and the twelve smaller books of prophetic writings, and some of the other Scriptures as well.[6] During this same period a number of diverse groups of Jews, living in the Land of Israel as well as in Babylonia to the east, and in Alexandria, in Egypt, to the west, took over these writings and interpreted them in diverse ways. Hence, during the period from the formation of the Torah-book to the destruction of the Second Temple, there were many Judaisms.

The destruction of Jerusalem in 586 BCE produced a crisis of faith, because ordinary folk supposed that the god of the conquerors had conquered the God of Israel. Israelite prophets saw matters otherwise. Israel had been punished for her sins, and it was God who had carried out the punishment. God was not conquered but vindicated. The pagans were merely his instruments. God could, moreover, be served anywhere, not only in the holy and promised land of Israel. Israel in Babylonian exile continued the cult of the Lord through worship, psalms, and festivals; the synagogue, a place where God was worshipped without sacrifice, took shape. The Sabbath became Israel's sanctuary, the seventh day of rest and sanctification for God. When, for political reasons, the Persians chose to restore Jewry to Palestine and many returned (ca. 500 BCE), the Jews were not surprised, for they had been led by prophecy to expect that, with the expiation of sin through suffering and atonement, God would once more show mercy and bring them homeward. The prophets' message was authenticated by historical events.

In the early years of the Second Temple (ca. 450 BCE), Ezra, the priest-scribe, came from Babylonia to Palestine and brought with him the Torah-book, the collection of ancient scrolls of law, prophecy, and narrative. Jews resolved to make the Torah the basis of national life. The Torah was publicly read on New Year's Day in 444 BCE, and those assembled pledged to keep it. Along with the canonical Scriptures, oral traditions, explanations, instructions on how to keep the law, and exegeses of Scripture were needed to apply the law to changing conditions of everyday life. A period of creative interpretation of the written Torah began, one that has yet to come to a conclusion in the history of Judaism. From that time forward, the history of Judaism became the history of the interpretation of the Torah and its message for each successive age.

The age of definition, beginning with the destruction of the Second Temple in 70 CE, saw the diverse Judaisms of the preceding period give way, over a long period of time, to a single Judaism. That was the system worked out by the sages who, after 70 CE, developed a system of Judaism, linked to Scripture but enriched by an autonomous corpus of holy writings in addition. This Judaism is marked by its doctrine of the dual media by which the Torah was formulated and transmitted, in writing on the one side, in formulation and transmission by memory, hence, orally, on the other.

We have already met the conception of the written and oral media by which the Torah of Sinai was handed on. The doctrine of the dual Torah, written and oral, then defined the canon of Judaism. The written Torah encompassed pretty much the same books that the world at large knows as the Old Testament. The oral Torah added the writings of the sages, beginning with the Mishnah, a philosophical law code produced at ca. 200 CE, two massive commentaries on the Mishnah, the two Talmuds, one produced in the Land of Israel and called the Yerushalmi, or Jerusalem Talmud (ca. 400 CE), the other in Babylonian and called the Bavli, or Talmud of Babylonia (ca. 600 CE).

In that same age, alongside Mishnah-commentary, systematic work on Scripture yielded works organized around particular books of the written Torah, parallel to works organized around particular tractates of the Mishnah. These encompassed Sifra, to the book of Leviticus, Sifré, to Numbers, another Sifré, to Deuteronomy, works containing statements attributed to the same authorities who stand behind the Mishnah (to be dated sometime between 200 and 400), as well as Genesis Rabbah and Leviticus Rabbah, discursive works on themes in Genesis and Leviticus (edited between 400 and 450), Pesiqta deRav Kahana, a profoundly eschatological treatment of topics in Pentateuchal writings (of about 450), and similar works. These writings all together, organized around, first, the Mishnah, and, then, Scripture, comprised the first works of the oral Torah. That is to say, the teachings of the sages, originally formulated and transmitted in memory, were the written down contents of the oral Torah that God had revealed – so the system maintained – to Moses at Sinai. During the age of definition, that Judaism of the dual Torah reached its literary statement and authoritative expression.

The age of cogency is characterized by the predominance, from the far west in Morocco, Spain and France, to Iran and India, and from Egypt to England, of the Judaism of the dual Torah. During this long period, the principal question facing Jews was how to explain the success of the successor-religions, Christianity and Islam, which claimed to replace the Judaism of Sinai with a new testament, on the one side, or a final and perfect prophecy, on the other. Both religions affirmed but then claimed to succeed Judaism, and the Judaism of the dual Torah enjoyed success, among Jews, in making sense of the then-subordinated status of the enduring people and faith of Sinai. While during this long period heresies took shape, the beliefs of the new systems responded to the structure of the established one, so that a principal doctrine, for example, the doctrine of the dual Torah, written and oral, or of the Messiah as a faithful sage, would take shape in opposition to the authoritative doctrines of the Judaism of the dual Torah.

The age of cogency ran on into the nineteenth century. That does not mean there were no other Judaic systems. It means that the Judaism of the dual Torah set the standard. A heresy selected its "false doctrine" by defining in a way different from the Judaism of the dual Torah a category emerging in that Judaism of the dual Torah. There were shifts and changes of all sorts. But the Judaism of the dual Torah absorbed into itself and its structure powerful movements, such as philosophy, on the one side, and mysticism (called Qabbalah), on the other, and found strength in both of them. The philosopher defended the way of life and world-view of the Judaism of the dual Torah. The mystic observed the faith defined by that same way of life as the vehicle for gaining his or her mystical experience.

So when we see the Judaism of the dual Torah as cogent for nineteen centuries, it is not because the system remained intact and unchanged, but because it was forever able to take within itself, treat as part of its system of values and beliefs, a wide variety of new concepts and customs. This is an amazingly long time for something so volatile as a religion to have remained essentially stable and to have endured without profound shifts in symbolic structure, ritual life, or modes of social organization for the religious community. The Judaism which predominated during that long period and which has continued to flourish in the nineteenth and twentieth centuries bears a number of names: *rabbinic* because of the nature of its principal authorities, who are rabbis; *talmudic* because of the name of its chief authoritative document after the Hebrew Scriptures, which is the Talmud; *classical* because of its basic quality of endurance and prominence; or, simply, *Judaism* because no other important alternative was explored by Jews.

What proved the stability and essential cogency of rabbinic Judaism during the long period of its predominance was the capacity of rabbinic Judaism – its modes of thought, its definitions of faith, worship, and the right way to live life – to take into itself and to turn into a support and a buttress for its own system a wide variety of separate and distinct modes of belief and thought. Of importance were, first, the philosophical movement, and, second, the mystical one. Both put forward modes of thought quite distinct from those of rabbinic Judaism.

Philosophers of Judaism raised a range of questions and dealt with those questions in ways essentially separate from the established and accepted rabbinic ways of thinking about religious issues. But all of the philosophers of Judaism not only lived in accord with the rabbinic way of life; all of them were entirely literate in the Talmud and related literature, and many of the greatest philosophers were also great Talmudists. The same is to be said of the mystics. Their ideas about the inner character of God, their quest for a fully realized experience of union with the presence of God in the world, their particular doctrines, with no basis in the talmudic literature produced by the early rabbis, and their intense spirituality, were all thoroughly "rabbinized" – that is, brought into conformity with the lessons and way of life taught by the Talmud. In the end, rabbinic Judaism received extraordinary reinforcement from the spiritual resources generated by the mystic quest. Both philosophy and mysticism found their way into the center of rabbinic Judaism. Both of them were shaped by minds that, to begin with, were infused with the content and spirit of rabbinic Judaism.

The second age of diversity is the one with which we deal in this book. It is marked not by the breaking apart of the received system, but by the development of competing systems of Judaism. In this period new Judaisms came into being that entirely ignored the categories and doctrines of the received system, not responding to its concerns but to other issues altogether. Now the principal question addressed by new systems concerned matters other than those found urgent by the received Judaism of the dual Torah, with its powerful explanation of the Jews' status in the divine economy. The particular points of stress, the self-evident answers to urgent questions, came at the interstices of individual life.

Specifically, Jews needed to explain to themselves how as individuals, able to make free choices on their own, they found a place, also, within the commanded realm of the holy way of life and world-view of the Torah of Judaism. The issue again was political, but it concerned not the group but the individual. Judaisms produced in modern times answered the urgent question of individual citizenship, just as the Judaism of the long period of Christian and Muslim hegemony in Europe, Africa, and Western Asia had taken up the (then equally pressing) question of a subordinated but, in its own view, holy society's standing as Israel in Islam or in Christendom.

Now let us turn to an account of the paramount issues of the Judaism of the dual Torah. We speak not of theology or philosophy of religion but of how the faith flourished in the everyday life of real people: Israel after the flesh who aspired to meet the standards of the Torah for Israel after the promise. Precisely what was at stake in the

Judaism of the dual Torah, and what issues did people find urgent –
and answered in its version of the Torah?

NOTES

1 Meaning throughout this book not the present-day Jewish state in the
   Land of Israel, but the Jewish people. As we noted in the Letter to the
   Student, Judaism in the State of Israel takes place in a completely
   different setting from the conditions of Judaism in the diaspora, European and American (North and South) alike. We do not in these pages
   deal with Judaism in the context of the Jews as an empowered, political
   entity forming a state.
2 Because no equivalent process revised the politics of the Islamic world,
   in general the issues facing the Jews there remained constant. Where a
   process of secularization of politics did get under way, as in Algeria and
   the other parts of Islam subject to European rule, there the received
   Judaic system met competition within Jewry. But, for the bulk of the Jews
   in Islam, the creation of the State of Israel and (for a great many)
   emigration from the Muslim to the Western countries, including the
   State of Israel, marked the beginning of the same processes that, for
   European and American Judaic systems, began with the American Constitution and the French Revolution. And, we must notice, those same
   processes of secularization and political change took place in a very
   different world from the one that defined the setting for the birth of the
   Judaic systems of Europe and America in the nineteenth and twentieth
   centuries. That is why the study of the Judaisms of the Jewries of North
   Africa and the Middle East, who now form the majority of the population of the State of Israel, today forms the single most interesting topic
   for the study of the history of Judaism. But that subject falls well outside
   of the framework of this book, for the simple reason that, for the larger
   part of the Jewries of the Islamic world, the Judaism of the dual Torah
   never died, as it progressively did for the bulk of the Jewries of
   Christendom from the eighteenth century onward.
3 The language is inherited; we should now say, "humanity as the
   measure . . ."
4 The role and standing of women in the history of the formation of Judaic
   systems in modern times form a subject awaiting systematic study. In
   general the new Judaisms redefined, also, the theory of the woman.
   Reform Judaism was first to ordain woman as rabbis, but that took place
   only in the 1970s. (The second woman to enter the rabbinical program
   of Hebrew Union College–Jewish Institute of Religion, the seminary for
   educating Reform rabbis, did her BA courses on Judaism with me in
   Brown University, and the years following saw one or two women
   annually enter Rabbinical School out of my courses. By the 1980s it was

routine for women to enter the Reform, and then the Conservative, seminaries, and Orthodoxy, for its part, was organizing yeshivas for women as well.) Much earlier, by contrast, both Jewish Socialism and Zionism in theory accorded to women equal responsibilities and rights. One of the many topics within the intersecting fields of women's studies and the study of the history of Judaism is provided by the present problem.

5   The Israeli counterpart, also a Judaism of Holocaust and Redemption, bears its own points of stress. It answers Israeli questions: why should I live here? It provides its own way of life. While it corresponds to the American Judaism of Holocaust and Redemption, it is in no important way cogent with it. And that is despite the fact that it appeals to the same symbolic vocabulary. Its way of life, for one thing, lays entirely different demands on the devotee from those placed upon the devotee of American Judaism. The Israeli who frames the world-view and way of life presented by the Israeli Judaism of Holocaust and Redemption lives in the State of Israel, and the American counterpart not only does not do so but also does not imagine why he or she has to do so.

6   See especially David Noel Freedman, *The Unity of the Hebrew Bible* (Ann Arbor, 1991: University of Michigan Press), and Sara Mandell and David Noel Freedman, *The Relationship between Herodotus' History and Primary History* (Atlanta, 1993: Scholars Press for South Florida Studies in the History of Judaism).

Chaim Grade
"Reb Simkha Feinerman's Sermon"

The most important book by the greatest Yiddish novelist of our time, Chaim Grade, portrays the life of what I have called "holy Israel," that is, the Israel formed by the Torah of Sinai and covenanted to live in accord with God's will and word. The Jews of which he writes lived in Poland between World War I and World War II, but neither Poland nor the catastrophic wars enter into the story. Here we read about Jews whose deepest concerns are formed in Heaven and address what God wants of them. For them the category "Judaism" contains nothing; the category "the Torah," everything. How do people think about the world, what sort of public statements do they make, when not the hostile environment on earth, but the insistent, demanding voice of Heaven, forms the dimensions of life?

In this brief passage, we hear how Grade formulates a sermon on the occasion of the prayer Kol Nidré ("all vows"), which is said at sundown on the eve of Yom Kippur, the Day of Atonement. Here is how Judaism looks when the Jews face upward to God, rather than outward to the gentile world. Then the issues are moral, theological, inward-facing. The theme is repentance, the critical concern, God's presence within humanity, God's judgment of us all, and how we are to overcome, with the help of the Torah, prayer, and deeds of compassion, our natural instinct to do evil. Here, where holy Israel is most singular and inward-facing, the universal issues of the human condition come to predominate. When the Jews appear most different from everybody else, they happen to work out, in their own terms and idiom, issues of a universal order. Here is that segregationist Judaism that would meet competition, in the nineteenth and twentieth centuries, from the integrationist ones. Seen in its own framework, segregationist Judaism turns out to address all of humanity through holy Israel.

Reb Simkha stopped and swayed in silence for a long time. His long, narrow red-gold beard hung over the prayer stand like the festive curtain that covered the Holy Ark on holidays. The room was filled with a charged, tense atmosphere. A yellowish mist covered the light bulbs, seemingly darkened by the exhaled heat of the scholars who awaited the stormy outburst – the rosh yeshiva's [sage's] exhortation for spiritual awakening. The students covered their eyes with their hands as if reciting the Shma Yisroel ["Hear, O Israel"], so as not to feel ashamed in case they wanted to cry. Reb Simkha began with a plaintive melody, and the crowd accompanied his remarks with a subdued hum.

"My teachers and colleagues, the Prophet Isaiah states, 'The wicked are like the troubled sea, for it cannot rest, and its waters cast up mire and dirt.' The stirred-up waves in the sea think that they can go farther up the shore than previous waves. But no wave has yet succeeded in going farther than the place assigned to the sea during the Six Days of Creation. The stormy waters cast up only dregs and silt. No matter how much a man exerts himself to achieve more than his predecessor, no one has yet left this world having achieved half of what he wanted. The Midrash [interpretation of Scripture] states that the path of repentance too may be compared to the sea. As the sea is open to all, so is the way to repentance constantly open to all. But woe unto the man who flees danger on land to save himself at sea–and then drowns. Woe unto him who stumbles on his way to repentance. He needs a new Yom Kippur to atone for the previous one."

The yeshiva students felt as if their clothes were being singed from all sides. Everyone moved closer to Reb Simkha and stood with wrinkled brow and glazed eyes. Permeated by the all-encompassing, electrifying hum that accompanied his plaintive melody, Reb Simkha soared even higher.

"My teachers and colleagues, no matter how much we do for a person, we do nothing for him if we disregard his world to come. No matter how great our sacrifice for a friend, we give him nothing if we don't give him eternity. If we can't console an anguished man that eternal life will be the reward for his suffering, with what then *can* we console him?

"My teachers and colleagues, the Old Man of Navaredok, Reb Yosef-Yoizl Hurwitz, always said that the worst sentence for a person is to be unable to renounce his own nature. But if a person tries hard to overcome his innate evil traits, heaven also comes to his aid. So let us ask for heavenly help in the words of the prayer: 'Our Father, our King, destroy the evil decree against us,'" the rosh yeshiva cried out, and the words were repeated by the entire congregation like thunder reverberating on a mountain where every abyss, ravine, and slope echoed the sounds a hundredfold.

"My teachers and colleagues" – Reb Simkha's voice was heard again, and the other voices began to recede and vanish as crumbling thunder dwindles into the distance – "We believe with perfect faith that the world is sustained by virtue of the saintly man – and we, we want to be saints. But at first glance some of us might think: Is it possible? *I* slave away to achieve perfection, *I* walk about disheveled and hungry, and the world that is sustained through me even makes fun of my ritual fringes! But whoever thinks thus is surely not one of the saints because of whom the world is sustained. The Talmud tells us about the sage Rabbi Hanania ben Dosa: 'Every day a heavenly voice is heard saying: "The entire world is sustained because of my son, Hanania, yet one measure of carob suffices Hanania from one Sabbath eve to the next."' The true man of perfection is satisfied with a pot of dried carob from one Sabbath eve to the next. He demands nothing and even lovingly accepts the humiliation of the world which is sustained on account of him. And so, my dear friends, with the strength of a vast multitude, let us come at least one step closer to the presence of Rabbi Hanania ben Dosa in Paradise. Now, in this hour of mercy, when the heavenly gate is open, let us pray once more for divine help: 'Our Father, our King, let us repent fully before you!'"

Part I
The Nineteenth Century

1

The Challenge of the Secular Age: Segregation or Integration and Three Integrationist Judaisms

In Christian Europe from the time of Constantine to the nineteenth century, Jewry was accorded the status of a segregated community. The Jewish people sustained itself as a recognized and ordinarily tolerated minority. True, the contradictory doctrines of Christianity – the Jews as Christ-killers to be punished, the Jews as witnesses to be kept alive and ultimately converted at the second coming of Christ – held in an uneasy balance. The pluralistic character of some societies (for instance, that in Spain when it was shared among Islam, Christianity, and Judaism), the welcome accorded entrepreneurs in opening territories (for instance, Norman England, Poland and Russia, White Russia and Ukraine) in the early centuries of development – these account still more than doctrine for the long-term survival of Jews in Christian Europe.

The Jews, like many others, formed not only a tolerated religious minority, but something akin to a guild, specializing in certain occupations, for example, crafts and commerce in the East. Economic calling, religion, language, clothing, marriage and family-life, political status – all joined together to define a well-differentiated and enduring entity and its social order, distinct from all others. The centuries of essentially ordinary existence in the West ended with the Crusades, from 1096 onward, which forced Jewry to migrate to the eastern, pioneering, newly Christianized frontiers of Europe, Poland, Ukraine, Lithuania, Hungary, Romania, Bohemia, Slovakia, and elsewhere. But the Jews remained a European people. That is, until the twentieth century, the Jews formed one of the peoples permanently settled in Europe, first in the West, later in the East. In that long period, the Jews, like many others among whom they lived, identified themselves not by reason of the territory that they occupied and where they predominated, but by the language, clothing, food, calendar, religion, and other distinctive elements of their distinctive identification. The Yiddish language, deriving from that which the German Jews spoke when driven out of the Rhineland to the east in the catastrophe of the Crusades, was one important mark; but then Poles spoke Polish, Lithuanians their language, Ukrainians and Belorussians theirs, and no one imagined a single language covered everybody. And while not a majority in any large territory, the Jews lived in areas where they formed a large and visible minority.

It was only in modern times that the Jews as a whole found, or even aspired to, a position equivalent to that of the majority population in European societies. Before that time the Jews found themselves subjected to legal restrictions as to where they might live and how they might earn a living. They enjoyed political and social rights of a most limited character. In the East, where most Jews lived, in many important aspects of life, they formed a disciplined society, with shared values and subject to the authority of their own sages and judges, and they governed their own communities through their own administration and law. They spoke their own language, Yiddish; wore distinctive clothing; ate only their own food; controlled their own sector of the larger economy and ventured outside of it only seldom; and, in all, formed a distinct and distinctive group. Commonly, the villages in which they lived found Jews and Christians living side by side, but in many of those villages Jews formed the majority of the population. These facts made for long-term stability and autonomy. In the West, the Jews formed only a tiny proportion of the population, but, until modern times, lived equally segregated from the rest of the country, behind the barriers of language, custom, and economic calling. So the Jews for a long time formed a caste, a distinct and clearly defined group – but within the hierarchy ordered by the castes of the society at hand.

In the nineteenth century sweeping changes in the political circumstances in which Jews made their lives as well as in the economic conditions in which they made their living made urgent issues that formerly had drawn slight attention. The Jews had formerly constituted a distinct group. Now in the West they formed part of an undifferentiated mass of citizens, all of them equal before the law, all of them subject to the same law. The Judaism of the dual Torah rested on the political premise that the Jews were governed by God's law and formed God's people. The two political premises – the one of the nation-state, the other of the Torah – scarcely permitted reconciliation. The Torah governed holy Israel, wherever it was located. True, the common law of a given empire or kingdom applied and would be not only obeyed but also honored: "the law of the kingdom is [valid] law," said a third-century Talmudic authority. But in the areas of life that really counted, how life was lived in a practical way, the law of the kingdom – whether Russia, Germany, or Austria-Hungary in the nineteenth century – scarcely pertained. Living deeply segregated lives, the Jews addressed issues of universal human concern, finding particular language to set forth profound and wise judgments upon the human condition.

In the nineteenth century (many) Jews formed the aspiration to take their place as citizens, integrated into the nation-states where they were located: first the USA, France, and Britain, then Germany and Austria-Hungary, and onward to the east. So the segregation of long centuries now competed with the integration of the new age. The three consequent integrationist Judaisms, Reform Judaism, Orthodox Judaism, positive Historical Judaism (in the USA: Conservative Judaism), each of them addressing issues regarded as acute and not merely chronic, in the nineteenth century sought to make the case that the long-segregated holy life could be authentically lived in the circumstance of citizenship and social integration. To make the case for authenticity, each in its own way alleged that it formed the natural next step in the unfolding of "the tradition," meaning the Judaic system of the dual Torah. The upshot is that, speaking in the name of the Torah or "tradition" or "Judaism," the nineteenth-century Judaic systems argued out of the past in favor of the changes of the present.

A process called "emancipation," part of a larger movement of emancipation of serfs, women, slaves, Catholics (in Protestant countries, for instance, England and Ireland), encompassed the Jews as well. Benzion Dinur defines this process of emancipation as follows:

> Jewish emancipation denotes the abolition of disabilities and inequities applied specially to Jews, the recognition of Jews as equal to other citizens, and the formal granting of the rights and duties of citizenship. Essentially the legal act of emancipation should have been simply the expression of the diminution of social hostility and psychological aversion toward Jews in the host nation . . . but the antipathy was not obliterated and constantly hampered the realization of equality even after it had been proclaimed by the state and included in the law.[1]

The political changes that fall into the process of the Jews' emancipation began in the eighteenth century, and in a half-century affected the long-term stability that had characterized the Jews' social and political life from Constantine onward. These political changes raised questions not previously found urgent, and, it follows, also precipitated reflection on problems formerly neglected. The answers to the questions flowed logically and necessarily from the character of the questions themselves.

Dinur traces three periods in the history of the Jews' emancipation, from 1740 to 1789, ending with the French Revolution, then from 1789 to 1878, from the French Revolution to the Congress of Berlin, and from 1878 to 1933, from the Congress of Berlin to the rise of the Nazis to power in Germany. The adoption of the American Constitution in 1787 confirmed the US position on the matter. Jewish males enjoyed the rights of citizens, along with all other whites. The first period marks the point at which the emancipation of the Jews first came under discussion, the second marked the period in which Western and Central European states accorded to the Jews the rights of citizens, and the third brought to the fore a period of new racism that in the end annihilated the Jews of Europe.

In the first period advocates of the Jews' emancipation maintained that religious intolerance accounted for the low caste-status assigned to the Jews. Liberating the Jews would mark another stage in overcoming religious intolerance. During this first period the original ideas of Reform Judaism came to expression, although the important changes in religious doctrine and practice were realized only in the earlier part of the nineteenth century. In the second period, the French Revolution brought Jews political rights in France, Belgium, the Netherlands, Italy, Germany, and Austria-Hungary. As Germany and Italy attained unification and Hungary independence, the Jews were accorded the rights and duties of citizenship. Dinur explains: "It was stressed that keeping the Jews in a politically limited and socially inferior status was incompatible with the principle of civic equality . . . 'it is the objective of every political organization to protect the natural rights of man,' hence, 'all citizens have the right to all the liberties and advantages of citizens, without exception.'"

Jews at that time entered the political and cultural life of the Western nations, including their overseas empires (hence Algerian Jews received French citizenship). During this second period Reform Judaism reached its first stage of development, beginning in Germany. It made it possible for Jews to hold together the two things they deemed inseparable: their desire to remain Jewish, and their wish also to be one with their "fellow citizens." By the middle of the nineteenth century, Reform had reached full expression and had won the support of a sizable part of German Jewry. In reaction against

Reform ("the excesses of . . ."), Orthodoxy came into existence. As we shall see, Orthodoxy no less than Reform asked how "Judaism" could co-exist with "German-ness," meaning citizenship in an undifferentiated republic of citizens.

A centrist position, mediating between Reform and Orthodoxy, was worked out by theologians in what was then called the Historical School, and what, in twentieth-century America, took the name of Conservative Judaism. The period from the French Revolution to the Congress of Berlin therefore saw the full efflorescence of all of the Judaisms of political modernization. All of these Judaisms characterized the Jews of Western Europe, and, later on, America. But in America, Reform, Orthodoxy, and the Historical School or Conservative Judaism radically changed in character, responding to the urgent issues of a different circumstance, producing self-evidently valid answers of a character not compatible with the nineteenth-century statements of those same systems.

In the third period, anti-Semitism as a political and social movement attained power. Jews began to realize that, in Dinur's words, "the state's legal recognition of Jewish civic and political equality does not automatically bring social recognition of this equality." The Jews continued to form a separate group; they were racially "inferior." The impact of the new racism would be felt in the twentieth century. As we shall see in the next part, the Judaisms of the twentieth century raised the questions of political repression and economic dislocation, as these faced the Jews of Eastern Europe and America.

Clearly, in the nineteenth century, particularly in Western countries, a new order revised the political settlement covering the Jews, in place for nearly the entire history of the West. From the time of Constantine forward, the Jews' essentially autonomous life as a protected minority had raised political questions that found answers of an essentially supernatural and theological character. But now the emancipation redefined those questions, asking about Jews not as a distinct group but Jews as part of some other polity altogether than the Jewish one. Those Jews who simply passed over retain no interest for us; Karl Marx, converted to Christianity at an early age, produced to ideas important in the study of Judaism(s). But vast numbers of Jews in the West determined to remain Jewish and also to become something else. Their urgent question addressed the issue of how to be both Jewish and something else: a citizen of Germany or France or Britain. That issue would not confront the Jews of the Russian Empire until World War I, and, together with the Jews of the Austro-

Hungarian Empire, Romania, and other Eastern European areas, these formed the vast majority of the whole.

The Jews of the West, preoccupied with change in their political position, formed only a small minority of the Jews of the world – the Western frontier (extending, to be sure, to California in the farthest west of all) of the Jewish people. But their confrontation with political change proved paradigmatic. They were the ones to invent the Judaisms of the nineteenth century. Each of these Judaic systems exhibited three characteristic traits. First, it asked how one could be both Jewish and something else, that is, also a citizen, a member of a nation. Second, it defined "Judaism" (that is, its system) as a religion, so leaving ample space for that something else, namely, nationality, whether German ("*Deutschtum und Judentum*," German-ness and Jewish-ness), or British, or French, or American. Third, it appealed to history to prove the continuity between its system and the received Judaism of the dual Torah. The resort to historical fact, the claim that the system at hand formed the linear development of the past, the natural increment of the entire "history" of Israel, the Jewish people, from the beginning to the new day – that essentially factual claim masked a profound conviction concerning self-evidence. The urgent question at hand – the political one – produced a self-evidently correct answer out of the history of politics constituted by historical narrative.

That appeal to history, particularly historical fact, characterizes all three Judaisms. The Reformers stated explicitly that theirs would be a Judaism built on fact. The facts of history, in particular, would guide Jews to the definition of what was essential and what could be dropped. History then formed the court of appeal – but also the necessary link, the critical point of continuity. The Historical School took the same position, but reached different conclusions. History would show how change could be effected, and the principles of historical change would then govern. Orthodoxy met the issue in a different way, maintaining that "Judaism" was above history, not a historical fact at all. But the Orthodox position would also appeal most forcefully to the past in its claim that Orthodoxy constituted the natural and complete continuation of "Judaism" in its true form.

The importance of "history" – the to us rather odd conception that if we know exactly what happened then, we also can find out precisely how things ought to be now – in the theological thought of the nineteenth-century Judaisms derives from the intellectual heritage of the age, with its stress on the nation-state as the definitive unit of society, and on history as the mode of defining the culture and character of the nation-state. History as an instrument of reform, further, had served the Protestant Reformation, with its appeal to Scripture as against (mere) tradition, its claim that it would restore Christianity to its (historical) purity. Finally and most important, the supernaturalism of the inherited Judaism of the dual Torah, its emphasis upon God's active intervention in history, on miracles, on a perpetual concern for the natural implications of the supernatural will and covenant – that supernaturalism contradicted the rationalism of the age. The one thing the Jewish thinkers wished to accomplish was to show the rationalism, the reason – the normality – of the Judaisms they constructed. Appealing to (mere) facts of history, as against the unbelievable claims of a Scripture, placed upon a positive and this-worldly foundation that religious view of the world that, in the received system of the dual Torah, rested upon a completely supernatural view of reality.

For the three Judaisms of the age, which we see as continuous in important ways, took as their task the demonstration of how they formed out of the received and unwanted old Judaism something new, different, and acceptable. That defined their theological problem and its solution. The Judaisms of the nineteenth century were born in the matrix of the received system of the dual Torah, among people who themselves grew up in a world in which *that* Judaism defined what people meant by Judaism. That is why the questions of analysis address the fact that the framers of the Judaisms of continuation could not evade the issue of continuity. They wished both to continue and also to innovate – and to justify innovation. And that desire affected Orthodoxy as much as Reform. In making changes, they appealed to the past for justification. But they pointed to those changes also as proof that they had overcome an unwanted past. The delicate balance between tradition and change attained by each of the Judaisms of continuation marks the genius of its inventors. All worked out the same equation: change but not too much, whatever the proportion a group found excessive.

When we analyze the Judaisms of continuity, each one alleging itself to form the necessary next step of history, we therefore want to know in what ways that allegation corresponds to fact. Do the Judaic systems that came into being in the nineteenth century claim to renew the received Judaism of the dual Torah or do they allege that they invent a Judaism? And if they allege that they stand as the natural next step in "the tradition," does that claim stand? Answers to these questions will guide us to an understanding of how the Judaisms of the nineteenth century testify – as I said in the introduction – to humanity's power of creative genius: making something out of nothing. The Judaic systems of the nineteenth century answered through (to devotees) self-evidently right doctrine questions that none can escape or ignore. And the questions before all three important Judaisms of the nineteenth century were the same, the answers of the three systems remarkably congruent to one another.

The view that the Judaisms of the nineteenth century from a later perspective look remarkably alike will have surprised their founders and framers. For they fought bitterly among themselves. But, as we have already noticed, the three Judaisms of continuity exhibit striking traits in common. All looked backward, at the received system of the dual Torah. All sought justification in precedent out of a holy and paradigmatic past. All viewed the documents of that system as canonical, differing, of course, on the relative merit of the several components. They concurred that texts to prove propositions deemed true should derive from those canonical writings (or from some of them). All took for granted the enduring, God-given authority of those writings. None doubted that God had revealed the (Written) Torah at Sinai. All looked for validating precedent in the received canon. Differing on issues important to both world-view and way of life, all three Judaisms concurred on the importance of literacy in the received writings, on the lasting relevance of the symbolic system at hand, on the pertinence of the way of life (in some, if not in every detail), on the power of the received Judaism of the dual Torah to stand in judgment on whatever, later, would serve to continue that Judaism.

True, the differences among the three Judaisms impressed their framers and with good reason. The Reformers rejected important components of the Judaism of the dual Torah and said so. Written Torah, yes, Oral Torah, no. The Orthodox explicitly denied the validity of changing anything, insisting on the facticity, the givenness, of the whole. The Conservatives, in appealing to historical precedent, shifted the premise of justification entirely. Written Torah, yes, Oral Torah, maybe. They sought what the Orthodox thought pointless and the Reform inconsequential, namely, justification for making some few changes in the present in continuation of the processes that had effected development in the past. None of these points of important difference proved trivial. But all of them, all together, should not obscure the powerful points of similarity that mark all three Judaisms as continuators of the Judaism of the dual Torah.

Continuators, but not lineal developments, not the natural next step, not the ineluctable increment of history, such as all claimed to be – each with good reason, and, of course, all wrong. The points at which each Judaism took its leave from the received system do not match. In the case of Reform, the break proved explicit: change carried out by articulate, conscious decision, thus change as a matter of policy, enjoys full legitimacy. And as for the positive Historical School and of its continuators in Conservative Judaism, the gulf between faith and fact took the measure of the difference between the received system of the dual Torah and the statement of mere historical facts that, for the Historical School, served to document the faith.

While the differences in the grounds of separation from the received system prove formidable, still more striking and fresh are the several arguments adduced once more to establish a firm connection to the Judaism of the dual Torah, or, more accurately, to "the tradition" or to "Judaism." For the Judaisms of continuation characteristically differ in the several ways in which each, on its own, proposed to establish its continuity with a past perceived as discontinuous. All three Judaisms enjoyed ample justification for the insistence, each in its way, that it carried forward the entire history of Judaism and took the necessary and ineluctable step beyond where matters had rested prior to its own formation. Reform in this regard found itself subjected to vigorous criticism, but in saying that "things have changed in the past, and we can change them too," Reform established its primary position. It too pointed to precedent, and implicitly conceded the power of the received system to stand in judgment. All the more so did the Orthodox and Conservative theologians affirm that same power and place themselves under the judgment of the Judaism of the dual Torah. In my view, all three established a firm position within the continuation of that Judaism. While the allegation made by each of priority as the next step in the linear and incremental history of Judaism scarcely demands serious analysis, the theory, for each one respectively, enjoys ample, if diverse, justification.

Before we examine the three Judaisms one by one, let us ask a question to all of them together: what exactly was accomplished by the framers of the three Judaic systems of the nineteenth century? If I had to specify the three Judaisms' single most striking trait in common, it is the power to endure. Orthodoxy, Reform, Conservative Judaism, as well as their variations and extensions, today continue to flourish. Nearly two hundred years have seen the birth and death of movements in the arts and philosophy, literature and music, and also religion. But the Judaisms of continuation retained, even to the beginning of the third century of Reform Judaism, the power to set the issues within Jewry and to sustain their institutions as well. We may readily lose sight of that fact and miss its surprising quality, until we realize that the more vigorous and popular movements of the twentieth century exhibited in common the opposite quality: their transience. True, one came to an end because of its success, and another perished along with its mass participants in the murder of European Jews in World War II and the cultural genocide practiced in Stalin's Soviet Union and into our own day. But if we set aside the adventitious effects of real history – as distinct from Jewish History – we realize that the Judaisms of continuation did endure, and other Judaisms did not. And, with their success, they preserved (and I would say, enhanced) that Judaism of the dual Torah that, in diverse ways, the continuator-systems made their own.

When we come to the three Judaisms of the twentieth century, we shall appreciate more vividly the meaning of that fact. The three systems that would reach prominence in the twentieth century laid no claim to continue the Judaism of the dual Torah, in no way placed themselves in relationship to it, implicitly denied all relevance, all right of judgment, to that Judaism. So in fact they formed essentially new Judaisms, none exhibiting the claim, or the mark, of continuity. True, as a matter of form or convention each claimed antecedents, even precedents, each adduced proof-texts. As we turn our attention to the mythic ideologies that took shape in the twentieth century, however, we find a new set of questions, a new body of proof-texts – above all, a new definition of imperatives confronting the Jews as a group.

What marks the shift from the nineteenth- to the twentieth-century Judaisms? It is the one thing that mattered to all the Judaisms of continuity but to none of the Jewish versions of socialism, nationalism, and American ethnicity: the issue of continuity. The nineteenth-century Judaisms outlined the grounds for establishing a single and continuous relationship with "the past," as the Conservatives would put it, the revealed, Written Torah, as the Reformers emphasized, or Sinai and God's will, as the Orthodox said. That mattered. So too did one other thing: all of the Judaisms of continuity paradoxically recognized their separation from the received tradition and proposed to account for it and to treat it as important, to be explained. So each composed a statement of a self-conscious explanation of who it was in relationship to the received system.

The systems of the future, coming in the twentieth century, discontinuous with the received system, found no urgency in such a self-conscious accounting but treated their several compositions –

world-views, ways of life, addressed to an identified Israel – as essentially self-evident. So the Judaisms of continuation responded to the knowledge of change with an account of the meaning of change, the self-aware explanation of how change gave way before continuity, whether of doctrine, or method, or historical force. The Judaisms that made the total break from the received system lost the perspective gained from the external point of viewing themselves. Appealing to the fully formed system of their own, they went in search not of proof-texts, whether in literature or in history, so critical to the Reform, Orthodox, and Conservative theologians, but of mere pretexts: rhetoric to conform to an available rhetoric. So if the prophets said what the Socialists or Zionists wished to hear, the prophets would provide the requisite texts, to be affixed, so to speak, to the door-posts of the houses and to the gates, but not to be bound on mind and heart. Of such self-evidence is made: of a myth become the medium for making meaning out of the messages of the twentieth century.

NOTE

1 Benzion Dinur, "Emancipation," *Encyclopaedia Judaica* (Jerusalem, 1971: Keter), 6: 696–718. Quotation: col. 696.

Chaim Grade
"The Yeshiva"

*In the two chapters of his classic account of the living Judaism of
Poland between World War I and World War II, Chaim Grade
captures in a delightful narrative many of the conflicts that swept
over the ancient, thousand-year-old life of Jewry in Eastern Europe.
Here we see in a vivid way how the ideas and abstract issues that we
take up in these pages play themselves out in the workaday affairs of
real people, living ordinary lives. The fact that all of the Jews whom
Grade portrays would be dead within less than two decades, murdered
in a systematic way in factories built to produce dead Jews, should not
divert our attention from the vitality of the faith before us: these are
people striving to live a holy life, somehow or other.*

*The conflicts are not among secular against religious Jews alone,
nor between integrationists and segregationists. They also are between
young and old, left and right, conflicting aspirations of people who,
all Jews to outsiders, formed an arena of conflict to insiders. We meet
the factory manager, a Jew, but a Hasid, a believer in a Judaic
system that identified saints on earth as channels to Heaven; non-
Hasidic Litvaks (Lithuanians) stressed a Judaic system that laid
emphasis on Torah-study and learning as the path to Heaven. "The
Valkenik youths" are the secular Jewish young people of the town of
Valkenik. The summer guests are Torah-scholars from nearby cities,
particularly Vilna, then a Polish city, now Lithuanian, which was
"the Jerusalem" of Lithuania, famed for its scholars. The Seventeenth of Tammuz and Tisha B'Av, that is, mid-July to early
August, form a period of mourning for the Temple of Jerusalem,
destroyed in the summer of 586 BCE by the Babylonians and in the
summer of 70 CE by the Romans. The town of Valkenik firemen form
yet another group – young people organized to fight fire, complete*

with a marching band of their own. Yet another group is made up of the "library demons," that is, free-thinkers, who organized to buy books and run a lending library. The books they bought concerned philosophy and history, not Torah-study. Then there are the Mizrachi party, Orthodox Jews who supported Zionism and wanted to build a Jewish state in what was then Palestine. They are opposed by the Agudah group, equally Orthodox, who opposed Zionism because only God can and will restore the Jewish state in the Land of Israel, when the Messiah comes. We meet Jews who observe the law and study the Torah, but also get themselves a secular education in science and history and philosophy. And they even learn the Hebrew language as it is coming back to life, using it for secular purposes, and speaking it in preference to Yiddish, which for most serves as the everyday language. So much for the Jews who wish to be Jewish in any of a dozen different and conflicting models. Then there are the Jews who wish to bury Judaism and assimilate the Jews into the working class. These are the Jewish Communists, who believed the propaganda of the Soviet Union and accepted its promise of a society of "all humanity" without differentiation. They despise religion and nationalism alike. They are represented by one person only, but he makes plenty of trouble, as we shall see.

Bands and parades violate the spirit of the three weeks of mourning – and the law of Judaism too. Riots break out. Everyone in the brawl is Jewish. The conflict comes when the fire fighters and the library group get together against the elders of the town, who stand for the Torah. It is timed for the Ninth of Av, when the pious fast. To join in the holy day, some village Jews make their way to the town. Now the mixture is complete: townsfolk and villagers, Communists and Torah scholars, Zionists and anti-Zionists, believers and atheists, musicians and intellectuals – everything and its opposite. Come on back, now, to Valkenik around 1930, and follow the fray as the various Judaisms meet, not in the pages of a book that reports on ideas dead folk held, but in the life of a great writer's reconstruction of a world he himself knew.

No sooner had the season for blackberries, sunny currants, and wine-red cherries ended than the time for the purple plums began. They were so cheap that they were sold by the pailful. But since pious Jews do not eat meat or new fruits – and do not go swimming, either – between the Seventeenth of Tammuz and the Tisha B'Av fast days, landlords reserved their butter, cheese, and sour cream for the summer visitors while they and their families made do with black bread soaked in sorrel soup thickened with a bit of milk. The days were hot, and the dust from the roads settled in one's throat. The peasants were working hard in the fields and didn't come to the village. The market place was deserted. The older generation sat on the sun-baked porches of the cottages and the steps of the shops. In their hearts the exiled Divine Presence murmured like a dove the opening words of the Book of Lamentations: "How doth the city sit forlorn . . ."

The younger generation was even more sober and subdued. The cardboard factory beyond the woods had no place to sell its merchandise. The saws no longer gasped all night; work had stopped on two of the three shifts. Having grown accustomed to the factory whistle, the town youths still awoke to the minute, even without the signal, but they heard only eerie silence from the forest. The factory was still in operation during the day, but except for ten older Jews, the manager kept only the village peasants on, because they would work for less and were not troublemakers. The factory manager, a young, black-bearded, fiery-eyed Hasid from Poland, argued that it was no mitzva to provide a livelihood for such Jewish sinners. Praying among the cold, stiff non-Hasidic Litvaks, he alone swayed like a tree in a storm. He liked to have guests at his table seven days a week, but he couldn't stand these inciters of labor unrest. The Valkenik youths who had been fired gossiped that he ran after gentile girls, and, hating him, they began to hate the town's pious Jews as well as the vacationing yeshiva scholars.

The summer guests sat on the porches eating juicy red radishes and scallions in sour cream. They coated their potatoes with butter and gobbled stacks of omelets, big and round and clear as the sun. They drank rich thick cocoa and ate little cheese-filled pastries and puffy cakes sprinkled with cinnamon and sugar. Heeding the advice of their landladies, they ate dozens of raw eggs. The women also bought tender chickens for them, blowing into the rear feathers of hens to see if they were fat enough. This caused consternation among the town Jews.

"Are Torah scholars eating meat during the three weeks between the Seventeenth of Tammuz and Tisha B'Av?"

To which the landladies answered, "Our lodgers are merely following doctors' orders, and we all know that, according to the Talmud, even the Sabbath may be violated to save one's life." The villagers then turned directly to the yeshiva scholars. The latter replied to their ignorant questioners, "Not eating meat during the Three Weeks is only a custom, not a law. In fact some scholars hold that the custom is valid only for the first nine days of Av and not for the entire Three Weeks."

A couple of Valkenik lads swore that in their aunt's house they had seen a group of yeshiva boys secretly eating on the fast of the Seventeenth of Tammuz, but these backbiters were quickly silenced. "They probably got permission from their rosh yeshivas. They study Torah – and studying, the holy books say, makes one weak. How can you compare yourselves to them? It's all right for the students."

"Then it's all right for us too," the youths answered, and they began to put their arms around their girl friends' waists in public. The girls would swing their broad hips and, their wanton eyes shining, laugh pertly into the faces of the bewigged old women who looked back at them disdainfully from their porches.

The daughters of Valkenik grew tall and full-bodied like ripe cucumbers under moonlight. Nubile girls with full breasts like pumpkins and faces like risen dough peered out from the curtained windows of their small houses. Like tiny flower pots holding rosebushes, these poor little cottages were too small for the Valkenik girls with their large bodies and thick, beribboned braids. With nothing to do and nowhere to go, the local girls stayed indoors from the moment they awoke, heads heavy and eyelids leaden. In the evening they went to the bridge to meet boys. They chewed sunflower seeds and spat the shells into the water. They heard the carters' jokes for the hundredth time and slapped their hands when they got fresh. The young men had no intention of falling in love and getting married. They dreamed of Brazil, they wanted to go to Australia – anywhere, just so they could get out of town. The young people strolled around the back lanes, watching the setting sun finally sink like a stone into the cold blue lakes – far off where the sky touched the earth and the roads strayed to the Lithuanian border. The youths were so bored that they even lost interest in dancing, so the girls danced among themselves, singing and keeping rhythm with their high heels. The brides without grooms would gather in a friend's house around the big speaker of a rusty phonograph. Like stuffed birds with glass eyes they would sit and listen to the cracked record grating out its wornout waltz, turning incessantly – just as the three Valkenik rivers turned, and just as their thoughts turned around the lost hope of getting married and managing a household. Finally the girls became too lazy to meet and dance. They sat at home, took their trousseaus out of their dressers, and counted tablecloths, sheets, towels, linens, and lace-embroidered underwear until dark. They held their trousseaus in their slack hands and wondered: For whom is all this prepared? Where are our bride-grooms?

With the arrival of the vacationing yeshiva students a hope stole into the girls' hearts: the scholars were so fine and gentle; they never let a vulgar word cross their lips. What harm was there in having a religious Jew for a husband? Who cared if he grew a beard a couple of years after the wedding? But the girls soon realized that they couldn't count on the summer visitors either. Torah students wouldn't even talk to a poor girl. They didn't seem to mind looking – their eyes devoured the girls' hips, their bare knees and legs; they longed to put a hand on a plump shoulder. Some of the scholars literally drooled. But as for marriage – they thought only of rich matches. To spite the community leaders as well as their own parents, the girls stayed out with the local youths till after midnight, inciting them against the pious idlers, those gluttonous summer guests.

Completely bored and angry with the whole world, the youths were spoiling for a fight with both the pious local Jews and the visiting band of "God's thieves," as they called the students. Depressed by the heat wave and by their annual gloom at the destruction of ancient Jerusalem, the religious townsmen in turn became increasingly angry with the impudent, irreligious youths who lolled about in the woods by day and in the high grass at the river's edge by night. The smoldering argument finally blazed up unexpectedly, precipitated by those responsible for putting fires out – the Valkenik firemen.

The heat wave had caused forest fires in the region. One fire destroyed all the dry underbrush and left tree stumps burning for days, then spread to a swampy region. It was almost to the point of burning itself out; only a little smoke curled slowly up into the blue sky. Then suddenly a wind came and blew the blaze into another section of the woods. And just then the Valkenik fire brigade got the wild notion of having a fire-fighting exercise. They set fire to a pile of wood on the river bank and then ran down with pumps, ladders, and axes. They swung the axes and sprayed the water hoses, shouting, "Tear the roof down! Break down the walls!" At first the older Valkenik onlookers made fun of them, and their barbed remarks fell like sparks on the exhausted firemen. Then, as though the devil had had a hand in it, along came a gust of wind, and a red sheen spread over the river. Women holding babies screamed, "Help!" and the men shouted, "Our houses are going to burn up!" The frightened firemen just barely managed to smother the smoldering chunks of wood. Infuriated at their humiliation, their smoke-blackened faces red with rage, they accosted the bearded Jews with axes in hand. "Hunchbacks, why are you shoving?" But the latter snapped, "Go to hell and take your antics with you!" After this incident the brigade assembled in secret and made plans to repair their tarnished reputation and get even with the pious elders.

One afternoon the townsmen were sitting on the steps of their houses or shops as usual, swaying in a doze. Drops of perspiration ran down behind their ears and from their foreheads to their chins, but they didn't lift a hand to wipe their wet faces or shoo away the flies perched on their noses in a Silent Devotion of buzzing. The heat made the yeshiva students drowsy over their Talmuds. Not a sound was heard from the beth medresh. Suddenly the boom of a bass drum and a resounding trumpet call broke the stillness. The fire brigade band was marching up one of the back lanes near the river, approaching Synagogue Street. The bandmaster walked backward, facing the musicians and conducting with his hands. One bandsman slid the trombone back and forth, a second moved his fingers on the keys of the clarinet, a third blew into a tuba, a fourth clanged the cymbals, and finally a short-legged fellow last in line pounded away at the drum. Following the band was the fire brigade commander, decked out in shiny boots and a sky-blue uniform adorned with silver threads and fringes plus a whistle and medals. The strap of his cocked hat was stretched tight under his raised chin like a Polish cavalryman's. Next came the helmeted, square-shouldered brigade of youths with their round, strong faces; they marched in step, axes hanging from the belts at their sides. One of them was wearing a Red Cross armband and carrying a first-aid kit. The helmets and the brass instruments flashed in the sun. There seemed to be a lively competition between the metallic sounds of the brass instruments and the cymbals and the thumping of the big bass drum to see which could make the greater racket and deafen the village.

Valkenik was stunned. The townsmen awoke from their drowse and gaped at the sky, as if Elijah the Prophet were up there riding in his chariot and blowing the ram's horn to herald the Messiah's coming, and before Tisha B'Av no less. From his house near the road the old slaughterer Lippa-Yosse ran out in his long underwear, pillow feathers clinging to his skullcap and the fear of death in his eyes, as if expecting a pogrom. Seeing the firemen, Lippa-Yosse thundered with all the strength of a pensioned-off slaughterer and cantor.

"Heathens! How dare you parade around with music during the days Jerusalem was destroyed!" His upraised hands trembled as if a bound ox had broken away from under his slaughterer's knife.

But the commander shouted to his brigade, "Forward march! One, two, three, four," as a signal to ignore everything. And with brisk march step the group headed for the market place, where on both sides of the street the villagers stood shouting abuse at them. The musicians played on, and the youths marched smartly without saying a word in reply. They were accomplishing what they had set out to do. The local people were now seeing that the fire fighters could carry off a secretly planned parade even more successfully than a mock fire exercise. Suddenly the band stopped playing and the marchers halted.

Swaying toward them with black silk umbrellas held aloft were the pious summer residents, on their way to the forest to breathe the fresh piny air and rock in their hammocks. Each umbrella carried by a rosh yeshiva was flanked by the lowered heads of two younger yeshiva students who looked like mushrooms in the shade of a spreading tree. Seeing the firemen surrounded by the local Jews, the vacationers stopped: the two camps faced each other. On one side stood helmeted youths in uniforms and boots, carrying axes like bayonets; on the other side were the Torah scholars in their gaberdines and soft hats. Ashamed to have the students witness their humiliation, the villagers shook their heads in mute complaint: You see our misfortune? These are our heirs, woe unto us! The yeshiva students remained silent and, smiling faintly, tried to walk around the crowd. But their cold, arrogant silence and their desire to slip away incited the firemen even more. The youths broke out of line and lunged at the vacationers.

"Spongers! Poor people give money for them to sit and study Torah, but instead they fatten themselves up in the country. Just look at their fat potbellies. They look like a herd of cows coming home from pasture with their udders full."

Frightened, the summer residents stopped dead in their tracks, hands and feet paralyzed. But the villagers attacked the firemen with fists flying. "Apostates! May the earth swallow you up!" At that the vacationing students took advantage of the confusion and ran to the forest, their lowered umbrellas bent and twisted like shot-down birds with wings outspread.

The feud that began that summer day encompassed all of Valkenik and, like the forest fires, lasted for weeks. One day it would flare intensely, another day it would be nearly out, and on a third it would flicker to life again. Most incensed at the firemen were the owners of the summer cottages and the carters who transported passengers from the train station. They were afraid the vacationers would leave early and not come back next year. Sroleyzer the bricklayer and his gang also opposed the firemen. During a dispute Sroleyzer and his pack usually sided with the religious community.

On the other hand, the youths who supported the secular library sided with the fire fighters. The "library demons," as they were called, were sharp-tongued, impudent brats and open heretics. They took no part in the constant conflict between the people who sided with the Mizrachi party and those who supported the Agudah. In their view, both were narrow-minded fanatics. While the village seethed with the drawn-out squabble as to who would be the new rabbi in Valkenik – an old-fashioned scholar or a secularly educated one – the library group had said that no matter who the new rabbi might be, he would in any case side with the speculators and blood-suckers. The villagers knew that the source of these words was the Bolshevik Meyerke Podval from Panashishok.

Panashishok was a Jewish village just across the Lithuanian border. Meyerke was an orphan from childhood who had been tossed from one Valkenik Talmud Torah to another until he grew up and could study on his own in the beth medresh. The Valkenik people said he had been a radical even as a youngster. Still, they had supported him because they saw signs of genius and had high hopes of his becoming a great scholar. But he had dropped his Torah studies and had gone to Vilna to work in a sawmill on the Viliye River. In Vilna he had befriended the leftists, was caught and imprisoned. After serving his sentence, he had returned to Valkenik and gone to work in the cardboard factory, where he immediately began to incite the workers. It was because of him that the manager, the Polish Hasid, had fired the Valkenik youths and kept the peasants on.

A short man, Meyerke Podval had a low, hairy forehead and an irascible glint in his half-closed eyes. When he debated with an opponent he would stand a hand's breadth away from him, one foot forward, head back, and both hands shoved into his trouser pockets. The Valkenik residents were more afraid of this gesture and the angry twinkle in his eyes than of his acerbic remarks. They sensed that Meyerke Podval could cold-bloodedly – and just for the fun of it – set the town ablaze.

On the Sabbath before Tisha B'Av the fire fighters and the library group stood behind the pulpit in the beth medresh laughing and talking. While the Reader was chanting verses from Isaiah in the traditional plaintive melody: "A seed of evil-doers, children who are corrupt," the congregation nodded in the direction of the heretics. That's exactly whom the prophet had in mind! But the youths laughed in their faces.

After services some of the town elders went to the firemen and said amiably, "You boors! The only things that used to interest you were having fire drills, spraying water from your hoses, and practicing your instruments. You never meddled in politics. Why did you suddenly give a concert during the Three Weeks before Tisha B'Av and furthermore attack the yeshiva students who provide a livelihood for our village? Tell us what you want."

The firemen scratched their necks, exchanged glances, and replied, "We want money for new water pumps, more brass instruments, and a big banquet. Why should only the Burial Society have a big feast every year? The Burial Society buries the dead; the Fire Fighters Society rescues the living."

Meanwhile Valkenik's leading citizen was approaching from his place along the eastern wall. Since the crowd had blocked Reb Hirshe Gordon's path, he stood listening with one ear cupped. The congregants gazed at him and waited for him to respond to the firemen.

"And what do *you* want?" Reb Hirshe turned to the library crowd.

Long, lanky Moshe Okun stepped forward. His height and his bulging eyes made him look like a skinny fish. No matter how loud he tried to speak, he couldn't make himself heard ten feet away. One merely saw him opening and closing his mouth. His gestures recalled the soft movements of water weeds and his rhetoric that of a public servant and chairman of conferences. After heated debates in all the Valkenik clubs, Moshe Okun would read interparty resolutions which he composed himself.

Now Moshe took the floor and declared, "On principle the library opposes a religious community, and especially the rule of the clergy. But until the community constitution is changed, the library presents three demands: First, one of our representatives must be included in a democratically elected commission that oversees the community finances. Second, the budget must include funds to support the Valkenik Dramatic Club. Third, the community must provide funds from its own resources for the purchase of new books."

"And what will you do if the community doesn't submit to these demands?" Reb Hirshe Gordon looked down over his glasses at the lanky youth.

"We'll keep on fighting till we win," Moshe Okun answered.

"Then fight," Reb Hirshe said and turned to the firemen. "You'll get money for a water pump and even for a banquet. And the community is prepared to give the library money – on condition that you buy wood and burn all the books."

Gordon left the beth medresh, followed by the congregants who sided with him. But his older brother-in-law, Eltzik Bloch, stayed in the beth medresh, fuming. "The Mizrachi *does* want to provide money to buy Hebrew books. Reb Hirshe Gordon has no right to speak for the entire community. He is not a councilman."

But Eltzik Bloch raged in vain. The congregants didn't hear what he had to say because they were so intent on looking at and listening to Meyerke Podval from Panashishok.

He spoke calmly, as usual, hands in his pockets and that glint in his half-closed eyes. "It's the Valkenik exploiters that the Prophet Isaiah had in mind when he used the phrase 'You rulers of Sodom.' And when that selfsame Isaiah said, 'When you make many prayers, I will not hear: your hands are full of blood,' he's once again referring to the Valkenik bloodsuckers. Your community leaders are a rebellious band of thieves. The pillars of the town are usurpers and crooks. Every one of you loves bribes and chases payoffs – every one of you loves to have his palm greased." Meyerke wanted to go on to cite Isaiah in connection with the way the Valkenikers treated orphans and widows. But the congregants slipped out of the beth medresh thinking: An orphan of his type had no business growing up. Nicer people were rotting in the earth.

On the morning of the Sabbath of Consolation, the week after Tisha B'Av, a group of twenty Jews made their way from their home in Dekshne to Valkenik. They wore peaked cloth caps, frayed gaberdines, and heavy, dust-covered boots. Their patched weekday prayer shawls were draped around their shoulders. No matter how these farmers tried to keep their belts snug, their sunken hips could hardly hold up their trousers. Their sparse gray beards looked like the skinny, sparse cornstalks in the stony Dekshne fields, and their emaciated faces were lined from hard work and worry. On this bright morning of the Sabbath of Consolation sadness darkened their eyes. The arid land that Czar Nicholas I had distributed among their grandfathers was still sucking the marrow from their bones. Despite their hard labor in the fields, the bread they reaped never lasted until the next harvest; nor were there enough potatoes and beets for the winter. The colonists felled trees in the forest and transported the big logs to the cardboard factory, and they also tried their hand at beekeeping and selling the honey. But each family's main source of income was caring for a mentally ill boarder.

The Dekshne patients were harmless, incurable melancholiacs; they came from well-to-do families who paid a monthly rent for their upkeep. Some of the lunatics had roved about in the village for more than thirty years. When a stranger came to Dekshne, the madmen would take the newcomer off to a corner. One would describe how his wife and children wanted to poison him; another would ask if the world was still insane. But visitors rarely strayed into the village, and the disturbed residents paid no attention to their landlords, so they usually smiled and gestured and talked to themselves. They would wander in a daze through the long village street, sit on heaps of refuse by the barns and on the steps of houses, making faces, until night came. From the time they had been normal one bright hour glimmered in the dimmed minds of these confused souls, like a stripe of light on the horizon when heaven and earth are all one darkness – but gradually even this single bright spot faded from the memories of these sick people. Sensing night covering their bodies like a wet, hairy beast, they would scream in terror. The second scream was wilder and more hair-raising. The third was accompanied by grating of teeth and raucous laughter that broke and crumbled as though their minds were falling apart. Having unburdened themselves of these shrieks, they would shudder, twitch, and shiver until paralysis beset them. Occasionally a landlord would find his lodger numb and stiff in the morning, like a beetle frozen during the night. The farmer would stand there looking numb too, and think how delighted the patient's relatives would be at the news that their payments could stop. And then, thinking of his wife and children, the farmer would realize that he and his family would have to suffer until he got another lodger.

Even though Dekshne had its own little shul, the colonists walked to the Valkenik beth medrash for festivals and important Sabbaths. For a couple of hours, at least, they liked to get away from their dismal settlement. Hence, in honor of the Sabbath of Consolation, they came to the Valkenik beth medresh and sat around the table at the western wall. But this time the Dekshners waited in vain to hear sweet melodies and cantorial trills. The beth medresh was in an uproar. The congregants were talking in every part of the room and the cantor Yudel rushed through the service. As the congregation grew, so did the tumult. When they reached the Shma Yisroel, the place buzzed like a market fair; during the Silent Devotion even the desk-pounding calls for silence were of no avail. The noise lessened only during the Torah reading, when the library group behind the pulpit went outside for a consultation.

The library club had a guest, Dan Dunietz. He was studying at a modern Jewish school in Vilna and had come to visit his parents in

Valkenik for a two-week vacation. Dan's father was a quiet man who tended orchards. He sat in a corner of the beth medresh keeping his eyes on the Siddur, as if feeling guilty for having a son who was his exact opposite in character and behavior. Dan Dunietz was talking, bursting with heat like an overboiled pot. As he spoke, a shock of black hair fell out from under his blue-and-white school cap. He gesticulated with his long hands, and his eyes glowed with the fever of the undrained swamps of pioneering Palestine. He laughed sarcastically at the pious Valkenik Jews who were waiting for a miracle to transport them to the Land of Israel as if it were an esrog in a silver container. "You want a land flowing with milk and honey. A Messiah who will come riding on a white mule over the refuse heap of the Valkenik synagogue courtyard. That's what you petty shopkeepers of Valkenik are waiting for."

Dan Dunietz didn't approve of the local youths either. There had once been a pioneer organization in the village but there was not one now because the illegal immigration to Palestine had stopped. Where was endurance, perseverance? Dan Dunietz asked. Nevertheless, he befriended the leftists of the library club, and they chose him to be their representative before the "masses" in the beth medresh. Since he had been educated at a modern school and spoke Hebrew, the provincials would trust him more. Moreover, he was a guest in town, and the congregants had no complaints about his uncivilized behavior as they had about that of the local youths. They merely warned him, "Don't get excited or people won't be able to understand you."

Everyone knew that the Sabbath of Consolation was a "Zionist Sabbath" and that Eltzik Bloch, the head of the pro-Zionist Mizrachi, should have the honor of chanting the Haftora. Instead, the honor had gone to his brother-in-law, the leader of the anti-Zionist Agudah, under the pretext that he was commemorating the Yohrzeit of a deceased grandfather or great-grandfather. Reb Hirshe Gordon chanted the chapter of Isaiah hoarsely and without melody. When he came to the verse, "O thou that tells Zion good tidings, get thee up into the high mountain," he broke into bitter tears. Eltzik Bloch actually jumped from his place. How could a man be so brazenly hypocritical? Reb Hirshe Gordon hated the Zionists! Reb Hirshe was weeping tears of anguish because the Mizrachi people were dragging the prophet Isaiah into their heathenish faction.

At that moment the library supporters marched in and, standing shoulder to shoulder, approached the Holy Ark as if taking up battle positions. Reb Hirshe peered at them over his glasses, which were dripping with tears, and continued reciting from the parchment in his hands until he finished the Haftora and then the blessings. The congregation knew that the library club wanted one of their members to be allowed to speak. The worshipers turned to the pulpit, curious to see how Reb Hirshe would handle the situation. To their amazement Reb Hirshe winked to the cantor not to take the Torah back to the Ark just yet. If these apostates wanted to talk, let them talk.

Dan Dunietz went up to the steps of the Holy Ark and began, "The Midrash says . . ."

Reb Hirshe Gordon had previously arranged with his supporters that the heretics should be allowed to say what they had to say and then the congregation could continue with the Musaf prayers undisturbed. And when the time came to provide money for books, they'd be put in their places. But Reb Hirshe had not expected Dunietz to have the gall to begin with a verse from the Midrash. The blood rushed to his temples; his face turned red.

"You're quoting the sages? First show me your fringes! Let me see that you have on ritual fringes like me and everybody else in this beth medresh," Gordon shouted and with both hands pulled the fringes out from beneath his gaberdine.

Dan Dunietz was bewildered. Even his shock of hair seemed afraid to peek from under his blue-and-white cap.

Meyerke Podval from Panashishok answered for him. "And are ritual fringes obligatory if one is wearing a tallis?"

"Whether they are or not, you're a Bolshevik and a convicted jailbird. You shouldn't have lived to get out of prison!" Reb Hirshe screamed. He pointed at Dan Dunietz. "Get him out of here!"

Sroleyzer the bricklayer and his gang of helpers suddenly materialized by the Holy Ark. Eltzik Bloch lunged at them. "Let him speak! The Mizrachi wants him to speak. The Mizrachi wants community funds allocated for Hebrew books. We're not asking Reb Hirshe's opinion. He's not a member of the community council."

But Gordon was now ranting at the highest pitch: "Drag that rebel down from there!" And his side chimed in, "Get him down, down!"

Dan Dunietz had recovered by now. He was fuming and waving his hands. "The Valkenik Jews would rather wail over the destruction of the Holy Temple than build up the Land of Israel. The main thing for them is to pray daily, 'Let us witness your return to Zion in mercy.' Those liars! Do they really mean it? They prefer the Exile in Valkenik, their Valkenik Diaspora, over the return to Zion."

But Dan Dunietz got no further. Hands stretched out to grab him, and in a flash he was flying down the steps. One of the town crooks jabbed five hard fingers into the cheek of the intellectual Moshe Okun. "You half-dead corpse! Who are you shoving?"

"I protest," Moshe Okun answered softly and, clawing with all his fingers, he bloodied the crook's face.

The fight spread. The red-eyed, iron-fisted roughnecks fought with silent, methodical anger. Their forceful blows were well aimed: a knee in the belly, a fist in the chest, a head butt to the chin. The library crowd returned the blows with blind fury, almost foaming at the mouth. They attacked with prayer stands and smacked heads with heavy Talmuds; they swung their elbows and kicked left and right. They were out for blood: to gouge out eyes, to lacerate faces, to bite into jugular veins. They wanted to murder the underworld crowd by beating them to death.

There was another commotion at the seats of the well-to-do worshipers; it sounded like the wheels of a water mill turning. Reb Hirshe's faction was squabbling with Eltzik Bloch, while other congregants shouted: "A plague on both your houses! Every Sabbath there's another to-do in the shul," they complained. "We have to eat stone-cold cholent because of these delays in the services. Let those rabble-rousers eat stones!" Two congregants almost came to blows. One shouted, "Why are you standing up for these heathens?" and the second shouted back, "Your talking and a dog's barking is all one to me. You consider *my* son a heathen?"

During all this the old ritual slaughterer Reb Lippa-Yosse was banging on the prayer stand and screaming with all his might, "You bastards! You're desecrating the Sabbath." Reb Yisroel the tailor and yeshiva supporter shut his eyes and groaned, "Woe unto the eyes that have seen this." The rabbi, Reb Mordekhai-Aaron Shapiro, was all hunched over; his small, sharp eyes darted about like those of a little animal in a trap. He cursed the day he decided to leave Shishlevitz for Valkenik. The rabbi realized that all the factions would later complain and ask why he had been afraid to intervene and silence the conflict.

Only one person derived pleasure from the fight: Yosef Varshever, wrapped in his silk tallis. It made no difference to him who was beating whom, so long as they kept beating and hurting one another. That's how much he hated Valkenik and all its residents. Varshever just barely managed to keep himself from shouting, "Good! Excellent!" His only regret was that his father-in-law, Gedalya Zondak, was not in the midst of the fray.

To everyone's amazement Sroleyzer's gang gradually retreated from the library group. The toughs were frightened by the intellectuals' murderous fury and their threats while exchanging blows: "Informers! We'll shoot every one of you down like dogs. . . . Horse

thieves! When the revolution comes, the proletariat will settle accounts with you." And some of the congregants were shouting at the
roughnecks from their seats: "You touch my son and there'll be
nothing left of you."

"Murderer! You'll rot in jail!"

"Cutthroat! Who are you waving your paws at? Youngsters!"

"People, help! Do something! They're making cripples out of our
children!"

"We're defending the holy Torah and now you're attacking us?"
the bloodied and tattered Sroleyzer spat at the congregants. "Damn
you all!" he shouted, and he ordered his bloody forces to withdraw.

The victors were also black and blue, with ribs battered, gasping,
and drenched with perspiration. They scarcely had time to draw a
breath before the disheveled Dan Dunietz pointed at Reb Hirshe
Gordon.

"He ordered me dragged away from the Holy Ark, so we'll drag
him off the pulpit." At which the entire band pounced at the pulpit
like a pack of wolves.

"Just try it!" Reb Hirshe removed his tallis, prepared to resist them
singlehandedly, like Samson against the Philistines. The noise increased. Someone shouted, "You're not going to hit the rabbi's son-
in-law?" Someone else put his hands to his head. "Help! They're
going to desecrate the Holy Scrolls."

From the rear benches came the carters, who could lift a laden
wagon with one shoulder; and butchers, who with their bare hands
could twist an ox's horn until he fell to the ground. They fell upon the
library supporters, shouting, "There'll be nothing left of you." The
youths fled to the door as though a cyclone had blown them off a
mountain. Fists fell upon their necks; blows rained down on their
sides. Before they could turn around they were thrown out into the
anteroom of the beth medresh. Dan Dunietz tore himself away from
a pair of hefty hands for a moment and shouted, "Fanatics! The
Prophet Isaiah who said 'comfort ye, comfort ye, my people,' was not
the Prophet Isaiah the son of Amoz, but another Isaiah. There were
two Isaiahs, three Isaiahs . . ."

"May you break your arms and legs!" The carter booted him out
of the beth medresh and slammed the door.

Throughout all this the Dekshners had sat still at the rear table.
When the congregation had quieted down and Reb Hirshe had given
the order to proceed with the Musaf service, one farmer turned to his
neighbor as if in a daze.

"Praying in our own little shul would have been more enjoyable."

The other man agreed. "Compared to these Valkenik loudmouths, our Dekshne madmen are a quiet sort." And the village Jews sank back into their gloomy silence.

2

Reform Judaism

Reform Judaism as a Judaism began in some modest changes in the forms of synagogue prayer and liturgy but ended up the single most important and most effective Judaism of the nineteenth century in Central Europe and of the later twentieth century in America. The reason is that Reform Judaism addressed the issue of integration and segregation and explained how, in a condition of social and political integration, (a) Judaism would flourish. Reform Judaism therefore forthrightly and articulately faced the political changes that redefined the conditions of Jews' lives and presented a Judaism, closely tied to the inherited system of the dual Torah, fully responsive to those changes. Constructive and intellectually vital in its day, Reform Judaism said what it would do and did it. Because it was a movement that confronted the issues of the day and the Jews' condition, Reform Judaism found itself able to change itself, its own deepest concerns and values. So that Judaism made itself into an instrument for what Jews wanted and needed it to be – whatever that was.

The full and authoritative statement of the Reform Judaic system – its world-view, with profound implications on its way of life, and its theory of who is Israel – came to expression not in Europe but in America, in an assembly in Pittsburgh in 1885 of Reform rabbis. At that meeting of the Central Conference of American Rabbis, the official body of Reform rabbis took up the issues that divided the Judaism and made an authoritative statement on them, one that most people could accept. The very fact that the Judaism before us could conceive of such a process of debate and formulation of a kind of creed tells us that this Judaism found urgent the specification of its systemic structure, testimony to a mature and self-aware frame of mind.

We look in vain for equivalent convocations to set public policy, for example, in the antecedent thousand years of the Judaism of the dual Torah. Statements of the world-view, as these would emerge in diverse expressions of the received system, did not take the form of a rabbis' platform, on the one side, and did not come about through democratic debate on public issues, on the other. That world-view percolated upward and represented a rarely articulated and essentially inchoate consensus about how things really are and should be. The received system came to expression in how things were done, what people found needless to make articulate at all: the piety of a milieu, not the proposition of a theological gathering. That contrast tells us not merely that Reform Judaism represented a new Judaism, but, of greater interest, that the methods and approaches of Reform Judaism enjoyed their own self-evident appropriateness.

We therefore meet Reform Judaism in Pittsburgh, Pennsylvania, in the USA, where this Judaism took root and would predominate, among rabbis who could point to three or even four generations of antecedents. These were not the founders of the new faith but the authorities of an established and enduring one. For the end of the nineteenth century found Reform Judaism a major component of the Judaic religious life of America as well as of Germany, and making inroads elsewhere as well. The American Reform rabbis, meeting in Pittsburgh in 1885, issued a clear and accessible statement of their Judaism. Critical to the Judaism of the dual Torah was its view of Israel as God's people, a supernatural polity, living out its social existence under God's Torah. The way of life, one of sanctification, and the world-view, one of persistent reference to the Torah for rules of conduct, on the one side, and of explanation of conduct, on the other, began in the basic conception of who is Israel. Here too, in Reform Judaism, we find emphasis on who is Israel, with that doctrine exposing for all to see the foundations of the way of life and world-view that these rabbis had formed for the Israel they conceived:

> We recognize in the Mosaic legislation a system of training the Jewish people for its mission during its national life in Palestine, and today we accept as binding only its moral laws and maintain only such ceremonies as elevate and sanctify our lives, but reject all such as are not adapted to the views and habits of modern civilization . . . We hold that all such Mosaic and rabbinical laws as regular diet, priestly purity, and dress originated in ages and under the influence of ideas entirely foreign to our present mental and spiritual state . . . Their observance in our days is apt rather to obstruct than to further modern spiritual

elevation . . . We recognize in the modern era of universal culture of heart and intellect the approaching of the realization of Israel's great messianic hope for the establishment of the kingdom of truth, justice, and peace among all men. We consider ourselves no longer a nation but a religious community and therefore expect neither a return to Palestine nor a sacrificial worship under the sons of Aaron nor the restoration of any of the laws concerning the Jewish state . . .

The Pittsburgh Platform takes up each component of the system in turn. Who is Israel? What is its way of life? How does it account for its existence as a distinct, and distinctive, group? Israel once was a nation ("during its national life") but today is not a nation. It once had a set of laws that regulate diet, clothing, and the like. These no longer apply, because Israel now is not what it was then. Israel forms an integral part of Western civilization. The reason to persist as a distinctive group was that the group has its work to do, namely, to realize the messianic hope for the establishment of a kingdom of truth, justice, and peace. For that purpose Israel no longer constitutes a nation. It now forms a religious community.

What that means is that individual Jews do live as citizens in other nations. Difference is acceptable at the level of religion, not nationality, a position that accords fully with the definition of citizenship of the Western democracies. The world-view then lays heavy emphasis on an as-yet unrealized but coming perfect age. The way of life admits to no important traits that distinguish Jews from others, since morality, in the nature of things, forms a universal category, applicable in the same way to everyone. The theory of Israel then forms the heart of matters, and what we learn is that Israel constitutes a "we," that is, that the Jews continue to form a group that, by its own indicators, holds together and constitutes a cogent social entity.

This system's Jews do not propose to eat or dress in distinctive ways. They do, however, seek a place within "modern spiritual elevation . . . universal culture of heart and intellect." They impute to that culture the realization of "the messianic hope" – a considerable stake. And, explicit to the whole, the Jews no longer constitute a nation. They therefore belong to some other nation(s). In this way, Reform Judaism took full measure of the Jews' position in the public polity of the several Christian European countries in which they lived. From the perspective of the political changes taking place from the American and French Revolutions onward, the received system of the Judaism of the dual Torah answered the wrong questions. For the issue no longer found definition in the claims of regnant Christianity. A new question, emerging from forces not contained within Christianity, demanded attention from Jews affected by those forces.

For those Jews, the fact of change derived its self-evidence from shifts in political circumstances. When the historians began to look for evidence of precedents for changing things, it was because their own circumstance had already persuaded them that change matters – change itself effects change (so to speak). What they sought, then, was a picture of a world in which they might find a place, and, it went without saying, that picture would include a portrait of a Judaic system – a way of life, a world-view, a definition of the Israel to live the one and believe the other. The issue confronting the new Judaism derived not from Christianity, therefore, but from political change brought about by forces of secular nationalism, which conceived of society not as the expression of God's will for the social order under the rule of Christ and his Church or his anointed king (emperor, tsar), but of popular will for the social order under the government of the people and their elected representatives, a considerable shift. When society does not form the aggregate of distinct groups, each with its place and definition, language and religion, but rather undifferentiated citizens (male, white, wealthy, to be sure), then the Judaism that Jews in such a society will have to work out also will account for difference of a different order altogether. That Judaism will have to frame a theory of who is Israel consonant with the social situation of Jews who will to be different, but not so different that they cannot also be citizens.

To the Reform rabbis in Pittsburgh, Christianity presented no urgent problems. The open society of America did. The self-evident definition of the social entity Israel therefore had to shift. We recall how the fourth-century rabbis balanced Israel against Rome, Jacob against Esau, the triumphant political messiah, seen as arrogant, against the Messiah of God, humble and sagacious. So Israel formed a supernatural entity and in due course would enter into that final era in God's division of time, in which Israel would reach its blessing. The supernatural entity, Israel, now formed no social presence. The Christian world, in which Christ ruled through popes and emperors, kings claimed divine right, and the will of the Church bore multiform consequences for society, and in which, by the way, Israel too was perceived in a supernatural framework – if a negative one – no longer existed. So the world at large no longer verified that category, Israel as supernatural entity, at all. Then the problem of the definition of what sort of entity Israel did constitute, and, by the way, what sort of way of life should characterize that Israel, what sort of world-view

explain it – that problem produced a new set of urgent and ineluctable questions, and, in the nature of things, also self-evidently true
answers, such as we find in Pittsburgh.

The Pittsburgh Platform came at the end of a century of development. Reform Judaism dates its beginnings to the nineteenth century
with changes, called reforms and regarded as the antecedents of
Reform, in trivial aspects of public worship in the synagogue.[1] The
motive for these changes derived from the simple fact that many Jews
rejected the received system. People were defecting from the synagogue. Since, it was taken for granted, giving up the faith meant
surrendering all ties to the group, the beginning of change made
reform and ultimately Reform address two issues at one time: (1)
making the synagogue more attractive so that (2) defectors would
return, and others would not leave. The reform of Judaism in its
manifestation in synagogue worship – the cutting edge of the faith –
therefore took cognizance of something that had already taken place.
And that was the loss for the received system – way of life, world-
view, addressed to a defined Israel – of its standing as self-evident
truth. That loss manifested itself in two ways. First, people were
simply leaving. Second and more important for the group, the many
who were staying looked in a new way on what, for so long, had
scarcely demanded examination at all. But, of course, the real issues
involved not the synagogue but society at large. It would take two
generations before Reform Judaism would find the strength to address that much larger issue, and a generation beyond for the power
of the ideas ultimately formulated in the Pittsburgh Platform to be
felt.

To begin with, the issue involved not politics but merely justification for changing anything at all. But framing the issue in terms of the
legitimacy of change simply asked the wrong question in the wrong
way. The Reformers maintained that change was all right because
historical precedent proved that change was all right. But change
long had defined the constant in the on-going life of the Judaism of
the dual Torah. Everybody knew that. The Judaism of the dual
Torah endured, never intact but always unimpaired, because of its
power to absorb and make its own the diverse happenings of culture
and society. So long as the structure of politics remained the same,
with Israel an autonomous entity, subordinated but recognized as a
cogent and legitimate social group in charge of some of its own
affairs, the system answered the paramount question. The trivial ones
could work their way through and become part of the consensus, to
be perceived in the end as "tradition" too. A catalogue of changes

that had taken place over fifteen hundred years, from the birth of Judaism to its death, therefore will list many more dramatic and decisive sorts of change than those matters of minor revision of liturgy – for example, sermons in the vernacular – that attracted attention at the dawn of the age of change become Reform.

We must wonder, therefore, what made the difference then, so that change could be perceived as reform and transformed into the Reform of Judaism, hence, Reform Judaism. Nothing in the earliest record of reform of liturgy tells us. The constructive efforts of the first generation focused, as I said, upon synagogue worship. The services were too long; the speeches were in a language foreign to participants; the singing was not aesthetic; the prayers were in a language no one understood. But that means some people recited the prayers as a matter of duty, not supplication; did not speak the language of the faith; formed other than received opinions on how to sing in synagogue; saw as alien what earlier had marked the home and hearth. Those people no longer lived in that same social world that had for so long found right and proper precisely the customs now seen as alien. Contrast their sense of things with the people you met in Chaim Grade's synagogue riot, and you see the difference. The one believed, the other carried out a duty.

When the heritage forms an unclaimed, unwanted legacy, out of duty people nonetheless accept it. So the reform that produced Reform Judaism introduced a shortened service, a sermon in the language people spoke, a choir and an organ, prayers in the vernacular. Clearly, a great deal of change had taken place prior to the recognition that something had changed. People no longer knew Hebrew; they no longer found pleasing received modes of saying the prayers. We look in vain to the consequent reforms for answers to the question of why people made these changes, and the reasons adduced by historians settle no interesting questions for us. The more interesting question concerns why the persistence of engagement and concern. For people always had the option, which many exercised, of abandoning the received Judaism of the two Torahs and all other Judaisms too. Among those for whom these cosmetic changes made a difference, much in the liturgy, and far more beyond, retained powerful appeal. The premise of change dictated that Jews would say the old prayers in essentially the old formulation. And that premise carried much else: the entire burden of the faith, the total commitment to the group, in some form, defined by some indicators, if not the familiar ones then some others. So we know that Reform Judaism, in its earliest manifestation in Germany in the early nineteenth century, constituted an essentially conservative, profoundly constructive effort to save for Jews the received Judaism by reforming it in some (to begin with) rather trivial ways.

Reform theologians justified change by claiming that their reforms represented the natural outcome of a single, linear Judaism. History showed change had been normal and constant. That is why the justification of change always invoked precedent. People who made changes had to show that the principle that guided what they did was not new, even though the specific things they did were. So to lay down a bridge between themselves and their past they laid out beams resting on deep-set piles. The foundation of change was formed of the bedrock of precedent. And more still: change restores, reverts to an unchanging ideal. Reform claims not to change at all, but only to regain the correct state of affairs, one that others, in the interval, themselves have changed. That forms the fundamental attitude of mind of the people who make changes and call the changes Reform. The appeal to history, a common mode of justification in the politics and theology of the nineteenth century, therefore defined the principal justification for the new Judaism: it was new because it renewed the old and enduring, the golden Judaism of a mythic age of perfection. Arguments on precedent drew the Reformers to the work of critical scholarship, as we shall see, as they settled all questions by appeal to the facts of history.

We cannot find surprising, therefore, the theory that Reform Judaism stood in a direct line with the prior history of Judaism. Judaism is one. Judaism has a history, that history is single and unitary, and it was always leading to its present outcome: Reform Judaism. Others later on would challenge these convictions. Orthodox Judaism would deny that Judaism has a history at all. Conservative, or positive Historical, Judaism would discover a different goal for history from that embodied by Reform Judaism. But the mode of argument, appealing to issues of a historical and factual character, and the premises of argument, insisting that history proved, or disproved, matters of theological conviction, characterized all the Judaisms of the nineteenth century. And that presents no surprises, since the Judaisms of the age took shape in the intellectual world of Germany, with its profoundly philosophical and historical mode of thought and argument. So the challenge of political change carried with it its own modes of intellectual response: in the academic, scholarly framework. The challenges of the twentieth century exhibited a different character altogether. They were not intellectual but wholly political, and they concerned not matters of political status, but issues of life or death. The Judaic systems of the age then would respond in their own way: through forming instrumentalities of collective action, political power, not theory. But we have moved ahead of our story.

To return to early nineteenth-century Germany and its Judaisms, we observe that the method of the Judaism aborning as Reform exhibited a certain congruence to the locale. Luther had effected his revolution in Christianity by calling for historical facts, deriving solely from Scripture, and how Christianity should or should not frame its doctrines and formulate its holy life. Whether Luther demanding reversion to the pure and primitive faith of the Gospels or the earliest generation of Reform leaders appealing to the Talmud as justification for rejecting what others thought the contemporary embodiment of the Talmud's requirements, the principle remains the same. Reform renews, recovers the true condition of the faith, selects, out of a diverse past, that age and that moment at which the faith attained its perfect definition and embodiment. Not change but restoration and renewal of the true modes, the recovery of the way things were in that perfect, paradigmatic time, that age that formed the model for all time – these deeply mythic modes of appeal formed the justification for change, transforming mere modification of this and that into Reform. But, confronted with dubious allegations as to matters of faith and fact, the leaders of change took on the mantle of Reform, for they revised not only a few lines of a prayer but the entire world-view expressed in the accepted liturgy.

The original changes, in the first decades of the nineteenth century, produced a new generation of rabbis. Some forty years into the century, these rabbis gave to the process of change the name of Reform and created those institutions of Reform Judaism that would endow the inchoate movement with a politics of its own. In the mid-1840s a number of rabbinical conferences brought together the new generation of rabbis. Trained in universities, rabbis who came to these gatherings turned backward, justifying the changes in prayer rites long in place, effecting some further, mostly cosmetic changes in the observance of the Sabbath and in the laws covering personal status through marriage and divorce. In 1845 a decision to adopt for some purposes German in place of Hebrew led to the departure of conservative Reformers, typified by Zacharias Frankel. But the Reformers appealed for their apologia to the received writings, persisting in their insistence that they formed a natural continuation of the processes of the "tradition." Indeed, that point of insistence – that Judaism formed, in Petuchowski's words in regard to Geiger, "a constantly evolving organism"[2] – formed the centerpiece of the nascent Judaism at hand.

Abraham Geiger enjoyed the advantage of the finest argumentative mind in Jewry in the nineteenth century. If we want to understand the new Judaisms of the age, therefore, we turn to the leading intellect to show us how people reached their conclusions, not merely what they said or why they found self-evident the positions that they took. Geiger's life presents facts of less interest than his work, and, in his work, his way of asking and answering questions tells us what matters in Reform Judaism. For that is the point at which we gain access to what people found self-evident on the one side, and urgent on the other. The urgency accounts for the questions, the self-evidence, the mode of discovering the answer. To those two matters, everything else takes second place.

The question Geiger found ineluctable takes simple form: how can we explain what has happened to us? The answer: what has taken place – change become Reform – forms the natural and necessary outcome of history. In his emphasis upon the probative status and value of the facts of history those self-evident principles lead us deep into the consciousness of the man and the Judaism he embodied. What Geiger took for granted – in our terms, held as self-evident – is that history proved propositions of theology. Whatever the particular matter of conviction or custom takes a secondary place. The primary source of verification, therefore, of appropriate and inappropriate traits in Judaism – that is to say, the origin of the reliable definition of Judaism – lies not in revealed records of God's will but in human accounts of humanity's works. To that principle, everywhere taken for granted, occasionally enunciated, but never systematically demonstrated, Geiger's mode of argument and inquiry took second place.

Since the earliest changes changed into reforms, and reforms of Judaism into Reform Judaism, to Geiger we address our principal questions: old or new? And how did people explain themselves? Abraham Geiger presented in clearest form the argument that Reform carried forward the historical processes of Judaism, hence in position both a single, linear Judaism and a Judaism affected by history, that is, by change. He appealed to the facts of history, beginning with the critical study of the Bible. The Reform theologian Jakob J. Petuchowski summarizes his view as follows:

> Judaism is a constantly evolving organism. Biblical Judaism was not identical with classical rabbinic Judaism. Similarly, the modern age calls for further evolution in consonance with the changed circum-

stances . . . The modern rabbis are entitled to adapt medieval Judaism, as the early rabbis had the right to adapt biblical Judaism . . . He found traces of evolution within the Bible itself. Yet for Geiger changes in Judaism had always been organic . . . The modern changes must develop out of the past, and not represent a revolutionary break with it.[3]

Geiger therefore recognized change as "traditional," meaning that changing represents the way things always were and so legitimately now go forward. The Jews change, having moved from constituting a nation to a different classification of social entity. The messiah-idea now addresses the whole of humanity, not only speaking of national restoration. Revelation then turns out to form a progressive, not a static fact. In these diverse ways Geiger – and with him, Reform Judaism through its history – appealed to history to verify its allegations and validate its positions. So facts turn into the evidence for faith.

Geiger was born in 1810 and died in 1874.[4] Growing up in Frankfurt, he undertook university studies at Heidelberg, then Bonn, with special interest in philosophy and Semitics. University study formed the exception, not the rule, for Jews. By definition, therefore, the change Geiger had to explain in fact came about through the decision of the former generation. Geiger explained change. His parents made it. But among the intellectual leaders in Geiger's day, not only he, but his arch-opponent, Samson Raphael Hirsch, founder of Orthodox Judaism, also acquired a university education. So Orthodox Judaism too emerged as the result of the decision of the generation prior to the age of the founders. To both sets of parents therefore the value of an education in the sciences of the West proved self-evident; the ways of harmonizing that education and its values with the education in the Judaic sciences considerably less clear. Earlier generations had not sent their sons to universities (and their daughters would have to wait until nearly our own day for a similar right). So before Geiger and Hirsch could reach the academy, their parents had to find self-evident the value of such an education. But before that generation, most parents found self-evident the value of education in the established institutions of the Judaism of the dual Torah – there alone. Knowledge of another sort, under other auspices, bore no value. So before the advent of the reformer, whether the great intellect of Reform Judaism or the courageous leader of Orthodoxy, change had already characterized modes of self-evident truth.

Geiger served a parlous life in synagogue pulpits, not always appreciated for the virtues he brought to them: flawless German and his questioning of routine.[5] What he did with most of his time, however, concerned not the local synagogue community but the constituency of Judaic learning. He lived for the long future; ideas mattered and would change the world. He was right. He produced a periodical, the *Scientific Journal for Jewish Theology*, from 1835 onward. The purpose of scientific knowledge Wiener epitomizes in the following statement: "They were convinced that, given the historical facts, it would be possible to draw the correct practical conclusions with regard to the means by which their religion could best be served and elevated to the level of contemporary culture."[6] That is to say, through systematic learning Judaism would undergo reform. Reform Judaism rested on deep foundations of scholarship of a certain sort, specifically, of a historical character.

What Geiger had in mind was to analyze the sources of Judaism and the evolution of Judaism. If science (used in its German sense, systematic learning) could uncover the sources of the Jewish "spirit," then, in Wiener's words, "the genius of his people and . . . its vocation" would serve "as a guide to the construction of a living present and future." Geiger's principle of Reform remained fixed. Reform had to emerge from *Wissenschaft*, "a term which he equated with the concept of the understanding of historical evolution."[7] To him "Judaism in its ideal form was religion per se, nothing but an expression of religious consciousness. Its outer shell was subject to change from one generation to another."[8] All things emerge out of time and of change. But when it comes to trace the history of time and change, contemporary categories assuredly defined the inquiry. Thus Geiger produced, out of ancient times, portraits suspiciously congruent to the issues of his own day.

For example, in his account of the Sadducees and Pharisees, the former enjoying a bad press, the latter, in Judaism, a good one, he identified the former with "the strict guardians of traditional institutions, while the latter spoke out in behalf of progress in both religion and politics."[9] Geiger's principal point is as follows:

> What Geiger sought to prove by this demonstration [that the text of Scripture was fluid] is quite obvious. It was not the Bible that created and molded the religious spirit of Judaism; instead, it was the spirit of Judaism that left the stamp of its own form and expression upon the Bible – Life, and its needs and strivings, change from age to age.[10]

What we learn from Wiener's and Petuchowski's accounts of Geiger concerns what Geiger found to be self-evident, truths beyond all appeal that formed the foundation of his life's work as the first and best historian of Judaism. These premises we identify not in the propositions he proposed to demonstrate, facts concerning change and the constancy of change.

Geiger represents Reform Judaism as a restoration of the past. It renews, it does not invent. There was, and is, only a single Judaism. In the current age, Reform undertakes the discovery of that definition. The answer to the question, On what basis does the claim stand? is clear. Reform lays its foundations on the basis of history, which is to say, tradition. Propositions of a theological character, for example, concerning the dual Torah revealed at Sinai, the sanctified and therefore supernatural character of Israel, the holy people, the coming Messiah-sage at the end of times – these take their place in the line of truths to be investigated through historical method, in historical sources. Some may see an incongruity between the propositions at hand and the allegations about the decisive, probative character of historical inquiry in evaluating them. For the facts of history hardly testify, one way or another, concerning the character of revelation at Sinai (though we may know what people recorded in that connection), the status and sanctity of Israel (though the social facts and political issues surely pertained to this-worldly Israel), let alone that event at the end, on the other side, of history altogether, the coming of the Messiah.

Clearly, Reform Judaism, once well under way, would have to situate itself in relationship to the past. Geiger's powerful appeal to precedent left no choice. For not all precedents sustained contemporary choices – the system as it had already emerged – and some of the more recent ones surely called it into question. So as learning rolled forward, the question emerged, Precisely what, in history, serves as a precedent for change become Reform? The answer came down to the appeal to continuing traits of change, the search for constants about change. To advance our understanding of Reform Judaism we move once more to America, the country in which Reform Judaism enjoyed massive success in the last half of the twentieth century. There we see in full and articulate formulation the world-view of Reform Judaism as it unfolded in a straight line from Geiger's day to our own.

Specifically, in his preface to Abraham Cronbach's *Reform Movements in Judaism*,[11] Jacob Rader Marcus, a principal voice in Reform Judaism in the twentieth century, provides a powerful statement of the place of the Reform view in history. Marcus recognizes that diverse Judaisms have flourished in the history of the Jews. What characterizes them all is that each began as a reform movement but then underwent a process we might characterize as "traditionalization." That is to say, change becomes not merely reform but tradition, and the only constant in the histories of Judaisms is that process of transformation of the new to the conventional, or, in theological language, the traditional. This process Marcus describes as follows:

> All [Judaisms] began as rebellions, as great reformations, but after receiving widespread acceptance, developed vested "priestly" interests, failed their people, and were forced to retreat before the onslaught of new rebellions, new philosophies, new challenges.

Nothing in Marcus's picture can have presented a surprise to Geiger. So the fundamental theological method of Reform Judaism in its initial phase, the appeal to facts of history for the validation of theological propositions, endures. But the claim that everything always changes yields a challenge, which Marcus forthrightly raises:

> Is there then nothing but change? Is change the end of all our history and all our striving? No, there is something else, the desire to be free ... In the end [the Jew] has always understood that changelessness is spiritual death. The Jew who would *live* must never completely surrender himself to one truth, but ... must reach out for the farther and faint horizons of an ever Greater God ... This is the meaning of Reform.

Marcus thus treats as self-evident – obvious because it is a fact of history – the persistence of change. And, denying that that is all there is to Reform, at the end he affirms the simple point that change sets the norm. It comes down to the same thing. The something else of Marcus's argument presents its own problems. Appeal to the facts of history fails at that point at which a constructive position demands articulation. "The desire to be free" bears a predicate: free of what? Free to do, to be, what? If Marcus fails to accomplish the whole of the theological task, however, he surely conveys the profoundly constructive vision that Reform Judaism afforded to its Israel.

For his part, Cronbach sets forth as the five precedents for the present movement the Deuteronomic Reformation, the Pentateuchal Reformation, the Pharisaic Reformation, the Karaite Reformation, and the Hasidic Reformation. His coming reformation appeals to social psychology and aims at tolerance: "Felicitous human relationships can be the goal of social welfare and of economic improvement ... Our Judaism of maturity would be dedicated to the ideal of freedom. Corollary of that ideal is what we have just observed about courtesy toward the people whose beliefs and practices we do not share ..."[12]

Reform Judaism attests to a shift in the character of issues found critical by Jews in Germany, the USA, Britain, and elsewhere in Western and Central Europe. The urgent problem was what is Israel in an age in which individual Jews had become something else, in addition to being Israel. Is Israel a nation? No, Israel does not fall into the same category as the nations. Jews are multiple beings: Israel in one dimension, part of France or Germany or America in a second. But if Israel is not a nation, then what of the way of life that had made the nation different, and what of the world-view that had made sense of the way of life? These now formed the questions people could not avoid. The answers constitute Reform Judaism. That Judaism does not carry forward an unbroken tradition and does not claim to. Reform Judaism knew as a matter of fact that Jews' political standing could no longer be tolerated. But how to define a politics appropriate both to Jewry and to the hopes and expectations of Jews in nineteenth-century Europe and twentieth-century America? That issue required a fair amount of picking and choosing.

The questions Reform Judaism confronted and could not evade pertained to the Jews' understanding of themselves as citizens of a state other than an (imaginary) Jewish one, a polity separate from, and in addition to, Israel. When Petuchowski states very simply that Reform Judaism came into existence to deal with political change in the status of Jews,[13] he leads us to the heart of the matter. Reform Judaism was not formed by incremental steps out of the received Judaism ("the tradition"), and it did not move onward along a path in a straight line from where Jews had been to where they wished to go.

Then what do we learn, from the earliest generations of Reform Jews, about the condition of humanity in modern times? The human achievement of Reform deserves a simple observation of what these people did and what they were. With acuity, perspicacity, and enormous courage, the Reformers, nineteenth and twentieth century alike, took the measure of the world and made ample use of the materials they had in hand in manufacturing something to fit it. And Reform did fit those Jews, and they were, and are, very many, to whom the issue of Israel as a supernatural entity remained vivid. For, after all, the centerpiece of Reform Judaism remained its powerful notion that Israel does have a task and a mission, on which account Israel should endure as Israel. Reform Judaism persuaded generations from the beginning to the present of the worth of human life lived in its Judaic system. Those who wanted out – assimilationists, not integrationists – left without difficulty. Reform Jews were Jews who did not want to abandon Judaism, but who also aspired to a place in the social order in which they found themselves. In Germany they were to be disappointed, but in the USA they found precisely what they hoped.

NOTES

1 Jakob J. Petuchowski, "Reform Judaism," *Encyclopaedia Judaica* (Jerusalem, 1971: Keter), 14: 23–8.
2 Petuchowski, "Reform Judaism," col. 25.
3 Ibid.
4 Max Wiener, *Abraham Geiger and Liberal Judaism: The Challenge of the Nineteenth Century*, trans. Ernst J. Schlochauer (1962: Jewish Publication Society of America).
5 Ibid., p. 11.
6 Ibid., p. 13.
7 Ibid., p. 40.
8 Ibid., p. 42.
9 Ibid., p. 50.
10 Ibid., p. 51.
11 New York, 1963: Bookman Associates. Quotations on pp. 7–9.
12 Cronbach, *Reform Movements in Judaism*, p. 132.
13 Petuchowski, "Reform Judaism."

Abraham Cronbach
"The Issues of Reform Judaism in the USA"

Since our picture of Reform Judaism stresses its origins in Germany, we turn now for an account of the life of a Judaism profoundly affected by the conditions of American life and the convictions of American civilization. Rabbi Cronbach surveys these in an authoritative way. Three definitive traits emerge. First, Reform Judaism in the USA takes a position on secular, political issues, trying to formulate out of its Judaic system, with stress on the teachings of the prophets, a truly moral policy. This effort ordinarily leads Reform Judaism to a liberal viewpoint and not infrequently identifies with the Torah the most current planks in the Democratic Party's platform. That Reform Judaism wishes to found its secular politics on the Torah forms a testimony to its deep commitments.

The second striking trait is its accommodation of, then its enthusiastic identification with, Zionism before 1948, and the pro-Israel position that succeeded it in the diaspora communities thereafter. And the third that Cronbach rightly points to is Reform "return to tradition," meaning its capacity to address in a fresh way rites that it formerly rejected. The processes of Reform then show how a Judaic system carries forward its original commitment to a fresh response to the received tradition. The matter has been formulated in a simple phrase by Leonard Fein, a social scientist who has studied Reform Judaism: "Reform is a Verb."

We note, also, in Rabbi Cronbach's account that Reform Judaism does propose to make normative statements on proper conduct, not only right belief. The questions that he lists tell us that in Reform Judaism rabbis still propose to frame teachings that define norms, rules to be obeyed, not just attitudes to be adopted or virtues to be emulated. That accounts for the interesting legal questions that he

> *catalogues. He shows us that Reform Judaism takes with great seriousness its commitment to a dialogue with what people call "the Tradition." Any representation of Reform Judaism as not integrationist but merely assimilationist – a way station out of the Jewish people – is contradicted by the character of Rabbi Cronbach's description of the modern life of that Judaic system.*

When the Central Conference of American Rabbis holds its annual assemblies, one of the numerous issues treated is that of social justice. Those rabbis have put themselves on the liberal side of such issues as collective bargaining, the living wage, arbitration of industrial disputes, employment exchanges, protection of wage-earning women, the abolition of child labor, housing for low income groups, social security, race relations, immigration, birth control, civil liberties, freedom of the press, world peace, the United Nations, the American Peace Corps. Also the Reform Jewish layfolk have officially voiced interest in such matters. The World Union for Progressive Judaism has singled out, for its special concern, international relations. Committees of the World Union channel support for the United Nations, for UNICEF, and for UNESCO.

A strident controversy in Reform Judaism has been that involving Zionism. For decades after the inception of the Zionist movement, Reform Jews stood overwhelmingly in opposition. Within recent decades this has changed. Among the Reform rabbis, the Zionists and the Zionist sympathizers now constitute a majority. A songbook recently issued by the Reform rabbis contains a number of Zionist hymns. When Zionism began to make inroads among the Reform Jewish laity, there came into being the American Council for Judaism, a militantly anti-Zionist fellowship. The American Council for Judaism maintains that there exists no Jewish body which can speak for all Jews. Though evoked by the Zionistic leanings and infiltrations of various Jewish organizations whose avowed objectives are other than Zionism, that protest has been extended by the American Council for Judaism until it applies not only to Zionism but to other issues as well, particularly to certain controversial issues of social and economic change.

A proposal recurrent in Reform Jewish gatherings has been that of increased resort to rituals, including the restoration of rituals which Reform had discarded. "We must retain the high drama of ceremonialism," we are told. "There has been a casting aside of much that was beautiful and accepted in Jewish ceremonial." This probably bespeaks the influence of the East European immigration which, cresting in the early years of the present century and having attained wealth and prestige, has entered the membership of Reform temples. Among the Reform rabbis, though hardly among the laity, there has asserted itself a growing emphasis upon the learning and the using of Hebrew.

On the whole, Reform rabbis are respected by their followers. Between the rabbis and the laity the relationship is usually one of cordiality and comradeship. Still the thinking of the laity sometimes fails to duplicate that of the rabbis. In matters of social justice the rabbinate tends to be the more progressive. In matters of ritual the rabbinate tends more than the laity to hark back to the traditional ways. This may be attributable to the fact that many a Reform rabbi originated in an Orthodox or Conservative family.

From its earliest days Reform Judaism has been coping with the problem of the Sabbath. The assertion has gone unchallenged that, if one were to exclude Sabbath violators from Judaism, one would have to exclude ninety-five percent of world Jewry. Admittedly, active men and women are busier on Saturday than on any other day of the week. Reform leaders have pondered various measures. It has been urged that the Sabbath be transferred to Sunday. A suggested and, in some instances, adopted expedient has been the Sunday service as a supplement to or a substitute for the Saturday service. We also meet vague references to "dignified and meaningful disciplines for the Sabbath."

Another issue among the Reform rabbis has been that of a Reform Jewish creed. Because the word "creed" carries some disquieting overtones – the word hints at some fettering of the intellect – "guiding principles" has been the more favored term. On various occasions such principles have been enunciated. Some were promulgated by the Charleston secessionists of 1824. Other pronouncements have emanated from gatherings of rabbis, pronouncements such as the Philadelphia Platform of 1869, the Pittsburgh Platform of 1885, and the Columbus Platform of 1937. In one or more of these platforms can be found each of the following traits: They declare that God is the Creator of the world, and that God is incorporeal. They dwell upon moral conduct as integral to religion. They urge social justice and international peace. While they reject the doctrine of bodily resurrection, they accept the doctrine of spiritual immortality. They believe in a divinely appointed mission of Israel, although their interpretation of that mission varies. They affirm divine revelation through Scripture and a continuing divine revelation through Jewish history. They stress the importance of prayer. They voice friendliness toward other religions and the willingness to accept proselytes. Some of the pronouncements take pains to convey that no conflict exists between Judaism and modern science.

In the Columbus Platform (1937) one senses a tendency to restore what earlier platforms rejected. The Columbus Platform confesses an obligation to aid in the upbuilding of Palestine; in the earlier platforms Jewish nationalism is spurned. The Philadelphia Platform and the Pittsburgh Platform expand upon the need of abandoning various of the old usages; the Columbus Platform pleads for the preservation of the Sabbath, the festivals, and various of the ceremonials. The Philadelphia Platform recognizes the need of supplanting Hebrew with the vernacular; the Columbus Platform urges that the cultivation and utilization of Hebrew be revived. The Columbus Platform alludes to "Jews who have become estranged," but it values some kind of bond between the estranged and those who are not estranged.

More widely considered, at least among the Reform rabbis, is a Reform code of practice. It is maintained that people need, in fact desire, some directive as regards which rituals to follow and which to ignore. Every convention of the Central Conference of American Rabbis listens to a report of its committee on responsa, responsa meaning replies to questions pertaining to ritual or to matters akin to ritual. There have also appeared some volumes on that topic. Here are some samples of questions for which responsa have been prepared:

Is it permissible to sue in court for the payment of pledges to a synagogue?

Is it intermarriage if the groom is a Jew and the bride is the daughter of a Jewish mother who has become converted to Christianity?

Is it permitted to hold a memorial service in the synagogue on the Sabbath?

Is it permissible to hold a business meeting of a congregation in the temple on a Friday evening after the service?

May discarded prayer books be burnt in the temple furnace?

Is it indispensable for a congregation to have a Hebrew name?

May funerals be held at night?

May Jewish children participate in Christmas celebrations held in public schools?

May a rabbi officiate at the burial of a Jewish person in a Christian cemetery?

May bride and groom see one another on the wedding day prior to the marriage ceremony?

Is it requisite that marriages be attended by at least ten onlookers?

Such questions are answered with a huge output of erudition drawing upon obscure Hebrew sources in a fully Orthodox Jewish manner although, when necessary, the answers are modified by reference to modern conditions.

All this betokens a waning of the conflict with Orthodoxy. Between the Reform group and the other two groups, namely the Orthodox and the Conservative, there has developed considerable *rapprochement* and cooperation. Some Reform rabbis have even envisaged a unification of all three groups, although others maintain that the differences are stimulating and that their effacement would entail a drawback. All of these groups have noticeably influenced one another. It happened once that the president of the Reform Temple Emanu-El in New York City was, at the same time, the board president of the Conservative Jewish Theological Seminary; such has been the degree of overlapping. The stress on Hebrew has been buttressed by the argument that Hebrew is the bond of union among Jews of all rubrics.

There has likewise developed not a little amenity between Reform Jewish leaders and the leaders of Christianity. Exchange of pulpits is frequent. For some decades now Reform temples in various parts of the country have arranged institutes for Christian ministers at which, before and after the hospitality of a luncheon, competent Jewish speakers hold forth on Jewish themes and reply to questions of Jewish import. There are Christian ministers in the student body of the Hebrew Union College–Jewish Institute of Religion, scholarships for such having been provided by Reform Jewish donors. The influence of Christmas is believed to account for the fact that *Hanukkah*, the Jewish festival of the winter solstice, has acquired a prominence unknown in the Jewish past. At the same time not entirely lacking is a little disdain for the "side-glance to see how the Gentile world reacts to the teachings and forms of our faith."

Among the Reform rabbis there has been revived a motif which, though vital in the Judaism of nineteen hundred years ago, has since that time dwindled, namely, the motif of gaining converts. Missions have been proposed for winning to Reform Judaism not the Jewish

Orthodox and not the Jewish Conservatives but the Jewish unaffili-
ated, indifferent, and drifting. Occasionally, though rarely, one hears
Reform Jewish proposals of proselytism for the conversion of Christians. We come upon an utterance like this:

> There is only one religion that could be of help to Western man today,
> and that is Judaism in its Liberal interpretation, for it has no dogmas
> unacceptable to the modern mind, and teaches a noble system of
> ethics. That is what modern man needs now.

The missionary spirit has expressed itself in prognostications. In
1898 Isaac M. Wise exclaimed: "Within twenty-five years all the
world will have accepted Reform Judaism." In 1948 an exuberant
young rabbi proposed "intensifying our mission to our own people
and setting a definite goal of a million Reform Jews for the next
decade." How enthusiasm outruns reality!

3

Orthodox Judaism

Orthodox Judaism among the modern Judaic systems is that integrationist Judaism that mediates between the received Judaism of the dual Torah and the requirements of living a life integrated in modern circumstances. Orthodoxy maintains the world-view of the received dual Torah, constantly citing its sayings and adhering with only trivial variations to the bulk of its norms for the everyday life. At the same time Orthodoxy holds that Jews adhering to the dual Torah may wear clothing that non-Jews wear and do not have to wear distinctively Jewish (even, Judaic) clothing, live within a common economy and not practice distinctively Jewish professions (however, in a given setting, these professions may be defined), and, in diverse ways, take up a life not readily distinguished in important characteristics from the life lived by people in general.

For integrationist Orthodoxy a portion of Israel's life may prove secular, in that the Torah does not dictate and so sanctify all details under all circumstances. Since the Judaism of the dual Torah presupposed not only the supernatural entity Israel, but also a way of life that in important ways distinguished that supernatural entity from the social world at large, the power of Orthodoxy to find an accommodation for Jews who valued the received way of life and world-view and also planned to make their lives in an essentially integrated social world proves formidable. The difference between Orthodoxy and the system of the dual Torah therefore comes to expression in social policy: integration, however circumscribed, versus the total separation of the holy people.

Many people reasonably identify all "traditional" or "observant" Judaism with Orthodoxy, and they furthermore take for granted that all traditional Judaisms are pretty much the same. But viewed from the perspective of differentiation between a Judaic system that accommodates and one that rejects integration, the Judaic systems that affirm the myth of the dual Torah and the authority of the Talmud for law and theology are to be distinguished from one another. The formation of Orthodox Judaism as an articulated Judaic system took place when integrationists proposed an alternative to Reform Judaism. They concurred with the Reformers on the basic social policy of integration, but they differed from them on how integration was to be worked out.

When Jews who kept the law of the Torah, for example, as it dictated food choices and use of leisure time (to speak of the Sabbath and festivals in secular terms), sent their children to secular schools, in addition to or instead of solely Jewish ones, or when, in Jewish schools, they included in the curriculum subjects outside of the sciences of the Torah, they crossed the boundary between the received and the new Judaism. For the notion that science or German or Latin or philosophy deserved serious study, while not alien to important exemplars of the received system of the dual Torah, in the nineteenth century struck as wrong those for whom the received system remained self-evidently right. Those Jews did not send their children to gentile schools, and in Jewish schools did not include in the curriculum other than Torah-study.

Exactly where and when did Orthodox Judaism come into being? It was in Germany, in the middle of the nineteenth century. Orthodox Judaism came to articulated expression among Jews who rejected Reform and made a self-conscious decision to remain within the way of life and world-view that they had known and cherished all their lives. They framed the issues in terms of change and history. The Reformers held that Judaism could change, and that Judaism was a product of history. The Orthodox opponents denied that Judaism could change and insisted that Judaism derived from God's will at Sinai and was eternal and supernatural, not historical and man-made. In these two convictions, of course, the Orthodox recapitulated the convictions of the received system. But in their appeal to the given, the traditional, they found more persuasive some components of that system than they did others, and in the picking and choosing, in the articulation of the view that Judaism formed a religion to be seen as distinct and autonomous of politics, society, "the rest of life," they entered that same world of self-conscious believing that the Reformers also explored.

Orthodoxy advanced as its most powerful argument the claim that it stood for "the Tradition," and that it alone defined authentic

Judaism. But it is when the system lost its power of self-evidence that it entered, among its other apologetic categories, the classification "the Tradition." And that came about when Orthodoxy met head-on the challenge of change become Reform. Just as the Reformers justified change, the Orthodox theologians denied that change was ever possible, so Walter Wurzburger: "Orthodoxy looks upon attempts to adjust Judaism to the 'spirit of the time' as utterly incompatible with the entire thrust of normative Judaism which holds that the revealed will of God rather than the values of any given age are the ultimate standard."[1] To begin with the issue important to the Reformers, the value of what was called "Emancipation," meaning the provision to Jews of civil rights, defined the debate.

When the Reform Judaic theologians took a wholly one-sided position affirming Emancipation, numerous Orthodox ones adopted the contrary view. The position outlined by those theologians followed the agenda laid forth by the Reformers. If the Reform made minor changes in liturgy and its conduct, the Orthodox rejected even those that, under other circumstances, might have found acceptance. Saying prayers in the vernacular, for example, provoked strong opposition. But everyone knew that some of the prayers, said in Aramaic, in fact were in the vernacular of the earlier age. The Orthodox thought that these changes, not reforms at all, represented only the first step of a process leading Jews out of the Judaic world altogether, so, as Wurzburger says, "the slightest tampering with tradition was condemned."

When we explain by reference to political and economic change the beginnings of Reform Judaism – in Central Europe, Germany and the Austro-Hungarian Empire – we also understand the point of origin of Orthodoxy as articulate, self-conscious, distinct and organized. Predictably, then, the beginnings of Orthodoxy took place in the areas where Reform made its way, hence in Germany and in Hungary. In Germany, where Reform attracted the majority of not a few Jewish communities, the Orthodox faced a challenge indeed. Critical to their conviction was the notion that "Israel," all of the Jews, bore responsibility to carry out the law of the Torah. But the community's institutions in the hands of the Reform did not obey the law of the Torah as the Orthodox understood it. So, in the end, Orthodoxy took that step that marked it as a self-conscious Judaism. Orthodoxy separated from the established community altogether. The Orthodox set up their own organization and seceded from the community at large. The next step prohibited Orthodox from participating in non-Orthodox organizations altogether. Isaac

Breuer, a leading theologian of Orthodoxy, would ultimately take the position that "refusal to espouse the cause of separation was interpreted as being equivalent to the rejection of the absolute sovereignty of God."[2]

The matter of accommodating to the world at large, of course, did not allow for so easy an answer as mere separation. The specific issue – integration or segregation – concerned preparation for life in the large politics and economic life of the country, and that meant secular education, involving not only language and science, but history and literature, matters of values. Orthodoxy proved diverse, with two wings to be distinguished, one rejecting secular learning as well as all dealing with non-Orthodox Jews, the other cooperating with non-Orthodox and secular Jews and accepting the value of secular education. That position in no way affected loyalty to the law of Judaism, for example, belief in God's revelation of the one whole Torah at Sinai. The point at which the received system and Orthodox split requires specification. In concrete terms we know the one from the other by the evaluation of secular education. Proponents of the received system never accommodated themselves to secular education, while the Orthodox in Germany and Hungary persistently affirmed it. That represents a remarkable shift, since central to the received system of the dual Torah is study of Torah – Torah, not philosophy.

Explaining where we find the one and the other, Katzburg works with the distinction we have already made, between an unbroken system and one that has undergone a serious caesura with the familiar condition of the past. He states:

> In Eastern Europe until World War I, Orthodoxy preserved without a break its traditional ways of life and the time-honored educational framework. In general, the mainstream of Jewish life was identified with Orthodoxy, while Haskalah [Jewish Enlightenment, which applied to the Judaic setting the skeptical attitudes of the French Enlightenment] and secularization were regarded as deviations. Hence there was no ground wherein a Western type of Orthodoxy could take root . . . European Orthodoxy in the 19th and the beginning of the 20th centuries was significantly influenced by the move from small settlements to urban centers . . . as well as by emigration. Within the small German communities there was a kind of popular Orthodoxy, deeply attached to tradition and to local customs, and when it moved to the large cities this element brought with it a vitality and rootedness to Jewish tradition . . .[3]

Katzburg's observations provide important guidance. He authoritatively defines the difference between Orthodoxy and "tradition." So he tells us how to distinguish the received system accepted as self-evident, and an essentially selective, therefore by definition new, system called Orthodoxy. In particular he guides us in telling the one from the other and where to expect to find, in particular, the articulated, therefore self-conscious, affirmation of "tradition" that characterizes Orthodoxy but does not occur in the world of the dual Torah as it glided in its eternal orbit of the seasons and of unchanging time.

If we ask, how new was the Orthodox system? we find ambiguous answers. In conviction, in way of life, in world-view, we may hardly call it new at all. For the bulk of its substantive positions found ample precedent in the received dual Torah. From its affirmation of God's revelation of a dual Torah to its acceptance of the detailed authority of the law and customs, from its strict observance of the law to its unwillingness to change a detail of public worship, Orthodoxy rightly pointed to its strong links with the chain of tradition. But Orthodoxy constituted a sect within the Jewish group. Its definition of the "Israel" to whom it wished to speak and the definition characteristic of the dual Torah hardly coincide. The Judaism of the dual Torah addressed all Jews, and Orthodoxy recognized that it could not do so. Orthodoxy acquiesced, however, in a situation that lay beyond the imagination of the framers of the Judaism of the dual Torah.

True, the Orthodox had no choice. Their seceding from the community and forming their own institutions ratified the simple fact that they could not work with the Reformers. But the upshot remains the same. That supernatural entity Israel gave up its place, and a natural Israel, a this-worldly political fact, succeeded in its stead. Pained though Orthodoxy was by the fact, it nonetheless accommodated the new social reality – and affirmed it by reshaping the sense of Israel in the supernatural dimension. Their Judaism no less than the Judaism of the Reformers stood for something new, a birth not a renewal – a political response to a new politics. True enough, for Orthodoxy the politics was that of the Jewish community, divided as it was among diverse visions of the political standing of Israel, the Jewish people. For the Reform, by contrast, the new politics derived from the establishment of the category of neutral citizenship in an encompassing nation-state. But the political shifts flowed from the same large-scale changes in Israel's consciousness and character, and, it follows, Orthodoxy as much as Reform represented a set of self-evident answers to political questions that none could evade.

This brings us to the distinction between the religious and the secular, which the Judaism of the dual Torah did not make, but which Orthodox Judaism found itself constrained to adopt. The category "religion," with its counterpart, "secular," recognizes as distinct from "all of life" matters having to do with the Church, the life of faith, the secular as against the sacred. Those distinctions were lost on the received system of the dual Torah, of course, which legislated for matters we should today regard as entirely secular or neutral, for example, the institution of state (such as king, priest, army). We have already noted that, in the received system as it took shape in Eastern and Central Europe, Jews wore garments regarded as distinctively Jewish, and some important traits of these garments indeed derived from the Torah. They pursued sciences that only Jews studied, for instance, the Talmud and its commentaries. In these and other ways, the Torah encompassed all of the life of Israel, the holy people. The recognition that Jews were like others, that the Torah fell into a category into which other and comparable matters fell – that recognition was long in coming.

For Christians it had become a commonplace in Germany and other Western countries to see "religion" as distinct from other components of the social and political system. While the Church in Russia identified with the tsarist state, or with the national aspirations of the Polish people, for example, in Germany two churches, Catholic and Protestant, competed. The terrible wars of the Reformation in the sixteenth and seventeenth centuries, which ruined Germany, had led to the uneasy compromise that the prince might choose the religion of his principality, and, from that self-aware choice, people understood that "the way of life and world-view" in fact constituted a religion, and that one religion might be compared with some other. By the nineteenth century, moreover, the separation of church and state ratified the important distinction between religion, where difference would be tolerated, and the secular, where citizens were pretty much the same.

That fact of political consciousness in the West reached the Judaic world only in the late eighteenth century for some intellectuals, and in the nineteenth century for large numbers of others. It registered, then, as a fundamental shift in the understanding and interpretation of "the Torah," now seen, among Orthodox as much as among Reform, as "Judaism," an -*ism* along with other -*isms*. A mark of the creative power of the Jews who formed the Orthodox Judaic system derives from their capacity to shift the fundamental category in which they framed their system. The basic shift in category is what made

Orthodoxy a Judaism on its own, not simply a restatement, essentially in established classifications, of the received system of the dual Torah.

If we ask how Orthodox Judaism, so profoundly rooted in the canonical writings and received convictions of the Judaism of the dual Torah, at the same time made provision for the issues of political and cultural change at hand, we recognize the importance of the shift in category contributed by Orthodoxy. Orthodox Judaism took the view that one could observe the rules of the Judaic system of the ages and at the same time keep the laws of the state. More important, Orthodox Judaism took full account of the duties of citizenship, so far as being a good citizen imposed the expectation of conformity in certain aspects of everyday life. So a category, "religion," could contain the Torah, and another category, "the secular," could allow Jews a place in the accepted civic life of the country. The importance of the category-shift therefore lies in its power to accommodate the political change so important, also, to Reform Judaism. The Jews' differences from others would fit into categories in which difference was (in Jews' minds, at any rate) acceptable, and would not violate those lines to which all citizens had to adhere.

To review the fundamental shift represented by the distinction between secular and religious, we recall our original observation that Jews no longer wished to wear distinctively Jewish clothing, for example, or to speak a Jewish language, or to pursue only Jewish learning under Jewish auspices. Yet the received system, giving expression to the rules of sanctification of the holy people, did entail wearing Jewish clothing, speaking a Jewish language, learning only, or mainly, Jewish sciences. So clothing, language, and education now fell into the category of the secular, while other equally important aspects of everyday life remained in the category of the sacred. Orthodox Judaism, as it came into existence in Germany and other Western countries, therefore found it possible by recognizing the category of the secular to accept the language, clothing, and learning of those countries. And these matters serve only to exemplify a larger acceptance of gentile ways, not all but enough to lessen the differences between the Holy People and the nations. Political change of a profound order, which made Jews call into question some aspects of the received system – if not most or all of them, as would be the case for Reform Judaism – presented to Jews who gave expression to Orthodox Judaism the issues at hand: how separate, how integrated? And the answers required picking and choosing, different things to be sure, just as much as, in principle, the Reform Jews picked and chose.

Both Judaisms understood that some things were sacred, others not, and that understanding marked these Judaisms off from the system of the dual Torah.

Once the category-shift had taken place, the difference was to be measured in degree, not kind. For Orthodox Jews maintained those distinctive beliefs, which Reform Jews rejected, of a political character in the future coming of the Messiah and the reconstitution of the Jewish nation in its own land. But, placing these convictions in the distant future, the Orthodox Jews nonetheless prepared for a protracted interim of life within the nation at hand – like the Reform, different in religion, not in nationality as represented by citizenship. What follows for our inquiry is that Orthodoxy, as much as Reform, signals remarkable changes in the Jews' political situation and – more important – aspiration. They did want to be different, but not so different as the received system would have made them.

Still, Orthodoxy in its nineteenth-century formulation laid claim to carry forward, in continuous and unbroken relationship, "the tradition." That claim assuredly demands a serious hearing, for the things that Orthodoxy taught, the way of life it required, the Israel to whom it spoke, the doctrines it deemed revealed by God to Moses at Sinai – all of these conformed more or less exactly to the system of the received Judaism of the dual Torah as people then knew it. So any consideration of the issue of a linear and incremental history of Judaism has to take at face value the character, and not merely the claim, of Orthodoxy. But we do not have without reflection to concede that claim. Each Judaism, after all, demands study not in categories defined by its own claims of continuity, but in those defined by its own distinctive and characteristic choices. For a system takes shape and then makes choices – in that order. But the issue facing us in Orthodoxy is whether or not Orthodoxy can be said to make choices at all. For is it not what it says it is, "just Judaism"? Indeed so, but the dual Torah of the received tradition hardly generated the base-category "Judaism." And "Judaism," Orthodox or otherwise, is not "Torah."

By adopting for themselves the category religion, and by recognizing a distinction between religion and the secular, the holy and other categories of existence, the founders of Orthodoxy performed an act of choice and selectivity. The Torah found itself transformed into an object, a thing out there, a matter of choice, deliberation, affirmation. In that sense Orthodoxy recognized a break in the line of the received "tradition;" and proposed to repair the break: a self-conscious, a modern decision. The issues addressed by Orthodoxy, the questions its framers found ineluctable – these take second place. The primary consideration in our assessment of the claim of Orthodoxy to carry forward, in a straight line, the incremental history of a single Judaism carries us to the fundamental categories within which Orthodoxy pursued its thought, but the Judaism of the dual Torah did not. The Judaism of the dual Torah had no word for Judaism, and Orthodoxy did (and does).

For nineteenth-century Reform and Orthodox theologians alike, the category "Judaism" defined what people said when they wished all together and all at once to describe what the Jews believe, or the Jewish religion, or similar matters covering religious ideas viewed as a system and as a whole. It therefore constituted a philosophical category, an *-ism*, instructing thinkers to seek the system and order and structure of ideas: the doctrine of this, the doctrine of that, in Juda-*ism*. The nineteenth-century Judaic religious thinkers invoked the category Judaism when they proposed to speak of the whole of Judaic religious existence. Available to the Judaism of the dual Torah are other categories, other words, to tell how to select and organize and order data: all together, all at once to speak of the whole.

To the Jews who abided within the received Judaism of the dual Torah, the discovery of Orthodoxy therefore represented an innovation, a shift from the perceivedly self-evident truths of the Torah. For their word for Judaism was Torah, and when they spoke of the whole all at once, they used the word Torah – and they also spoke of different things from the things encompassed by Judaism. For the received Judaism of the dual Torah did not use the word the nineteenth-century theologians used when speaking of the things of which they spoke when they said Juda-*ism*. The received system not only used a different word, but in fact referred to different things. The two categories – Judaism and Torah – which are supposed to refer to the same data in the same social world, in fact encompass different data from those taken in categorically by Judaism. So we contrast the two distinct categories, Judaism and Torah.

Let me spell out what is at stake here. *Judaism* falls into the classification of a philosophical or ideological or theological one, a logos: a word, while *Torah* fell into the classification of a symbol, that is, a symbol that in itself encompassed the whole of the system that the category at hand was meant to describe. The species *-ism* falls into the classification of the genus, logos, while the species Torah, while using words, transcends words. It falls into a different classification, a species of the genus symbol. How so? The *-ism*-category does not invoke an encompassing symbol but a system of thought.

Judaism is an it, an object, a classification, an action. Torah, for its part, is an everything in one thing, a symbol. I cannot imagine a more separate and unlike set of categories than Judaism and Torah, even though both encompassed the same way of life and world-view and addressed the same social group. So Torah as a category serves as a symbol, everywhere present in detail and holding all the details together. Judaism as a category serves as a statement of the main points: the intellectual substrate of it all.

The conception of Judaism as an organized body of doctrine, as in the sentence *Judaism teaches*, or *Judaism says*, derives from an age in which people further had determined that Judaism belonged to the category of religion, and, of still more definitive importance, a religion was something that *teaches* or *says*. That is to say, Judaism is a religion, and a religion to begin with is (whatever else it is) a composition of beliefs. That age is the one at hand, the nineteenth century, and the category of religion as a distinct entity emerges from Protestant theological thought. For in Protestant theological terms, one is saved by faith. But the very components of that sentence – one (individual, not the people or holy nation), saved (personally, not in history, and saved, not sanctified), faith (not *mitzvot*) – in fact prove incomprehensible in the categories constructed by Torah. Constructions of Judaic dogmas, the specification of a right doctrine – an ortho-doxy – and the insistence that one can speak of religion apart from such adventitious matters as clothing and education (for the Orthodox of Germany who dressed like other Germans and studied in universities, not only in yeshivas) or food (for the Reform), testify to the same fact: the end of self-evidence, the substitution of the distinction between religion and secularity, the creation of *Judaism* as the definitive category.

In fact in the idiomatic language of Torah-speech one cannot make such a statement in that way about, or in the name of, Judaism – not an operative category at all. In accord with the modes of thought and speech of the received Judaism of the dual Torah, one has to speak of Israel, not the private person, to address not only individual life but all of historical time. Not only so, but one native to the speech of the Torah will use the words of *mitzvot*, commanded deeds, not of faith alone. So the sentence serves for Protestant Christianity but not for the Torah. Of course "Judaism," Orthodox or Reform, for its part will also teach things and lay down doctrines, even dogmas.

The counterpart, in the realm of self-evidence comprised by the received Judaism of the dual Torah, of the statement *Judaism teaches*, can only be, *the Torah requires*, and the predicate of such a sentence would be not . . . *that God is one*, but, . . . *that you say a blessing before eating bread*. The category Judaism encompasses, classifies, and organizes doctrines: the faith, which, by the way, an individual adopts and professes. The category Torah teaches what "we," God's holy people, are and what "we" must do. The counterpart to the statement of Judaism "God is one" then is, ". . . who has sanctified us by his commandments and commanded us to . . ." The one teaches, that is, speaks of intellectual matters and beliefs, the latter demands – social actions and deeds of us, matters of public consequence – including, by the way, affirming such doctrines as God's unity, the resurrection of the dead, the coming of the Messiah, the revelation of the Torah at Sinai, and on and on: "we" can rival the Protestants in heroic deeds of faith. So it is true, the faith demands deeds, and deeds presuppose faith. But, categorically, the emphasis is what it is: Torah on God's revelation, the canon, to Israel and its social way of life, Judaism on a system of belief. That is a significant difference between the two categories, which, as I said, serve a single purpose, namely, to state the thing as a whole.

Equally true, one would (speaking systemically) also *study Torah*. But what one studied was not an intellectual system of theology or philosophy, rather a document of revealed Scripture and law. That is not to suggest that the theologians of Judaism, Orthodox or Reform, of the nineteenth century did not believe that God is one, or that the philosophers who taught that "Judaism teaches ethical monotheism" did not concur that, on that account, one has to say a blessing before eating bread. But the categories are different, and, in consequence, so too are the composites of knowledge. A book on Judaism explains the doctrines, the theology or philosophy, of Judaism. A book of the holy Torah expounds God's will as revealed in "the one whole Torah of Moses, our rabbi," as sages teach and embody God's will. I cannot imagine two more different books, and the reason is that they represent totally different categories of intelligible discourse and of knowledge. Proof, of course, is that the latter books are literally unreadable. They form part of a genuinely oral exercise, to be cited sentence by sentence and expounded in the setting of other sentences, from other books, the whole made cogent by the speaker. That process of homogenization is how Torah works as a generative category. It obscures other lines of structure and order.

True, the two distinct categories come to bear upon the same body of data, the same holy books. But the consequent compositions – selections of facts, ordering of facts, analyses of facts, statements of conclusion and interpretation, and, above all, modes of public discourse, meaning who says what to whom – bear no relationship to one another, none whatsoever. Indeed, the compositions more likely than not do not even adduce the same facts, or even refer to them.

How is it that the category I see as imposed, extrinsic, and deductive, namely, "Judaism," attained the status of self-evidence? Categories serve because they are self-evident to a large group of people. In the case at hand, therefore, Judaism serves because it enjoys self-evidence as part of a larger set of categories that are equally self-evident. In all of these categories, religion constitutes a statement of belief distinct from other aspects and dimensions of human existence, so religions form a body of well-composed -isms. So whence the category "Judaism"? The source of the categorical power of "Judaism" derives from the Protestant philosophical heritage that has defined scholarship, including category formation, from the time of Kant onward. "*Juda*" + "*ism*" do not constitute self-evident, let alone definitive, categories – except where they do. Judaism constitutes a category asymmetrical to the evidence adduced in its study. The category does not work because the principle of formation is philosophical and does not emerge from an unmediated encounter with the Torah. Orthodoxy can have come into existence only in Germany, and, indeed, only in that part of Germany in which the philosophical heritage of Kant and Hegel defined the categories of thought, also, for religion. And this brings us to Samson Raphael Hirsch, who defined Orthodox Judaism.

The importance of Hirsch (1808–88), first great intellect of Orthodoxy, derives from his philosophy of joining Torah with secular education, producing a synthesis of Torah and modern culture. He represents the strikingly new Judaism at hand, exhibiting both its strong tie to the received system and also its innovative and essentially new character. Sometimes called "neo-Orthodox,"[4] Hirsch's position laid stress on the possibility of living in the secular world and, by sustaining a fully Orthodox life, rallied the Jews of the counter-reformation. But Hirsch and his followers took over one principal position of Reform, the possibility of integrating Jews in modern society. What made Hirsch significant was that he took that view not only on utilitarian grounds, as Samet says, "but also through the acceptance of its scale of values, aiming at creating a symbiosis between traditional Orthodoxy and modern German-European culture; both in theory and in practice this meant abandonment of Torah study for its own sake and adopting instead an increased concentration on practical halakhah."[5] On that basis we rightly identify Orthodoxy as a distinct Judaism from the system of the dual Torah. Hirsch himself studied at the University of Bonn, specializing in classical languages, history, and philosophy.[6] So, as we noted, he did not think one had to spend all his time studying Torah, and in going to a university he implicitly affirmed that he could not define, within Torah-study, all modes of learning. Gentile professors knew things worth knowing. But continuators of the Judaism of the dual Torah thought exactly the opposite: whatever is worth knowing is in the Torah.

In his rabbinical posts, Hirsch published a number of works to appeal to the younger generation. His ideal for them was the formation of a personality that would be both enlightened and observant, that is to say, educated in Western knowledge and observant of the Judaic way of life. This ideal took shape through an educational program that encompassed Hebrew language and holy literature, and also German, mathematics, sciences, and the like. In this way he proposed to respond to the Reformers' view that Judaism in its received form constituted a barrier between Jews and German society. The Reformers saw the received way of life as an obstacle to the sort of integration they thought wholesome and good. Hirsch concurred in the ideal and differed on detail. Distinctive Jewish clothing, in Hirsch's view, enjoyed a low priority. Quite to the contrary, he himself wore a ministerial gown at public worship, which did not win the approbation of the traditionalists, and when he preached, he encompassed not only the law of the Torah but other biblical matters, equally an innovation. Hirsch argued that Judaism and secular education could form a union. This would require the recognition of externals, which could be set aside, and the emphasis on the principles, which would not change. So Hirsch espoused what, in the ideas of those fully within the mentality of self-evidence, constituted selective piety, and, while the details differed, therefore fell within the classification of reform.

In his selections Hirsch included changes in the conduct of the liturgy, involving a choir, congregational singing, sermons in the vernacular – a generation earlier sure marks of Reform. He required prayers to be said only in Hebrew and Jewish subjects to be taught in that language. He opposed all changes in the Prayer Book. At the same time he sustained organizational relationships with the Reformers and tried to avoid schism. By mid-career, however, toward the middle of the century, Hirsch could not tolerate the Reformers' abrogation of the dietary laws and those affecting marital relationships, and he made his break, accusing the Reformers of disrupting

Israel's unity. In the following decades he encouraged Orthodox Jews to leave the congregations dominated by Reform, even if, in the locale, such was the only synagogue. Separationist synagogues formed in the larger community.

We come now to Hirsch's framing of issues of doctrine. He constructed an affirmative system, not a negative one. His principal argument stressed that the teachings of the Torah constitute facts beyond all doubt, as much as the facts of nature do not allow for doubt. This view of the essential facticity – the absolute givenness – of the Torah led to the further conviction that human beings may not deny the Torah's teachings even when they do not grasp the Torah's meaning. Wisdom is contained within the Torah, God's will is to be found there. Just as the physical laws of nature are not conditioned by human search, so the rules of God's wisdom are unaffected by human search. The Torah constitutes an objective reality, and, in Katz's words, its laws form "an objective disposition of an established order that is not dependent on the will of the individual or society, and hence not even on historical processes."[7] Humanity nonetheless may through time gain religious truth.

What makes Israel different is that they gain access to the truth not through experience but through direct revelation. Gentile truth is truth, but derives from observation and experience. What Israel knows through the Torah comes through a different medium. That people then stands outside of history and does not have to learn religious truth through the passage of history and changes over time. Israel then forms a supernatural entity, a view certainly in accord with the Judaism of the dual Torah. But when it came to explaining the way of life at hand, Hirsch went his own way. Hirsch pursued a theory of the practice of the religious life through concrete deeds – the commandments – in a highly speculative and philosophical way. What he maintained was that each of the deeds of the way of life represented something beyond itself, served as a symbol, not as an end in itself. So when a Jew carries out a holy deed, the deed serves to make concrete a revealed truth. This mode of thought transforms the way of life into an exercise in applied theology and practical, practiced belief.

Hirsch's theory of who is Israel stood at the opposite pole from that of Geiger and the Reformers. To them, as we have seen, Israel fell into the classification of a religious community, that alone. To Hirsch Israel constituted a people, not a religious congregation, and Hirsch spoke of "national Jewish consciousness": "The Jewish people, though it carries the Torah with it in all the lands of its dispersion, will never find its table and lamp except in the Holy Land." Israel performs a mission among the nations, to teach "that God is the source of blessing." Israel then falls between, forming its own category, because it has a state system, in the land, but also a life outside.[8] In outlining this position, Hirsch of course reaffirmed the theory of the supernatural Israel laid forth in the dual Torah. The power of the national ideal for Hirsch lay in its polemical force against the assimilationists and Reformers, whom he treated as indistinguishable:

> The contempt with which the assimilationists treat David's [fallen] tabernacle and the prayer for the sacrificial service clearly reveals the extent of their rebellion against Torah and their complete disavowal of the entire realm of Judaism. They gather the ignorant about them to whom the Book of Books, the Divine national document of their Jewish past and future, is closed with seven seals. With a conceit engendered by stupidity and a perfidy born from hatred they point to God's Temple and the Divine Service in Zion as the unholy center of the "bloody cult of sacrifices." Consequently, they make certain to eliminate any reference to the restoration of the Temple service from our prayers . . . The "cultured, refined" sons and daughters of our time must turn away with utter disgust from their "pre-historic, crude" ancestors who worship their god with bloody sacrifices . . .

Hirsch reviews the long line of exalted leaders who affirmed sacrifice and who were not crude, for example, Moses, Isaiah, Jeremiah, and on. Then he concludes:

> The Jewish sacrifice expresses the highest ideal of man's and the nation's moral challenge. Blood and kidney, head and limbs symbolize our service of God with every drop of blood, every emotion, every particle of our being. By performing the act of sacrifice at the place chosen by God as the site of His Law, we proclaim our determination to fulfill our lofty moral and ethical tasks to enable God to bless the site of the national vow with the presence of this glory and with the fullness of this love and grace.[9]

Hirsch's spiritualization of the sacrifices, in an ample tradition of precedent, to be sure, derives from the challenge of Reform. Demanding an acceptance at face value of the Torah as the revelation of God's wisdom, Hirsch nonetheless made the effort to appeal to more than the givenness of the Torah and its commandments.

On the contrary, he entered into argument in the same terms – spiritualization, lofty moral and ethical tasks – as did the Reformers.

That marks his thought as new and responsive to a fresh set of issues. As to the Reformers, he met them on their ground, as he had to, and his principal points of insistence to begin with derived from the issues defined by others. That is why we may find for him a suitable place in the larger setting of discourse among the Judaisms of the nineteenth century, all of them products of the end of self-evidence and the beginning of a self-conscious explanation for what had formerly, and elsewhere in the age at hand, the authority of the absolutely given. We see that fact most clearly when we take up a single stunning instance of the possibility of locating the several Judaisms on a single continuum: the doctrine of the Torah, what it is, where it comes from.

The Judaism of the dual Torah by definition maintained that not only the Hebrew Scriptures ("Old Testament") but also the entire canon of rabbinic writings constituted that one whole Torah that Moses received at Sinai. The three Judaisms of the nineteenth century met that issue head on. Each of the possibilities – only Scripture, everything, some things but not others – found proponents. The consequent theory of revelation had to explain the origin and authority of each of the components of the received canon. And, further, that theory of revelation had to explain what, precisely, revelation meant. The position of Orthodoxy on this matter takes on significance only in the larger context of the debate with Reform. Reform through Geiger took the view that revelation was progressive. The Bible derived from "the religious genius of the Jewish people." Orthodoxy through Hirsch as the example saw the Torah as wholly and completely God's word. A middle position, represented by Conservative Judaism, espoused both views. God revealed the written Torah, which was supplemented by "the ongoing revelation manifesting itself throughout history in the spirit of the Jewish people."[10]

Orthodoxy of course could not concur. The issue pertained to the historical identification of those responsible for the rabbinic writings. The Conservatives, in the person of Zechariah Frankel, a contemporary of Hirsch, maintained that the whole of the rabbinic corpus derived from scribes and their successors. These authorities adapted the system of Scripture by inventing the notion of the Oral Torah. The Orthodox could not concede such a break. The positive historical school, in Wurzburger's description, held that "the religious consciousness of the Jewish people provided the supreme religious authority, [while] the Orthodox position rested upon the belief in the supernatural origin of the Torah which was addressed to a 'Chosen People.'" So the theory of who is Israel joined to the issue of revelation: how, what, when? The Orthodox position, as outlined by Hirsch, saw Israel as a supernatural people that has in hand a supernatural revelation. The entirety of the dual Torah and the writings flowing from it constitute that revelation. Quite how this notion of a long sequence of revealed documents differs from the conception of a progressive revelation is not entirely clear, but in context it made a considerable difference. For in his affirmation of the entirety of the Torah, written and oral, as the revealed will of God, Hirsch marked the boundaries of Orthodoxy and made them coincide with the precise boundaries of the received dual Torah. Whether those to whom the supernatural character of Israel and the entirety of Torah formed self-evident truths will have understood Hirsch's careful explanations of matters outside of the received modes of apologetics, however, must come under doubt. For the one thing the traditionalist grasped, the absolute givenness of the whole, Hirsch could not concede. How do we know it? Because he explained and explained and explained.

Hirsch spent much energy defending the practice of the religious duties called commandments, such as circumcision, the wearing of fringes on garments, the use, in morning worship, of *tefillin* (commonly translated phylacteries), and the sacrificial cult and Temple. These he treats not as utter data – givens of the holy life. Rather, he transforms them into symbols of a meaning beyond. And that exercise, in his context, testifies to the utter self-consciousness of the Judaism at hand, hence to the formation of a new Judaism out of received materials, no less than Reform Judaism constituted a new Judaism out of those same received materials. For the sole necessity for making up such symbolic explanations derived from decision: defend these, at all costs. Equivalent explanations and a counterpart process of articulated defense of the holy way of life hardly struck as equivalently urgent the contemporaries of Hirsch living in the villages of the East.

When, therefore, Hirsch invoked the parallel, to which we have already alluded, between the study of nature and the study of the Torah, he expressed the freshness, the inventiveness, of his own system, thereby testifying to the self-consciousness at hand. A sizable abstract provides a good view of Hirsch's excellent mode of thought and argument:

> One word here concerning the proper method of Torah investigation. Two revelations are open before us, that is, nature and the Torah. In nature all phenomena stand before us as indisputable facts, and we can

only endeavor *a posteriori* to ascertain the law of each and the connection of all. Abstract demonstration of the truth, or rather, the probability of theoretical explanations of the acts of nature, is an unnatural proceeding. The right method is to verify our assumptions by the known facts, and the highest attainable degree of certainty is to be able to say: "The facts agree with our assumption" – that is, all the phenomena observed can be explained according to our theory. A single contradictory phenomenon will make our theory untenable. We must, therefore, acquire all the knowledge possible concerning the object of our investigation and know it, if possible, in its totality. If, however, all efforts should fail in disclosing the inner law and connection of phenomena revealed to us as facts in nature, the facts remain, nevertheless, undeniable and cannot be reasoned away.

The same principles must be applied to the investigation of the Torah. In the Torah, even as in nature, God is the ultimate cause. In the Torah, even as in nature, no fact may be denied, even though the reason and the connection may not be understood. What is true in nature is true also in the Torah: the traces of divine wisdom must ever be sought. Its ordinances must be accepted in their entirety as undeniable phenomena and must be studied in accordance with their connection to each other, and the subject to which they relate. Our conjectures must be tested by their precepts, and our highest certainty here also can only be that everything stands in harmony with our theory.

In nature the phenomena are recognized as facts, though their cause and relationship to each other may not be understood and are independent of our investigation. So too the ordinances of the Torah must be law for us, even if we do not comprehend the reason and the purpose of a single one. Our fulfillment of the commandments must not depend on our investigations.[11]

Here we have the counterpart, in argument, to Hirsch's theory of Torah and worldly learning. Just as Hirsch maintained the union of the two, so in the deepest structure of his thought he worked out that same union. Natural science dictated rules of inquiry, specifically, the requirement that we explain phenomena through a theory that we can test. The phenomenon is the given. Then, for the Torah, the requirements of the Torah constitute the givens, which demand explanation, but which must be accepted as facts even when explanation fails. Clearly, Hirsch addressed an audience that had come to doubt the facticity of the facts of the Torah in a way in which none doubted the facticity of the facts of nature.

Once we compare the Torah to nature, the Torah no longer defines the world-view and the way of life at hand. Rather, the Torah takes its place as part of a larger world-view and way of life, one in which the Israelite-human being (in Hirsch's happy concept) has to accommodate both the received of the Torah and the given of nature. The insistence that the process of accommodation – "studied in accordance with their connection . . . and the subject to which they relate" – testifies to a world-view essentially distinct from the one of the received system of the dual Torah. In this new world-view the Torah demands explanation, its rules find themselves reduced to the lesser dimensions of an apologia of symbolism, so that they form not givens in an enduring and eternal way of life, but objects of analysis, defense, above all, reasoned decision. True, Hirsch insisted, "our fulfillment of the commandments must not depend on our investigations." But the investigations must go forward, and that, in and of itself, tells us we deal with a new Judaism.

Orthodoxy never claimed to mark the natural next step in the history of Judaism. Orthodoxy saw itself as nothing other than Judaism. In its near-total symmetry with the received system, Orthodoxy surely made a powerful case for that claim. But the fact that the case had to be made, the context and conditions of contention – these form the indicators that another Judaism was coming into being. The asymmetrical points, moreover, demand attention, though, on their own, they should not decisively refute the position of Orthodoxy. What does is the existence of an Orthodoxy at all. Orthodoxy defends propositions that, in the received system, scarcely reached a level of articulated discourse, for instance, the absolute necessity to conform to the holy way of life of the Torah. The necessity for making such an argument testifies to the fact that people, within Orthodoxy, thought they confronted the need to choose and did choose. True, the choices, from the viewpoint of Orthodoxy, fell in the right direction. But Orthodoxy formed an act of restoration and renewal, therefore an act of innovation.

The modes of argument of Hirsch, representative as they are of the mentality of the Orthodoxy he defined, call into question the linear descent of Orthodoxy from what people called "tradition." An incremental progress, perhaps, but a lineal and unbroken journey, no. But even the incremental theory of the history of Judaism, which, in the case of Orthodoxy, identifies Hirsch's Orthodoxy with the system of the dual Torah, fails to take note of facts, and, as Hirsch himself argues, that failure suffices. The facts are that people, Hirsch included, made clear-cut choices, identifying some things as essential, others not (clothing, for one important instance). If the piety of Reform proved selective, the selections that Hirsch made place him into the classification, also, of one who sorted out change and made

changes. Just as the Reformers of the nineteenth century laid emphasis on the points of continuity they located between themselves and
the past, so, of course, did the Orthodox (and, from their perspective,
with better reason). Just as the Orthodox of the nineteenth century
specify what mattered more than something else, so, of course, did
the Reform (and, from their perspective, with greater relevance to the
situation at hand).

Piety selected is by definition piety invented, and Hirsch emerges
as one of the intellectually powerful creators of a Judaism. "Torah
and secular learning" defined a new world-view, dictated a new way
of life, and addressed a different Israel from the Judaism of the dual
Torah. To those who received that dual Torah as self-evident, what
the Torah did not accommodate was secular learning. The Torah as
they received it did not approve changes in the familiar way of life,
and did not know an Israel other than the one at hand. So the perfect
faith of Orthodoxy sustained a wonderfully selective piety. What
accounts for the human greatness of Hirsch and the large number of
Jews who found self-evident the possibility of living the dual life of
Jew and German or Jew and American? It lay in the power of the
imagination to locate, in a new circumstance, a rationale for inventing tradition.

NOTES

1   Nathaniel Katzburg and Walter S. Wurzburger, "Orthodoxy,"
    Encyclopaedia Judaica (Jerusalem, 1971: Keter), 12: 1486–93. Quota-
    tion: col. 1487.
2   Ibid., col. 1488.
3   Ibid., col. 1490.
4   Moshe Shraga Samet, "Neo-Orthodoxy," *Encyclopaedia Judaica*
    (Jerusalem, 1971: Keter), 12: 956–8.
5   Ibid., col. 957.
6   Simha Katz, "Samson (ben) Raphael Hirsch," *Encyclopaedia Judaica*
    (Jerusalem, 1971: Keter), 8: 508–15.
7   Ibid., col. 512–13.
8   Ibid., col. 514.
9   Samson Raphael Hirsch, *The Collected Writings* (New York and Jerusa-
    lem, 1984: Philipp Feldheim), 1: 388–9.
10 Katzburg and Wurzburger, "Orthodoxy," col. 1489.
11 Samson Raphael Hirsch, *The Collected Writings* (New York and Jerusa-
    lem, 1984: Philipp Feldheim), III: *Jewish Symbolism*, pp. xiii–xiv.

Charles Liebman
"Religion and the Chaos of Modernity: The Case of Contemporary Judaism"

People ordinarily distinguish Judaisms into three wings, Reform, Orthodox, and Conservative. But while a single and homogeneous Reform Judaism and Conservative Judaism may be identified in the USA, and Reform and Liberal Judaism in Britain agree on much, Orthodoxy is comprised of many Judaisms, all of them Orthodox in conviction and in practice, yet each of them different from the others in a variety of ways. Distinguishing one from the other becomes feasible when we ask some fundamental questions. For one example, does this Orthodox Judaism provide for Jews to live among gentiles, or does it wish to separate them from gentiles? That is, some Orthodox Judaisms are segregationist, others, integrationist. For example, in the USA the Orthodox Judaism organized around Yeshiva University and the Rabbinical Council of America affirms secular education and teaches that Jews may participate in the everyday life of the country but also preserve the holy way of life of the faith. But in the USA Orthodox Judaisms also flourish that want the Jews to speak their own language, Yiddish, and to associate with gentiles, if at all, only in the secular workplace. Again, some Orthodox Judaisms possess beliefs in addition to those common to all of Orthodoxy, the Hasidic Judaisms with their special doctrines about the special holiness of the rebbe being good illustrations of that point. Some Orthodox Judaisms are anti-Zionist and reject the State of Israel; some are non-Zionist and accommodate the State; and some are Zionist, the third group organized around Bar Ilan University and the Zionist-Religious political parties of the State of Israel. In these and other ways, Orthodoxy produces the most complex and nuanced set of Judaisms of any of the modern formulations of the ancient Torah. In the present framework, Charles Liebman, the Israeli sociologist of

Judaism, analyzes the adaptationist Orthodox Judaism that began with Hirsch and flourishes today in both Zionist Orthodox Judaism in the State of Israel and US Orthodox Judaism centered on Yeshiva University and the United Synagogue Orthodox of Great Britain.

The adaptationist response to modernity is to affirm that the basic values of the modern world are not only compatible with Judaism but partake of its essence. Freedom, individual autonomy, equality of man, rationalism, science, rule of law, etc., are all found to be inherent in the Jewish tradition. Secular study is affirmed as a positive religious value – an instrument whereby man might learn more of God's creation. Not least important, adaptationism includes an effort to reinterpret the tradition including those aspects of the law which seem to stand in opposition to modern values.

Adaptationism characterizes some early leaders associated with what is today known as Conservative Judaism (Davis, 1963; Siegel, 1978). Until recently, when more radical and self-conscious reinterpretations of Jewish law and conscious deviations from its norms have become pronounced, the label "adaptationism" suited leadership groups within the Conservative movement in particular. In fact, until the last few years, that which distinguished Orthodox adaptationists from some leadership groups within the Conservative movement was institutional, familial, and social ties no less than the degree of adaptation.

Orthodox adaptationists were ready to affirm the spirit and values of modernity but were far more cautious in the realm of religious behavior. Some, however, countenanced dancing, "mixed" swimming, married women uncovering their hair, and some degree of leniency in Sabbath observance law. There are Israeli religious authorities (Chief Rabbi Goren is an example) whose rulings tend to be adaptationist, without any ideological self-consciousness or philosophical underpinning. Emanuel Rackman, whose work is best known in the United States though he now resides in Israel, is the leading theoretical exponent of Orthodox adaptationism. He writes that:

> The only authentic Halakhic approach must be that which approximates the philosophy of the teleological jurist. The teleological jurist asks: what are the ends of the law which God or nature ordained and how can we be guided by these ideal ends in developing the law? (Rackman, 1961: 14).

The results, Rackman says, must not only meet the challenge of revelation but of history and of Jewish life in the present. By way of example he notes that:

> If rabbis have no sympathy whatever with the demands of modern women for equal status in the Jewish law of marriage and divorce, they will find texts adequate to support their intransigence. If, however, they feel that the present situation is simply intolerable and an insult to God and God's law, they will be vociferous and militant in making use of the halakhic authorities and the texts available to propose revisions in the *halakhah*. They are no less "Orthodox" than their colleagues, and indeed, they may even be more halakhically "authentic" (Rackman, 1976: 143).

There are limits to the extent to which adaptationists can affirm every aspect of modernity; they do not adapt Judaism to everything that is in current vogue; nor is everything which is in current vogue a necessary concomitant of modernity. There is an apologetic as well as an adaptive side to Orthodox reform. As in other religions (Smith, 1970: 3) family law and relations between the sexes evoke the most conservative sentiments. (Though, even here, adaptationists are far more accommodating than neotraditionalists). Nor is there any record of those associated with an adaptationist response directly confronting the problem of modern consciousness, the choices and alternatives which break down the taken-for-grantedness of Jewish identity. Instead, there is an implicit assumption that, given a really free choice, intelligent, well-meaning, and honest Jews will choose a Jewish-Orthodox identity. But, in fact, the Orthodox adaptationists have acquiesced in and even promoted an educational system structured to inculcate the values of Orthodoxy, paying lip service to the style of modernity.

Adaptationism's strength is also its weakness. It appeals to Jews who want to be or who are in fact "modern"; that is, Jews whose occupations, education, interests, and proclivities orient them toward the values of modernity. Adaptationism is, therefore, the most comfortable and convenient Orthodox response to modernity for many Jews, and this in itself raises problems about its religious authenticity. In addition, the adaptationists suffer from the classical dilemma of all liberal religion. The affirmation of modernity, the acceptance of its assumptions about the nature of reality, undermines religious faith and the belief in the efficacy of religious practice. Once religion legitimates the assumptions of modernity, it negates its own presup-

positions. Of course, many modern Jews seek to retain their allegiance and identity with the Jewish people, Jewish customs, and
Jewish tradition while living in the "modern" world. But, in such
cases, adaptationism is not their only alternative. Non-Orthodox
interpretations of Judaism which reinterpret Jewish law in more radical fashion or deny its binding authority or substitute Jewish culture
or Jewish social concern or Zionism for religion are more palatable
options than adaptationism.

On the other hand, the adaptationist response, other things being
equal, appears compromising and lacking authenticity to many modern Orthodox Jews. We must remember that Orthodoxy defines
proper Jewish life as adherence to Jewish law. Hence, the more
precisely one adheres to such laws, the better Jew one becomes.
While the adaptationists argue that their interpretation of Jewish law
is no less valid than that of the strict constructionists, their case is
weak. First of all, no recognized Talmudic authorities are identified
with their approach. Hence adaptationists must not only engage in a
fight over the interpretation of the Judaic tradition in which the logic
of their position might or might not be persuasive but in an argument
over the nature of rabbinic authority in which, as in any religious
argument, the conservative side has a clear advantage. Second, it is
difficult for them to escape the charge that their "reforms" are motivated by their attraction to the modern secular world rather than
by their commitment to what is authentically Jewish. Third, the
adaptationists are at a competitive disadvantage with other Orthodox
interpretations. The former recognize the legitimacy of the latter's
interpretation of Jewish law but demand legitimacy for their interpretation as well. In other words, they pose a pluralist model of interpretation. Other Orthodox leaders, on the other hand, deny the
legitimacy of the adaptationists' conceptions. This provides them
with a distinct psychological advantage.

In countries such as the United States where other religious interpretations of Judaism are found, the Orthodox adaptationists had to
be self-conscious about distinguishing themselves from, for example,
Conservative Judaism. As long as the adaptationists continued to
identify institutionally with Orthodoxy, they had to look over their
shoulders at what others were saying about them. But in Israel,
particularly in the early years of statehood, when non-Orthodox
religious interpretations of Judaism were almost unknown and the
Orthodox establishment was weak and divided, there was room for a
more radical development of adaptationism. Furthermore, the need
for an adaptationist response was also more evident because the

creation of a Jewish state raised questions without precedent in the tradition. A few, led by Israel's first minister of religion, Judah Leib Maimon (1875–1962), favored a reconstituted Sanhedrin, a tribunal of legal authorities which was the ultimate legislative authority for Jewish law in the period of the Second Temple. A Sanhedrin would presumably have the authority to legitimate the kind of change in Jewish law which many Orthodox Jews felt was necessary to adapt that law to the needs of a modern political society. Yet Maimon, despite his personal influence and the power of his office, never attracted enough support for his proposal to permit its implementation. The most radical proposal of reform in Jewish law, offered by Yeshayahu Leibowitz, would transfer the right to legitimate change from rabbinic authorities to the community of Jews committed to Jewish law, a community

> acting in accordance with its understanding of Torah and with the honest intent to preserve it. In other words, the changes are made from the need and necessity to maintain the Torah and not for the convenience of people or the gratification of their personal desires (Leibowitz, 1975: 53).

Leibowitz, for example, suggested the need to reform the laws of Sabbath observance to permit work by those engaged in providing services which any state must provide. Such work, he argued, would be the fulfillment of a religious obligation. He criticized those who believed they could extend religious law to include the whole of Israeli society without acknowledging that this required the introduction of changes in the law itself. Leibowitz's proposals evoked little positive response within Israeli Orthodoxy.

The founders of the religious kibbutzim (collective settlements) were also adaptationists in their orientation (Fishman, 1975: 184–248). Indeed, they called the ideology of religious labor Zionism "the holy revolt." But in the final analysis they shied away from the boldest step – seeking to legitimate their interpretation of Judaism in the absence of rabbinical authority. A number of explanations have been offered for their reticence. Not least important, I suspect, was their fear that once one questions the authority of recognized religious leaders it is easy to fall into an atmosphere of laxity and permissiveness out of indifference and laziness rather than principle. In order for adaptationism to survive as an authentic religious response, in order that it not degenerate into an excuse for religious laxity, it requires an enormous degree of religious enthusiasm and self-discipline because, by definition, it lacks the fixed and rigid framework of religious authority. But religious enthusiasts tend to be attracted to more rigorous and demanding forms of religious expression than that which adaptationism cultivates.

Nevertheless, adaptationism, for all its signs of weakness in the United States (Liebman, 1979), remains an attractive option for many Jews. Some of the largest Orthodox synagogues and some of the most prominent Orthodox rabbis are best characterized by an adaptationist approach, though they might be reluctant to admit it. In Israel, where the self-conscious adaptationist approach has also been declining in recent years (Liebman, 1982), a group of Orthodox intellectuals, joined by members of religious kibbutzim, have organized a group called Neemaney Torah V'avodah (Faithful to Torah and Labor – "Torah and Labor" was the slogan of the religious labor Zionist movement) to counter the tendency away from adaptationism and toward what they call religious extremism.

REFERENCES

Davis, Moshe. 1963. *The Emergence of Conservative Judaism.* Philadelphia: The Jewish Publication Society.
Fishman, Aryei. 1975. "The Religious Kibbutz" (Hebrew). Jerusalem: Ph.D. diss., Hebrew University.
Leibowitz, Yeshayahu. 1975. *Judaism, Jewish People and the State of Israel* (Hebrew). Jerusalem: Schocken.
Liebman, Charles. 1979. "Orthodox Judaism Today." *Midstream* 25 (August–September): 19–26.
———. 1982. "The Growth of Neo-Traditionalism among Orthodox Jews in Israel" (Hebrew). *Megamot* 27: 233–50.
Rackman, Emanuel. 1961. "Sabbaths and Festivals in the Modern Age." *Studies in Torah Judaism.* New York: Yeshiva University.
———. 1976. "Halakhah: Orthodox Approaches." *Encyclopaedia Britannica, 1976 Yearbook.*
Siegel, Seymour, ed. 1978. *Conservative Judaism and Jewish Law.* New York: Ktav.
Smith, Donald E. 1970. *Religion and Political Development.* Boston: Little, Brown.

4

Conservative Judaism

Reform Judaism precipitated the formation of Orthodox Judaism, which in turn called forth a mediating system, called the Historical School in Germany and Conservative Judaism in the USA. Between Reform and Orthodoxy, the Historical School, a group of nineteenth-century German scholars, and Conservative Judaism, a twentieth-century Judaism in America, took the middle position, each in its own context. We treat them as a single Judaism, because they share a single viewpoint. The Historical School began among German-Jewish theologians who advocated change but found Reform extreme. They parted company with Reform on some specific issues of practice and doctrine, observance of the dietary laws and belief in the coming of the Messiah, for example. But they also found Orthodoxy immobile. Conservative Judaism in America in the twentieth century carried forward this same centrist position and turned a viewpoint of intellectuals into a Judaism: a way of life, a world-view, addressed to an Israel. The Historical School shaped the world-view, and Conservative Judaism later on brought that view into full realization as a way of life characteristic of a large group of Jews, nearly half of all American Jews by the middle of the twentieth century.

The Historical School in Germany and Conservative Judaism in America affirmed a far broader part of the received way of life than Reform, while rejecting a much larger part than did Orthodoxy of the world-view of the system of the dual Torah. Calling itself "the Historical School,"[1] the Judaism at hand concurred with the Reformers in their basic position. The Reformers had held that change was permissible and claimed that historical scholarship would show what change was acceptable and what was not. But the proponents of the Historical School differed in matters of detail. The emphasis on historical research in settling theological debates explains the name of the group. Arguing that its positions represent matters of historical fact rather than theological conviction, Conservative Judaism maintained that "positive historical scholarship" will prove capable, on the basis of historical facts, of purifying and clarifying the faith, joined to far stricter observance of the law than the Reformers required.

Toward the end of the nineteenth century rabbis of this same centrist persuasion organized the Jewish Theological Seminary of America, in 1886, and from that rabbinical school the Conservative Movement developed. The order of the formation of the several Judaisms of the nineteenth century therefore is, first Reform, then Orthodoxy, finally Conservatism – the two extremes, then the middle. Reform defined the tasks of the next two Judaisms to come into being. Orthodoxy framed the clearer of the two positions in reaction to Reform, but, in intellectual terms, the Historical School in Germany met the issues of Reform in a more direct way.

The stress of the Historical School in Europe and Conservative Judaism in America lay on two matters, first, scholarship, with historical research assigned the task of discovering those facts of which the faith would be composed, second, observance of the rules of the received Judaism. A professedly free approach to the study of the Torah, specifically through what was called "critical scholarship," therefore would yield an accurate account of the essentials of the faith. But the scholars and lay people alike would keep and practice nearly the whole of the tradition just as the Orthodox did. The ambivalence of Conservative Judaism, speaking in part for intellectuals deeply loyal to the received way of life but profoundly dubious of the inherited world-view, came to full expression in the odd slogan: "eat kosher and think *traif*." That statement meant people should keep the rules of the holy way of life but ignore the convictions that made sense of them. Orthopraxy is the word that refers to correct action and unfettered belief, as against Orthodoxy, right doctrine. Some would then classify Conservative Judaism in America as an orthoprax Judaism defined through works, not doctrine.

The middle position then derived in equal measures from the two extremes. The way of life was congruent in most aspects with that other Orthodox, the world, with that of the Reform. The two held together in the doctrine of Israel which covered everyone. Conservative Judaism saw the Jews as a people, not merely a religious community, and celebrated the ethnic as much as the more narrowly religious side to the Jews' common life. Orthodoxy took a separatist and segregationist position, leaving the organized Jewish community in Germany as that community fell into the hands of Reform Jews. Reform Judaism, for its part, rejected the position that the Jews constitute a people, not merely a religious community. Conservative Judaism emphasized the importance of the unity of the community as a whole and took a stand in favor of Zionism as soon as that movement got under way. What separated Conservative Judaism from Reform was the matter of observance. Fundamental loyalty to the received way of life distinguished the Historical School in Germany and Conservative Judaism in America from Reform Judaism in both countries. When considering the continued validity of a traditional religious practice, the Reform asked why, the Conservatives, why not. The Orthodox, of course, would ask no questions to begin with.

The fundamental principle, that the world-view of the Judaism under construction would rest upon (mere) historical facts, came from Reform Judaism. Orthodoxy could never have concurred. The contrast to the powerful faith despite the world, exhibited by Hirsch's stress on the utter facticity of the Torah, presents in a clear light the positivism of the Conservatives, who, indeed, adopted the name "the *Positive* Historical School."

The emphasis on research as the route to historical fact, and on historical fact as the foundation for both change and, also, the definition of what was truly authentic in the tradition, further tells us that the Historical School was made up of intellectuals. In America, too, a pattern developed in which essentially non-observant congregations of Jews called upon rabbis whom they expected to be observant of the rules of the religion. As a result many of the intellectual problems that occupied public debate concerned rabbis more than lay people, since the rabbis bore responsibility – so the community maintained – for not only teaching the faith but, on their own, embodying it.

An observer described this Judaism as "Orthodox rabbis serving Conservative synagogues made up of Reform Jews." But in a more traditional liturgy, in an emphasis upon observance of the dietary taboos and the Sabbath and festivals – which did, and still does, characterize homes of Conservative more than of Reform Jews – Conservative Judaism in its way of life as much as in its world-view did establish an essentially mediating position between Orthodoxy and Reform Judaism. And the conception that Conservative Judaism is a Judaism for Conservative rabbis in no way accords with the truth. That Judaism for a long time enjoyed the loyalty of fully half of the Jews in America and today retains the center and the influential position of Judaism in that country. The viewpoint of the center predominates even in the more traditional circles of Reform and the more modernist sectors of Orthodoxy.

The adoption, by the Reform rabbis, of the Pittsburgh Platform of 1885, cited above, marked the beginning of Conservative Judaism. At that point a number of European rabbis now settled in America determined to break from Reform and establish what they hoped would be simply "traditional" Judaism in America. In 1886 they founded the Jewish Theological Seminary of America, and that is the point at which Conservative Judaism as a religious movement began. The actual event was simple. The final break between the more traditional and the more radical rabbis among the non-Orthodox camp produced the formation of a group to sponsor a new rabbinical school for "the knowledge and practice of historical Judaism."[2] The power of Reform Judaism to create and define its opposition – Orthodoxy in Germany, Conservative Judaism in America – tells us how accurately Reform had outlined the urgent questions of the age.

Reform, after all, had treated as compelling the issue of citizenship ("Emancipation") and raised the heart of the matter: how could Jews aspire to return to the Holy Land and form a nation and at the same time take up citizenship in the lands of their birth and loyalty? Jews lived a way of life different from that of their neighbors with whom they wished to associate. A Judaism had to explain that difference. The answers of all three Judaisms accepted the premises framed, to begin with, by Reform. Orthodoxy maintained one could accept citizenship and accommodate political change, but also adhere loyally to the Torah. To Orthodoxy, certain changes, necessary in context, represented trivial and unimportant matters, even though, as we have noted, these matters – secular education being the most striking – did not strike other "traditionalists" as trivial at all. Conservative Judaism in its German formulation took up a mid-position, specifying as essential fewer aspects of the received way of life than did Orthodoxy, more than Reform. In many ways therefore Reform Judaism defined the agenda for all of the Judaisms of the nineteenth century, and its success lies in imposing its fundamental perspective on its competition.

Both in Germany in the middle of the century and in America at the end, the emphasis throughout lay on "knowledge and practice of historical Judaism as ordained in the law of Moses expounded by the prophets and sages in Israel in Biblical and Talmudic writings," so the articles of Incorporation of the Jewish Theological Seminary of America Association stated in 1887. Calling themselves "traditionalists" rather than "Orthodox," the Conservative adherents accepted for most Judaic subjects the principles of modern critical scholarship. Conservative Judaism therefore exhibited traits that linked it to Reform but also to Orthodoxy, a movement very much in the middle. Precisely how the Historical School related to the other systems of its day – the mid- and later nineteenth century requires attention to that scholarship that, apologists insisted, marked the Historical School off from Orthodoxy.

The principal argument in validation of the approach of the Historical School and Conservative Judaism derived from these same facts of history. Change now would restore the way things had been at that golden age that set the norm and defined the standard. So, by changing, Jews would regain that true Judaism that, in the passage of time, had been lost. Reform added up to more than mere change to accommodate the new age, as the Reforms claimed. This kind of reform would conserve, recover, restore. That is what accounts for the basic claim that the centrists would discover how things had always been. By finding out how things had been done, what had been found essential as faith, in that original and generative time, scholarship would dictate the character of the Judaic system. It would say what it was and therefore what it should again become, and, it followed, Conservative Judaism then would be "simply Judaism."

Reform identified its Judaism as the linear and incremental next step in the unfolding of the Torah. The Historical School and Conservative Judaism later on regarded its Judaism as the reversion to the authentic Judaism that in time had been lost. Change was legitimate, as the Reform said, but only that kind of change that restored things to the condition of the original and correct Judaism. That position formed a powerful apologetic, because it addressed the Orthodox view that Orthodoxy constituted the linear and incremental outgrowth of "the Torah" or "the tradition," hence, the sole legitimate Judaism. It also addressed the Reform view that change was all right. Conservative Judaism established a firm criterion for what change was all right: the kind that was, really, no change at all. For the premise of the Conservative position was that things should become the way they had always been.

Scholarship would tell how things had always been and dictate those changes that would restore the correct way of life, the true world-view, for the Israel composed of pretty much all the Jews – the center. Historical research therefore provided a powerful apologetic against both sides. That is why the weapon of history in the nineteenth century was ultimate in the struggle among the Judaisms of the age. We therefore understand how much was meant by the name "the Historical School" in the Germany of the mid-nineteenth century. The claim to replicate how things always had been and should remain thus defined as the ultimate weapon historical research, of a sort. That was, specifically, a critical scholarship that did not accept at face value as history the stories of holy books, but asked whether and how they were true, and in what detail they were not true. That characteristically critical approach to historical study would then serve as the instrument for the definition of Conservative Judaism, the Judaism that would conserve the true faith, but also omit those elements, accretions of later times, that marred that true faith.

At issue in historical research, out of which the correct way of life and world-view would be defined, was the study of the talmudic literature, that is, the Oral Torah. The Hebrew Scriptures enjoyed immunity. Both the Reformers and the Historical School theologians stipulated that the Written Torah was God given. The Conservatives and Reformers concurred that God gave the Written Torah, man made the Oral Torah. So the two parties of change, Reformers and Historical School alike, chose the field of battle, declaring the Hebrew Scriptures to be sacred and outside the war. They insisted that what was to be reformed was the shape of Judaism imparted by the Talmud, specifically, and preserved in their own day by the rabbis whose qualification consisted in learning in the Talmud and approval by those knowledgeable therein. That agreement on the arena for critical scholarship is hardly an accident. The Reform and Historical School theologians revered Scripture.

Wanting to justify parting company from Orthodox and the received tradition of the Oral Torah, they focused on the Talmud because the Talmud formed the sole and complete statement of the one whole Torah of Moses our rabbi, to which Orthodoxy and, of course, the traditionalists of the East, appealed. Hence in bringing critical and skeptical questions to the Talmud, but not to the Hebrew Scriptures, the Conservatives and Reformers addressed scholarship where they wished, and preserved as revealed truth what they in any event affirmed as God's will. That is why the intellectual program of the Historical School in Germany and Conservative Judaism in America consisted of turning the Talmud, studied historically, into a weapon directed against two sides: against the excessive credulity of the Orthodox, but also against the specific proposals and conceptions of the Reformers.

The role of scholarship being critical, Conservative Judaism looked to history to show which changes could be made in the light of biblical and rabbinic precedent, "for they viewed the entire history of Judaism as such a succession of changes," Arthur Hertzberg explains.[3] The continuity in history derives from the on-going people. The basic policy from the beginning, however, dictated considerable reluctance at making changes in the received forms and teachings of the Judaism of the dual Torah. The basic commitments to the Hebrew language in worship, the dietary laws, and the keeping of the Sabbath and festivals distinguished the Historical School in Europe and Conservative Judaism in America from Reform Judaism. The willingness to accept change and to affirm the political emancipation of the Jews as a positive step marked the group as different from the Orthodox. So far as Orthodoxy claimed to oppose all changes of all kinds, Conservative Judaism did take a position in the middle of the three.

Who joined Historical Judaism in Europe and Conservative Judaism in America? The answer is, scholars – men who had an Orthodox education but Reform aspirations. Since nearly all of the first three generations of Conservative Jews in America and adherents of the Historical School in Europe had made their way out of the yeshivas that formed education within the received system of the dual Torah, the motivation for the deeply conservative approach to the received system requires attention. Indeed, once scholar-theologians maintained that the oral part of the Torah derived from mortals, not God, disagreements with Reformers on matters of change can have made little difference. For by admitting to the human origin and authority of the documents of the Oral Torah, the historian-theologians had accomplished the break with the Orthodox as well as with the received system. Then differences with Reform were of degree, not kind. But these differences sustained a Judaism for a very long time, a Judaism that would compose its world-view, its way of life, its audience of Israel, in terms that marked off that system from the other two successor-Judaisms we have already considered. Where and how did the differences emerge? To answer the question, we turn to two Europeans turned Americans, who typify the first mature generation of Conservative Judaism.

A professor at the Jewish Theological Seminary of America for the first half of the twentieth century, Louis Ginzberg, forms the counterpart to Abraham Geiger and Samson Raphael Hirsch. To him, keeping the way of life of the received tradition, because of upbringing and association, would define the way of life of Conservative Judaism. Ignoring the intellectual substance of the received system and striking out in new directions would define the method of thought, the world-view. The inherited way of life exercised profound power over the heart of the Conservative Jew of the early generation. The received viewpoint persuaded no one. So keep what could not be let go, and relinquish what no longer possessed value. To justify both sides, historical scholarship would find reassuring precedents, teaching that change is not Reform after all. But no precedent could provide verification for orthopraxy, the most novel, the most interesting reform among the Judaisms of continuation.

Louis Ginzberg (1873–1953)[4] typifies the entire group of theologian-historians, in that he grew up within the heartland of the Jewish world of Eastern Europe, but left for the West. In that important respect he stands for the experience of departure and of alienation from roots that characterized the generality of earlier Reformers, the earliest generations of Conservative theologians, and – if we substitute distance from alienation – the Orthodox of the age as well. Later on some of these figures would lay down the rule that, to be a scholar in Judaism, one had to grow up in a yeshiva – and leave! That counsel raised alienation to a norm. Obviously, it bore no relationship whatsoever to the received system of the dual Torah. None of the representative figures in the early generations found urgent the replication of the way of life and world-view in which he[5] grew up. The policy of orthopraxy then formed a mode of mediating between upbringing and adult commitment – that is, of coping with change.

Ginzberg himself traced his descent to the Vilna Gaon Elijah, a formidable and legendary figure in the life of the communities of the dual Torah. But while born and brought up in Lithuania, heartland of the intellectual giants of the received system, Ginzberg left. He went to Berlin and Strasbourg, where he studied with Semitists, historians, and philosophers – practitioners of disciplines unknown in the sciences of the dual Torah. Ginzberg's next move, from the Central European universities, brought him to the USA, where, in 1899, he found employment at Hebrew Union College. But the appointment he had received was cancelled when Ginzberg's position on biblical criticism became known.

Specifically, Ginzberg affirmed the validity of critical approaches to the Hebrew Scriptures, and that fact made him unacceptable at the Reform seminary. As we noted above, critical scholarship flourished within carefully circumscribed borders; within the frontier lay the Oral Torah, outside – and beyond permissible criticism – the Written. That distinction, central to Reform and Conservative positive-historical scholarship, placed Ginzberg outside of the camp for Reform seminaries. Instead, in 1900 he found employment at the

Jewish Encyclopedia, and, in 1903, he accepted an appointment in Talmud at the Jewish Theological Seminary of America, yet another of the founding faculty collected by Solomon Schechter. Why Schechter found Ginzberg's views on biblical scholarship acceptable I do not know, but, of course, Ginzberg taught Talmud, not Scriptures. He remained at the Jewish Theological Seminary for fifty years. Ginzberg is called by Hertzberg[6] simply "a principal architect of the Conservative movement."

His scholarly work covered the classical documents of the Oral Torah, with special interest in subjects not commonly emphasized in the centers of learning which he had left. So the subject changed, and changed radically. But the mode of learning remained constant. Ginzberg's work emphasized massive erudition, a great deal of collecting and arranging, together with episodic and *ad hoc* solutions to difficult problems of exegesis. But the work remained primarily textual and exegetical, and, when Ginzberg ventured into historical questions, the received mode of talmudic discourse – deductive reasoning, *ad hoc* arguments – predominated. So, for example, he propounded the theory – famous in its day – that differences on issues of the law represented class differences ("The Significance of the Halakhah for Jewish History," 1929). In this essay the repeated enunciation of the thesis followed by exemplifications of how the thesis might explain differences of opinion took the place of rigorous analysis and cool testing of the thesis at hand. So Ginzberg maintained that the liberals expressed the class interests of the lower classes, the conservatives of the upper classes. He then found in details of the law as two parties debated it ample exemplifications of this same theory. Just as in the yeshiva world Ginzberg had left, enthusiastic argument took the place of sustained analysis and critical exercise of testing, so in the world Ginzberg chose to build, the same mode of thought persisted, changed in context, unchanged in character.

However traditional in character, it was not Orthodoxy. And that explains the orthopraxy of formative Conservative Judaism, captured in the saying "eat kosher and think *traif.*" While such inconsistency of belief and practice may strike some as difficult to sustain, in fact for those who hold the position the world-view, imputing to religious practice enormous value while ignoring the received mythic basis for the practice in favor of some other, provides ample explanation for the way of life at hand. The story is reported by Ginzberg's son that, when he visited Hebrew Union College, "they inquired of young Ginzberg whether he was observant and he replied affirmatively; they next asked whether he 'believed' and the reply was in the negative."[7] Both answers, in that context, were the wrong ones.

Ginzberg very explicitly stressed that Judaism "teaches a way of life and not a theology."[8] At the same time he conceded that theological systems do "expound the value and meaning of religion in propositional form," but doctrines follow practices: "Theological doctrines are like the bones of the body, the outcome of the life-process itself and also the means by which it gives firmness, stability, and definiteness of outline to the animal organism." So Ginzberg rejected "the dogma of a dogma-less Judaism." Religious experience, in context meaning observance of the way of life, comes first and generates all theological reflection. The role of history: "Fact, says a great thinker, is the ground of all that is divine in religion and religion can only be presented in history – in truth it must become a continuous and living history."

This extreme statement of the Positive Historical School provides a guide to the character of Conservative Judaism in the context of the changes of the nineteenth and twentieth century. The appeal to fact in place of faith, the stress on practice to the subordination of belief – these form responses to the difficult situation of sensitive intellectuals brought up in one world but living in another. Ginzberg's judgment placed experience prior to thought: "Religious phenomena are essentially reactions of the mind upon the experienced world, and their specific character is not due to the material environment but to the human consciousness."[9] Ginzberg's capacity for a lucid statement of his own theological views belied his insistence that theology followed upon, and modestly responded to, what he called "religious experience," but what, in fact, was simply the pattern of religious actions that he learned in his childhood to revere.

So orthopraxy eased the transition from one world to another. The next generation found no need to make such a move; it took as normal, not to say normative, the stress on deed to the near-exclusion of intellect that, for Ginzberg and the Positive Historical School, as much as for Orthodoxy, explained why and how to keep in balance a world-view now utterly beyond belief and a way of life very much in evidence. His address in 1917 to the United Synagogue of America, of which he served as president, provides a stunning statement of his system of Judaism:

> Looking at Judaism from an historical point of view, we become convinced that there is no one aspect deep enough to exhaust the content of such a complex phenomenon as Judaism, no one term or

proposition which will serve to define it. Judaism is national and universal, individual and social, legal and mystic, dogmatic and practical at once, yet it has a unity and individuality just as a mathematical curve has its own laws and expression. By insisting upon historical Judaism we express further our conviction that for us Judaism is no theory of the study or school, no matter of private opinion or deduction, but a fact . . . If we look upon Jewish History in its integrity as a simple and uniform power, though marked in portions by temporary casual parenthetical interruptions, we find that it was the Torah which stood forth throughout the history of Israel as the guiding star of his civilization.[10]

While some may find this statement gibberish, affirming as it does everything and its opposite, we nonetheless discern a serious effort at a statement of deeply held convictions. The key to much else lies in the capital H assigned to the word History, the view that History possesses "integrity as a simple and uniform power." What we have is none other than the familiar notion that history – fact – proves theological propositions.

That position cannot surprise us when we remember that the facts of the way of life impressed Ginzberg far more than the faith that, in the context of the dual Torah, made sense of those facts and formed of the whole a Judaism. In fact Ginzberg did not possess the intellectual tools for the expression of what he had in mind, which is why he found adequate resort to a rather inchoate rhetoric. Assuming that he intended no merely political platform, broad enough to accommodate everyone whom he hoped would stand on it, we reach a single conclusion. Conservative Judaism stood for the received way of life, modified in only minor detail, along with the complete indifference to the received world-view. To take the place of the missing explanation – theology – "Jewish History" would have to make do. That history, of course, supplied a set of theological propositions; but these demanded not faith, merely assent to what were deemed ineluctable truths of history: mere facts. At what price the positivism of the founding generation? The intellectual paralysis that would follow. But to what benefit? The possibility of defining a position in the middle, between the Reform, with its forthright rejection of the received way of life, and the Orthodox, with the equally forthright rejection of the new mode of thought.

In its formative century Conservative Judaism carried forward the received way of life, hence, a Judaism professedly continuous with its past. But in its forthright insistence that no world-view one could delimit and define accompanied that way of life, Conservative Judaism imposed a still more radical break than did Reform Judaism between itself and the received tradition. Above all, Conservative Judaism denied the central fact of its system: its novelty. The change involved not a scarcely articulated change of attitude, as we found with Hirsch, but a fully spelled out change of doctrine. For the one thing that Hirsch, all the more so his critics in the traditionalist world, could not concede proves central to Ginzberg's case: "Judaism" is everything and its opposite, so long as Jewish History defines the matter.

Conservative Judaism formed a deeply original response to a difficult human circumstance. In its formative century it solved the problem of alienation: people who had grown up in one place, under one set of circumstances, now lived somewhere else, in a different world. They cherished the past, but they themselves had initiated the changes they now confronted. In the doctrine of orthopraxy they held on to the part of the past they found profoundly affecting, and they made space for the part of their present circumstance they did not, and could not, reject. A Judaism that joined strict observance to free thinking kept opposed weights in equilibrium – to be sure, in an unsteady balance. By definition such a delicate juxtaposition could not hold. Papered over by a thick layer of words, the abyss between the way of life, resting on supernatural premises of the facticity of the Torah (as Hirsch rightly understood), and the world-view, calling into question at every point the intellectual foundations of that way of life, remained. But how did the successor generation propose to bridge the gap, so to compose a structure resting on secure foundations?

We look for the answer to a representative Conservative theologian of the second generation, beyond Ginzberg. The claim of Reform Judaism to constitute an increment of Judaism, we recall, rested on the position that the only constant in "Judaism" is change. The counterpart for Conservative Judaism comes to expression in the writings of Robert Gordis, since, for their day, they set the standard and defined the position of the center of the religion. Specifically, we seek Gordis's picture of the Judaism that came before and how he proposes to relate Conservative Judaism to that prior system. We find a forthright account of "the basic characteristics of Jewish tradition" as follows:

> The principle of development in all areas of culture and society is a fundamental element of the modern outlook. It is all the more noteworthy that the Talmud . . . clearly recognized the vast extent to which

rabbinic Judaism had grown beyond the Bible, as well as the organic character of this process of growth . . . For the Talmud, tradition is not static – nor does this dynamic quality contravene either its *divine origin* or its *organic continuity* [all italics his] . . . Our concern here is with the historical fact, intuitively grasped by the Talmud, that *tradition grows*.[11]

Gordis's appeal is to historical precedent. But the precedent derives from a Talmudic story – which by itself is scarcely historical at all. The story, as Gordis reads it, recognizes that tradition is not static. Let us read the story in Gordis's words and ask whether that is, in fact, its point:

Moses found God adding decorative crowns to the letters of the Torah. When he asked the reason for this, the lawgiver was told: "In a future generation, a man named Akiba son of Joseph is destined to arise, who will derive multitudes of laws from each of these marks." Deeply interested, Moses asked to be permitted to see him in action, and he was admitted to the reason of the schoolhouse where Akiba was lecturing. To Moses' deep distress, however, he found that he could not understand what the scholars were saying and his spirit grew faint within him. As the session drew to a close, Akiba concluded: "This ordinance which we are discussing is a law derived from Moses on Sinai." When Moses heard this, his spirit revived![12]

While Gordis's view, that the story "clearly recognized the vast extent to which rabbinic Judaism had grown beyond the Bible, as well as the organic character of this process of growth," certainly enjoys ample basis in the sense of the tale itself, his interpretation hardly impressed the Orthodox and traditionalists who read the same story.

More important, if we did not know that "the principle of development . . . is fundamental," we should not have necessarily read the story in that context at all. For its emphasis, not adduced as a proof-text for the Conservative position, lies on the origin at Sinai of everything later on. And that point sustains the principal polemic at hand: the divine origin of the Oral Torah, inclusive, even, of the most minor details adduced by the living sage. We know, of course, the issue urgent to the story-tellers of both the Talmud of the Land of Israel and that of Babylonia, namely, the place of the sages' teachings in the Torah. And that polemic, fully exposed here, took the position that everything sages said derived from Sinai – which is precisely the opposite of the meaning imputed to the story by Gordis. That is not to suggest Gordis has "misinterpreted" the story, only that he has interpreted it in a framework of his own, not in the system which, to begin with, created the tale. That forms evidence of creativity and innovation, an imaginative and powerful mind proposing to make use of a received tradition for fresh purpose: not incremental but a new birth.

This small excursus on talmudic exegesis serves only to underline the fresh and creative character of Conservative Judaism. For without the slightest concern for anachronism, the Conservative theologians found in the tradition ample proof for precisely what they proposed to do, which was, in Gordis's accurate picture, to preserve in a single system the beliefs in both the divine origin and the "organic continuity" of the Torah: that middle-ground position, between Orthodoxy and Reform, that Conservative Judaism so vastly occupied. For Gordis's generation the argument directed itself against both Orthodoxy and Reform. In the confrontation with Orthodoxy, Gordis points to new values, institutions, and laws "created as a result of new experiences and new felt needs." But to Reform, Gordis points out "instances of accretion and of reinterpretation, which . . . constitute the major modes of development in Jewish tradition." That is to say, change comes about historically, gradually, over time, and change does not take place by the decree of rabbinical convocations. The emphasis of the Positive Historical School upon the probative value of historical events, we now recognize, serves the polemic against Reform as much as against Orthodoxy. To the latter, history proves change, to the former, history dictates modes of appropriate change.

Gordis thus argues that change deserves ratification after the fact, not deliberation beforehand: "Advancing religious and ethical ideals were inner processes, often imperceptible except after the passage of centuries." Gordis, to his credit, explicitly claims on behalf of Conservative Judaism origin an incremental and continuous, linear history of Judaism. He does so in an appeal to analogy:

> If tradition means development and change . . . how can we speak of the continuity or the spirit of Jewish tradition? An analogy may help supply the answer. Biologists have discovered that in any living organism, cells are constantly dying and being replaced by new ones . . . If that be true, why is a person the same individual after the passage of . . . years? The answer is twofold. In the first instance, the process of change is gradual . . . In the second instance, the growth follows the laws of his being. At no point do the changes violate the basic personality pattern. The organic character and unit of the personality reside

in this continuity of the individual and in the development of the physical and spiritual traits inherent in him, which persist in spite of the modifications introduced by time. This recognition of the organic character of growth highlights the importance of maintaining the method by which Jewish tradition . . . continued to develop.[13]

The incremental theory follows the modes of thought of Reform, with their stress on the continuity of process, that alone. Here too, just as Marcus saw the permanence of change as the sole continuity, so Gordis sees the on-going process of change as permanent. The substance of the issues, however, accords with the stress of Orthodoxy on the persistence of a fundamental character to Judaism. The method of Reform then produces the result of Orthodoxy, at least so far as practice of the way of life would go forward.

Conservative Judaism claimed to mark the natural next step in the slow evolution of "the tradition," an evolution within the lines and rules set forth by "the tradition" itself. Appeals to facts proved by scholars underline the self-evidence claimed on behalf of the system in its fully articulated form. The incapacity to discern one's own anachronistic reading of the past in line with contemporary concerns further sustains the claim that, at hand, we deal with a system of self-evidence. And yet, when we realize the enormous abyss between Louis Ginzberg and his ancestor, not to mention the striking difference between the viewpoint of the Talmud's story-teller and the reading of the story by Gordis, the fact becomes clear. What truths Conservative theologians hold to be self-evident they have uncovered through a process of articulated inquiry. The answers may strike them as self-evident, us as strident and invented. But they themselves invented the questions. And they knew it.

The appeal to an incremental and linear history, a history bonded by a sustained method and enduring principles that govern change, comes long after the fact of change. Assuredly, Conservative Judaism forms a fresh system, a new creation, quite properly seeking continuity with a past that has, to begin with, been abandoned. For processes of change discerned after the fact and in the light of change already made or contemplated are processes not discovered but defined, then imputed by a process of deduction to historical sources that, read in other ways, scarcely sustain the claim at hand. The powerful scholarship of Conservative Judaism appealed to a reconstructed past, an invented history: a perfect faith in a new and innovative system, a Judaism discovered by its own inventors.

NOTES

1   Arthur Hertzberg, "Conservative Judaism," *Encyclopaedia Judaica* (Jerusalem, 1971: Keter), 5: 901–6.
2   Ibid., col. 902.
3   Ibid., col. 901.
4   Arthur Hertzberg, "Louis Ginzberg," *Encyclopaedia Judaica* (Jerusalem, 1971: Keter), 7: 584–6.
5   There were no women of note; a century would have to pass before women found their rightful place in the life of Judaisms.
6   Ibid., col. 584.
7   Eli Ginzberg, *Keeper of the Law: Louis Ginzberg* (Philadelphia, 1966: Jewish Publication Society of America), p. 82.
8   Ibid., p. 145.
9   Ibid., p. 148.
10 Ibid., pp. 159–60.
11 Robert Gordis, *Understanding Conservative Judaism*, ed. Max Gelb (New York, 1978: Rabbinical Assembly), pp. 26–7.
12 Ibid., p. 26.
13 Ibid., pp. 39–40.

Seymour Siegel
"The Meaning of Jewish Law in Conservative Judaism"

Since the principal interest in Conservative Judaism in its first century concerned the justification for changing the law while honoring and keeping it, we take up the statement of an authoritative figure on the basis for legitimate change. Rabbi Seymour Siegel was professor at the Jewish Theological Seminary of America through most of the second half of the twentieth century and studied with the principal figures in the first. He here expresses the normative position of that school and the religious movement that in his time took shape around it. In this systematic account he stresses the difference between Conservative and Reform Judaism, on the one side, and Conservative and Orthodox Judaism, on the other. His stress is on the meeting of "the divine" and the human in the Torah. He sees the Torah as a human response to an act of God: "Scripture . . . is not literally revelation . . . [but] the human recording of the experience of revelation. Therefore Scripture is both divine and human." This position of his allows for Conservative Judaism to accommodate critical scholarship, which it so prized in Siegel's time, together with the authority of the law recorded in the Torah. But, it goes without saying, what human beings have made, other human beings may change, and that is the central motif throughout. That becomes explicit in Siegel's insistence that the needs of the time may well take over. And the same consideration comes into play when the Torah is viewed as a historical, not a supernatural, document. Most interesting in Siegel's presentation of the Conservative Judaic theory of law is his introduction of "aggadah," or lore, inclusive of theology, and ethics. The law must be placed into judgment before theology; the law must give way to ethical considerations. At the same time, the character of the Jewish community must be taken into account. Here, then, is an authoritative account of how a position between Orthodoxy and Reform Judaism is worked out by a leading spokesman.

The second part of the program of Conservative Judaism was to legitimate changes from the accepted practice. The legitimation of modification was established by means of the following principles: a nonfundamentalist view of revelation; discernment of the needs of the time; a recognition of historical development; the need for perspective; the demands of the aggadic and ethical aspects of Judaism; and the acceptance of pluralism in the religious community.

I   Doctrine of Revelation

The basic question concerning Jewish law involves a doctrine of Revelation. All forms of Judaism accept the notion of God's communicating with man in general and the Jewish people in particular. Most Orthodox thinkers argue that the traditional doctrine of *Torah MiSinai* (the Torah coming from Sinai) posits that God literally commanded everything written in the Torah. This, in their view, makes Jewish law immutable, and change can take place only within the most narrow limits. The Reform thinkers believed that the moral and ethical demands of Judaism were revealed, and that the ritual laws (which means most of the corpus of Jewish law) were the products of human legislation, reflecting various social conditions of the time. This means that *halachah* is not binding today. In recent times, Conservative Judaism has tried to find a third way in which revelation could be taken seriously but not literally. Most thinkers have relied on the thinking of Franz Rosenzweig. Rosenzweig argued that revelation is not the transmittal of concrete directives. Revelation means that man and God have met each other. Revelation means the self-uncovering of the Divine in relation to man. It is the transmission to man of God's love and concern. It is a miracle that God does reveal Himself to man. God could have hidden behind Creation and its iron laws. God is partially hidden so as to make man's acceptance of God the result of free will and not compulsion. But out of the hiding comes the Living God. When God reveals His love and concern, we are called upon to respond with love toward Him and our fellowman. We love with the love with which we are loved. This revelation happens to individuals. It happened to the whole people of

Israel, who perceived in their history and destiny the hand of the Living God. Scripture and its interpretation in the rabbinic writings are not *literally* revelation. They are the human recordings of the experience of revelation. Therefore, Scripture is both divine and human. The words contain the divine initiative and the human response to it. In each word the two – the divine and the human – are joined and cannot be separated. Therefore, Scripture and Talmud are infinitely precious – for through them the Divine is revealed. Scripture and Talmud contain the human response – and therefore are not infallible.

As a result of this encounter with the divine, many laws and customs were instituted as expressions of the demands of God as perceived by those who experienced God. Old customs that the Israelites had always observed were infused with new meanings. The Bible is not only the result of revelation. It is also the vehicle of revelation, for by imaginatively confronting the record, we have the chance to come into contact with the Being behind the text. This means that in differing circumstances, new demands will be discerned, and old ones changed. This is the essence of *midrash*, the attempt to relive the revelation and to realize the implications of this event for the here-and-now. The history of Judaism is a history of the interpretation of revelation. In Heschel's striking sentence: "Judaism is a minimum of revelation and a maximum of interpretation." This interpretation is what is included in *midrash* and what is included in whatever a diligent student in the future will discover. The crucible out of which Jewish law is created is the encounter with the record of revelation, by the people of revelation, who attempt ever anew to hear God's voice through the text and attempt to decide what they must do now. This, of course, means that there will be change and modification. It is true, for example, that God countenanced slavery, as is evident in Scripture, when there was no possibility of abolishing the institution. The aim of Jewish law was to humanize the institution until it could be abolished. Though God may have wanted slavery in antiquity, He certainly does not want it now. It is true that God once wanted the law of an "eye for an eye" to be applied literally. He certainly does not want it now. It is possible that God once wanted women to limit themselves to their roles as princesses whose grandeur consisted of being concealed. He probably does not want that now. Total subjectivity is avoided because of the presence of the community and because of the character of Catholic Israel. The concrete laws are not to be viewed as if they were Platonic Ideas eternally residing in the world of Forms. They are dynamic concepts – subject to the dynamic voice of God, which encounters us anew at all times.

II The Needs of the Time

The need for change in Jewish law is the result of a profound contact with the needs of the Jews in this particular time and place. This contact, born out of a shared destiny and sensitivity to the best that is within our time and place, frequently results in a need to modify existing norms. When the Conservative movement came into being, there was a need to change the synagogue service so that the people coming into the House of God could be moved by the worship and understand it. The customary way of doing things, especially in the ritual of the synagogue, with its mixture of law and customs, had to be modified so that the whole could stand. The synagogue would have to accommodate families as whole units, not segregate women in special sections or in balconies; the service had to introduce some prayers in the vernacular; the rabbis had to be educated enough to deliver sermons reflecting secular training; and the prayerbook would have to be shortened to remove redundant and un-understandable poems and *piyyutim*. These voices demanding change, so resonant in the Conservative movement, came not out of systematic considerations – but because there was a discernment of the desperate needs of the time. Sometimes these changes were not really needed. It is time to reexamine some of the changes that were instituted. But when one realizes the situation, the desire for change is very demanding.

III The Historical Approach

As was stated previously, Conservative Judaism recognizes that which is the basis of scholarship: the historical nature of Jewish tradition. In the previous section we showed that this historical sense validated Jewish observance. However, it is also evident that a historical sense validates necessary change. Though the Laws are the reflection of the divine will, they are influenced by economic, scientific, political, and even textual influences. Even as reluctant a law-changer as the late Professor Boaz Cohen, in the selection included in this volume, writes:

> We conceive of Jewish law as a body of practices and regulations that have undergone a long development since the time of Moses . . . when we are asked what is the Jewish law on this or that point, we do not answer fully by referring to this or that code, commentary, or *responsum* for no single code is the complete expression of the law. The origin, the transformations of the rule, its archaic features, discarded elements, temporary expedients, idealistic aspirations, as well as its present interpretations are all part of the majestic structure.

With this recognition of the historical character of Jewish law, we find the methodology to affect change today. Thus, for example, if it could be shown that the separation of the sexes in houses of worship was the result of the desire to preserve decorum in the Temple and that this decorum was disturbed when the two sexes were in the place without a separation, it is, then, perfectly obvious that in today's society, where the relationships of men and women in society are so much different, and where the family unit is so important, it is a good thing to have mixed seating rather than segregated seating. Of course, it is necessary to avoid the "genetic fallacy," which sees institutions and concepts only as they originated and not in their historical development. However, the historical sense does legitimate changes when such changes are necessary.

IV   The Need for Perspective

One of the basic principles of the Conservative interpretation of Jewish law is the attempt to take into consideration the whole corpus of Jewish law, not just one summary of it – such as the *Shulchan Aruch*. If necessary, it is possible to rely on precedents which are found in other codes or which appear in the Talmud and were not made normative in the later compilations of Jewish law. Professor Boaz Cohen, in the chapter from his writings appearing in this volume, cites the following example of the application of this principle. In the procedure for the conversion of a female proselyte, the author of the *Shulchan Aruch* (*Yoreh Deah*, 268: 2) requires the *tevilah* to take place in the presence of three men. "While the regulation can be traced to Maimonides' code, the *Mishnah Torah*, it is not required by the Talmud where the requirement of witnesses was waived for reasons of delicacy. Apparently Maimonides incorporated the stricter rule from some early source now lost . . . there should be no compunction in reverting to the more ancient practice customary in talmudic times."

V   Aggadah and Ethics

Most important in Conservative Judaism's view of the interpretation of Jewish law is the introduction of the aggadic and ethical component. Since the Law is the expression of the covenant, and a basic aim of the covenantal obligation is the practice of justice and compassion, we cannot sustain the authority of any norm which results in unethical outcomes. When the *halachah* cannot adequately express the *aggadah*, it must be modified. Thus we do not practice the exclusion of *mamzerim* (children born of an incestuous or adulterous relationship) because it is an unfair law. We do not defend the laws of slavery because they are not up to our ethical standards; we accept the marriage of a divorcee and a *kohen* because we feel that the notion of a divorcee being somehow flawed and therefore not worthy of a *kohen* does not square with our notions of what is right and wrong. This does not mean that we are ethically more sensitive than our forebearers. It means that in our situation, certain ethical considerations are present that may not have been present in ancient times. These ethical perceptions come out of our tradition and are applied to the tradition as a whole. Of course, there will be differences of opinion as to the ethical thing to do, and therefore different conceptions about outcomes, but the principle remains.

VI   Religious Pluralism

Because of the above considerations, there will be a variety of practice in the community. Since perceptions of what is needed, what is ethical, etc., will differ, there will be differences in decisions made in different places by different authorities. Thus, if women are not to be given *aliyot* because to do so might offend the congregation (*kevod hatzibbur*), there will be legitimate differences of opinion as to whether this is still true or not. Thus a very traditional congregation, where the worshippers would be outraged by women being called to the Torah, should take this outrage into consideration in determining whether a change should be instituted or not. In other congregations, the *kevod hatzibbur* would be affected by not giving women *aliyot*. As long as the pluralistic practices are born out of serious considerations, and as long as they do not offend the broad consensus of our movement, we are willing to countenance and grant legitimacy to varying practices.

Part II
The Twentieth Century

5

The Challenge of the "Post-Christian" Century and the Response of Three "Post-Christian" Judaisms

The twentieth century is called "post-Christian"[1] because it is a century in which principal public events in no way responded to the teachings of Christianity; it has been the first anti-Christian century in the history of humanity from antiquity. Christianity's public, political competition came from secularism, nationalism, and Communism. Christianity's competition in the West – Europe and its overseas diaspora, now covering most of the world – yielded the age of total war and the degradation of humanity in a hitherto unthinkable manner. The militantly secular nation-state, formed around ever diminishing territories of uniform populations, each conceiving itself pure and aspiring to remove impurities from its midst, the Communist Empire, with its so-called scientific materialism, the profoundly anti-Christian politics of the German National Socialist Workers Party (the Nazis) – all three rejected every fundamental conviction of Christianity. It goes without saying that they took as primary enemy Judaism too. In both instances they were right. For the conviction of both Christianity and Judaism celebrate humanity in God's image, after God's likeness, and Nazism, Communism, and militant secularism all put forth a very different vision of humanity. Everyone now has seen the result of that vision.

Accordingly, the twentieth century was called "post-Christian" – just as it also was "post-Judaic" – because its history was shaped by other ideals for humanity than the Christian and Judaic ones. The Nazi, Communist, and secular counterparts to Christianity and Judaism each in its way brought about the massive repudiation of the basic worth of human life that has characterized a century of perpetual war, on the one side, alongside the celebration of the all-powerful state, on the other. We cannot find surprising, therefore, that the first "post-Christian" century also marked the last century of Judaism in most of Europe. At the end of the twentieth century, except for Britain and France,[2] Judaism the religion is dead in Europe. Militantly atheistic Communism and explicitly anti-Christian and anti-Judaic Nazism joined together to annihilate Judaism and the Jewish people, respectively, the one in the Soviet Union, the other in the whole of continental Europe. The story of Judaism in the twentieth century portrays how Judaic systems attempted to cope with the age of Holocaust.

The contrast between the nineteenth- and twentieth-century systems should be drawn. The Judaisms of the nineteenth century retained close and nurturing ties to the Judaism of the dual Torah. All three – Reform, Orthodoxy, Conservative Judaism – confronted its issues, drew heavily on its symbolic system, cited its texts as prooftexts, eagerly referred to its sources in justification for the new formations. All of them looked backward and assumed responsibility toward that long past of the Judaism of the dual Torah, acknowledging its authority, accepting its program of thought, acceding to its way of life – if only by way of explicit rejection. While the nineteenth-century Judaisms made constant reference to the received system of the dual Torah, its writings, its values, its requirements, its viewpoints, its way of life, the twentieth-century Judaisms did not. True, each Judaism born in the nineteenth century faced the task of validating change. But all of the new Judaisms of the nineteenth century articulated a principle of change guiding relationships within the received system, which continued to define the agenda of law and theology alike. All the Judaisms of that age recognized themselves as answerable to something they deemed the tradition.

We cannot point to a similar relationship between the received Judaism of the dual Torah and the new Judaisms of the twentieth century. For none of them made much use of the intellectual resources of that system, none found important issues deemed urgent within that system, none even regarded itself as answerable to the Judaism of the dual Torah. Between the twentieth-century Judaisms and the nineteenth-century ones lay a century – and the difference between the nineteenth and the twentieth centuries. That made part of the difference.

And the full explanation for the character of the Judaisms of the twentieth century derives from what was going on in that worst of all centuries in the history of humanity, the "post-Christian" age of total death. Confronting the urgent and inescapable questions of the twentieth century, the system-makers of Judaisms in the end came up with no self-evident, enduring answers. The twenty-first century inherits much from the nineteenth, nothing from the twentieth, in Judaisms. In response to the challenge of the twentieth century, there was no self-evidently valid answer to the urgent question of the age. There could have been none. What is there to say in the face of "extermination" – that is, of the murder of human beings because they were Jews? And what system could have answered the urgent question of life in the time and place of factories constructed to produce death?

Three Judaisms were born in the twentieth century. The first was Jewish Socialism and Yiddishism, the second, Zionism, and the third, three generations later, the American Judaic system of Holocaust and Redemption. Jewish Socialism took shape in the Bund, a Jewish union organized in Poland in 1897. Zionism was founded in the World Zionist Organization, created in Basel, also in 1897. American Judaism in the formulation under discussion came to powerful expression in the aftermath of the 1967 War in the Middle East. All three Judaic systems answered narrowly political questions, not those of sanctification and salvation that religious Judaic systems addressed. Their agenda attended to the status of the Jews as a group (Zionism, American Judaism), the definition of the Jews in the context of larger political and social change (Jewish Socialism, Zionism). It follows that the urgent questions addressed by the twentieth-century Judaisms differed in kind from those found acute in the nineteenth century. In the twentieth century powerful forces for social and economic change took political form, in movements meant to shape government to the interests of particular classes or groups – the working classes or racial or ethnic entities, for instance. The Judaic systems of the century responded in kind:

ZIONISM The definition of citizenship, encompassing ethnic and genealogical traits, presented the Jews with the problem of how they were to find a place in a nation-state that understood itself in an exclusionary and exclusive, racist way – whether Nazi Germany or nationalist Poland or Hungary or Romania or revanchist and irredentist France. Zionism declared the Jews "a people, one people," and proposed as its purpose the creation of the Jewish State.

JEWISH SOCIALISM AND YIDDISHISM Here is presented a Judaic system congruent to the political task of economic reform through state action. The Jews would form unions and engage in mass activity of an economic and, ultimately therefore, of a political character.

AMERICAN JUDAISM OF HOLOCAUST AND REDEMPTION In this formulation we deal with a narrowly ethnic, not a religious, system.

Shifting currents in American politics, a renewed ethnicism and emphasis on intrinsic traits of birth, rather than extrinsic ones of ability, called into question Jews' identification with the democratic system of America as that system defined permissible difference. A Jewish ethnicism, counterpart to the search for roots among diverse ethnic groups, responded with a tale of Jewish "uniqueness" – unique suffering – and unique Jewish ethnic salvation, redemption in the Jewish State – far away, to be sure.

So three powerful and attractive movements, Jewish Socialism and Zionism and American Judaism, presented answers to critical issues confronting groups of Jews. All of these movements addressed political questions and responded with essentially political programs. Zionism wanted to create a Jewish State, American Judaism wanted the Jews to form an active political community on their own, and Jewish Socialism in its day framed the Jews into political, as much as economic, organizations, seeing the two as one, a single and inseparable mode of defining economic activity and public policy.

These Judaisms were not at all like the ones that came to formation in the nineteenth century. That is for two reasons. First of all, on the surface the three Judaic systems of the twentieth century took up political, social, economic, but not theological questions. Second, while the nineteenth-century Judaisms addressed issues particular to Jews, the matters of public policy of the twentieth-century Judaic systems concerned everyone, not only Jews. Judaisms of the nineteenth century spoke in Judaic language about particularly Judaic problems, with which, to be sure, others could identify. Judaisms of the twentieth century addressed common problems in a Jewish framework and proposed in a Jewish idiom and circumstance solutions comparable with those that served everywhere else. So none of the Judaisms of the twentieth century proves congruent in details of structure to the continuator-Judaisms of the nineteenth. All of the new Judaisms intersected with comparable systems – like in character, unlike in content – among other Europeans and Americans. Socialism then is the genus, Jewish Socialism the species, American ethnic assertion the genus, American Judaism the species.

Accordingly, we move from a set of Judaisms that form species of a single genus – the Judaism of the dual Torah – to a set of Judaisms that bear less in common among themselves than they do between themselves and systems wholly autonomous of Judaic world-views and ways of life. It is hard to imagine how matters could have been otherwise. For the issues addressed by the Judaisms of the twentieth century, the crises that made those issues urgent, did not affect Jews alone or mainly. The crises in common derived from economic dislocation, which generated socialism, and also Jewish Socialism; the reorganization of political entities, which formed the foundation of nationalism, and also Zionism; and the reconsideration of the theory of American society, which produced, alongside the total homogenization of American life, renewed interest in ethnic origins, and also American Judaism. So, as is clear, the point of origin of the nineteenth-century Judaisms locates perspective from the dual Torah. Jews in the twentieth century had other things on their minds.

The nineteenth-century Judaisms made constant reference to the received system of the dual Torah, its writings, its values, its requirements, its viewpoints, its way of life. The twentieth-century Judaisms did not. True, each Judaism born in the nineteenth century faced the task of validating change that all of the aborning Judaisms in one way or another affirmed. But all of the new Judaisms articulated a principle of change guiding relationships with the received system, which continued to define the agenda of law and theology alike, and to which, in diverse ways to be sure, all the Judaisms recognized themselves as answerable. We cannot point to a similar relationship between the new Judaisms of the twentieth century and the received Judaism of the dual Torah. For none of them made much use of the intellectual resources of that system, found important issues deemed urgent within that system, or even regarded itself as answerable to the Judaism of the dual Torah.

For the twentieth-century systems took shape within another matrix altogether, for Jewish Socialism and Yiddishism, the larger world of socialism and linguistic nationalism; for Zionism, the realm of the nationalisms of the smaller peoples of Europe, rejecting the government of the international empires of Central and Eastern Europe; for American Judaism, the reframing, in American culture, of the policy governing social and ethnic difference. None of these Judaic systems of believing and behaving drew extensively on the received Judaic system of the dual Torah, and all of them for a time vastly overshadowed, in acceptance among the Jewish group, the Judaisms that did. So the passage of time, from the eighteenth to the twentieth century, had produced a radical attenuation of the bonds that joined the Jews of Zionism, Socialism, and Holocaust and Redemption, to the Judaism of the dual Torah.[3]

The difference between the twentieth-century Judaisms and the nineteenth-century ones was a century. For a hundred years from the beginning of political change separated the principal twentieth-century Judaisms from the point at which the self-evidence of the received system of the dual Torah gave way to self-consciousness about continuing that system one way or another. Since scarcely a generation intervened between Reform and Orthodox Judaisms and that same turning point, we wonder what, if any, difference the passage of time made.

The answer is simple. The Judaisms of the nineteenth century retained close and nurturing ties to the Judaism of the dual Torah. All three confronted its issues, drew heavily on its symbolic system, cited its texts as proof-texts, eagerly referred to its sources in justification for the new formations. All of them looked backward and assumed responsibility toward that long past of the Judaism of the dual Torah, acknowledging its authority, accepting its program of thought, acceding to its way of life – if only by way of explicit rejection.

The new Judaisms of the twentieth century in common treated with entire disinterest the same received Judaism of the dual Torah. They looked forward, and they drew heavily upon contemporary systems of belief and behavior. But they turned to the received system of the dual Torah merely opportunistically, in a cynical search for proof-texts for positions framed outside of the Torah altogether. For that received Judaism provided not reasons but excuses. Appealing to its proof-texts provided not authority for what people wanted to do anyhow, but mere entry to the mind and imagination of Jews themselves not far separated from the world that took for granted the truth of Scripture and the wisdom of the Oral Torah. So the shift from the Judaisms that responded to the received system and those that essentially ignored it, except (at most) after the fact, marked the true beginning of the modern age, that is, the point at which the old system held to be a set of self-evident truths gave way to a new set of systems, all of them equally self-evident to their adherents. What intervened was a span of self-consciousness, in which people saw choices and made decisions about what had formerly appeared obvious and beyond argument.

Is it correct to study as Judaic systems three political and ethnic systems? The continuators of the Judaism of the dual Torah developed systems of belief and behavior that invariably fell into the category of religions, in our setting, Judaisms. Clearly, Jewish Socialism and Zionism provided deep meaning for the lives of millions of Jews, so, defining ways of life and world-views and the Israel subject to realize both, they functioned entirely as did the religions, the

Judaisms, of the nineteenth century and of the twentieth as well. One may argue that the secular Judaic systems functioned as did the religious ones.

But Socialism-Yiddishism and Zionism differ from the continuator-Judaisms, because neither invoked a supernatural God, revelation of God's will in the Torah, belief in Providence, or any other indicators of the presence of the family of closely related religions, the Judaisms; and, moreover, their framers and founders did not claim otherwise. The Socialists took a position actively hostile to religion in all forms, as Chaim Grade's account has shown us. The Zionists compromised with the religious Judaisms of the day but in no way conceded that theirs was a competing Judaism. As to American Judaism, that forms a separate set of problems; but it suffices to observe that, in its contemporary form, in its appeal to the salvific myth of Holocaust and Redemption, it crosses the border between a genuinely religious and an entirely secular system addressed to Jews, falling on both sides of the not-unmarked boundary between the one and the other.

The difference between the twentieth-century Judaisms and the nineteenth-century ones was much more than a century. It was the difference between the civilization of the West in its Christian form and that same civilization as it took new forms altogether. What pertinence the Judaism formed in response to Christianity, with its interest in Scripture, Messiah, the long trends of history and salvation? The new world imposed its own categories: class and class struggle, the nation-state composed of homogeneous cultural and ethnic units – the lowest common denominator of bonding for a society, the search, among diverse and rootless people, for ethnic identity. These issues characterized a world that had cast loose moorings long able to hold things firm and whole.

In that same context, a second difference is noteworthy. The theological systems of Christianity and the Judaism of the dual Torah took up questions of enduring human concern: life and death, sanctification and salvation, for example. But the ideological Judaisms of the twentieth century addressed transient moments and treat as particular and unique what are structural, permanent problems. Take Zionism, for example. For not more than three generations Zionism thrived as an ideal for life and a solution to urgent problems. It essentially solved the meagre "Jewish problem" that was left by World War II to be solved and, with the creation of the State of Israel, passed on into institutional continuations bereft of all ideological interest.

Socialism and Yiddishism turn out to have expressed the ideals of exactly that sector of Jewry to which they spoke, the Yiddish-speaking workers. When the vast Yiddish-speaking populations were murdered, between 1941 and 1945, Yiddishism lost its natural constituency. Jewish Socialism in the USA thrived for that one generation, the immigrant one, which worked in factories; the Jewish unions then folded into the larger amalgam of unionism and lost their distinctive ethnic character; the Jewish voters, originally socialist or radical, found a comfortable home in New Deal Democracy in America. The Jewish Communists of Poland and the USSR in Stalin's time only with difficulty survived their revolution's success. In the 1930s, as part of his obliteration of the founding generation of Bolsheviks, Stalin eliminated the Jewish Section of the Communist Party. Disqualified by perfect faith in what they were doing, most of the survivors lost out to the bureaucrats that made the new order permanent. The Polish Communist Party exiled its Jewish members – they were not very numerous – in 1967. And so it went across Europe.

Of American Judaism we may scarcely speak; it is the birth of a single generation. Its power to mediate between a generation out of touch with its roots and a society willing to affirm ethnic difference – on carefully defined and limited bases, to be sure – remains to be tested. As an explanation to young Jews on why they should remain Jewish – different in some way from other people – the Judaism of Holocaust and Redemption failed in the USA. For in the quarter-century after its ascendency as the principal Judaism of the Jewish community there, the rate of intermarriage between Jews and gentiles rose to unprecedented proportions. That indicated that young Jews were not persuaded by the Judaism of Holocaust and Redemption that they should continue the endogamous definition of the Jewish community; by marrying gentiles, they were taught they married out of the community, and yet they did so. So whatever the power of self-evidence of the Judaism that explained why gentiles should be avoided in marriage, it had no effect upon the coming generation.

The Judaism of Holocaust and Redemption, Socialism, Yiddishism, and Zionism all share a transient character. Each came into existence for a generation that found itself in the middle, unable to continue what it had inherited, unable to hand on what it created. Anita Shapira tells us about the founders of Zionism:

> Theirs was the generation of the great leap; their parental homes were pervaded with religion, with innocent faith and hallowed custom; the homes of their children were detached from Jewish tradition, rooted in

a secular life style and alienated from the Jewish past. They themselves were affected by the ambivalence which comes from being bred in one society and living in another. Wherever they went and whatever they did, they were influenced . . . by the society from which they emerged . . . All . . . cast off the burden of Jewish religion at an early age . . .[4]

The twentieth-century Judaisms form systems for a very particular moment indeed.

They also did little to define the life of Jews in a way that markedly differed from the life of Christians and other gentiles. The way of life defined by Judaic systems of the twentieth century differed in yet a second way from the way of life of the Judaic systems of the nineteenth century. A devotee of a Judaism of the nineteenth century would do deeds that differed in quality and character from a devotee of another system altogether, for example, either a Christian or a socialist one. The way of life in definition (not merely by definition) differed from any other; the categories were distinctive to the system. The ways of life of the twentieth-century movements, whether essentially political, as in Zionism, or fundamentally economic, as in the Jewish labor unions of Jewish Socialism, or in category basically ethnic and cultural, as in American Judaism – all produced a culture of organizations, each such culture fitting comfortably into the category that encompassed all of them. So when I try to describe the way of life of a given system, I find it difficult to do more than specify the name of the organization one joined because of adherence to that system.

What the one who joined then did was pretty much what he or she would have done in any other organization: the flags had different colors, but the flag poles were all made of the same wood. We shall find difficult the identification of *systemically distinctive* ways of life that differ among the Judaic systems at hand. All of them call for actions of a single kind: the building of organizations, institutions, bureaucracies, institutions of collective action. The contribution of the individual is to the support of the bureaucracy.

Every way of life requires action of the same order as every other way of life, and each system treats the devotee as a specialist in the doing of some few deeds. None any longer is a generalist, doing everything on his or her own. The labor of the individual in one system therefore hardly differs from the role of the individual in another. Ordinarily what is asked for by all systems is the same thing: money, attendance at meetings, repeating of the viewpoint of the system. Yet that description misses the point, because it treats as trivial what to the participants meant life. In attending meetings, in giving money, people gave what, in the circumstances, they had to give. They went to meetings because they believed their presence mattered, to others and to themselves, as much as in attending services in worship of God pious people considered their presence important – holy. Paying dues marked identification with not the organization but the ideal and goal of the organization. So the way of life bore that same weight of profound commitment that the holy way of life had earlier sustained.

The three Judaisms are alike in yet another way. The several Judaisms in common share enormously emotional appeals to the (self-evidently probative) experiences of history, meaning, what is happening today. Each framed a grievance for itself, a doctrine of resentment. For Zionism, statelessness, for Jewish Socialism and Yiddishism, economic deprivation; for American Judaism, a sense of alienation expressed that grievance, bringing to words the underlying feeling of resentment. The ideologies of the twentieth-century Judaisms came after the fact of experience and emotion and explained the fact, rather than transforming feeling into sensibility and sentiment into an intellectual explanation of the world. The systems in common appeal to a self-evidence deriving from a visceral response to intolerable experience, near at hand. Unemployment and starvation made entirely credible the world-view and explanation of Jewish Socialism, made compelling the program of activity, the way of life, demanded thereby. Zionism formed into a single whole the experiences of remarkably diverse people living in widely separated places, showing that all those experiences formed a single fact, the experience of a single sort – exclusion, victimization, anti-Semitism – which Zionism could confront. American Judaism linked to an inchoate past the aspirations of a third and fourth generation of Jews who wanted desperately to be Jewish but in its own experience and intellectual resources could find slight access to something to be called "Jewish."

Emotion – the emotion of resentment in particular – sentimentality and nostalgia and resentment – these formed the road within: strong feeling about suffering and redemption, for American Judaism; a powerful appeal to concrete deed in the here and now by people who thought themselves helpless, for Zionism; an outlet for the rage of the dispossessed, for the suffering workers of tzarist Russia and turn-of-the-century America alike, for Jewish Socialism. So the power and appeal of the three ideological systems, all of them enjoying self-evidence for those for whom they answered basic questions, proved not only uniform, but also apt. For the problems taken up for solution – political, cultural, social, economic – raised for deep reflection the everyday and the factitious. What, after all, preoccupied the Jews in the twentieth century? Politics, economics, the crumbling of connection to a thousand-year-old culture, the Yiddish one, and a fifteen-hundred-year-old way of life and world-view, the Judaism of the dual Torah. These were, as a matter of fact, things the most sanguine person could not ignore, experiences of the hour, education in the streets.

The Judaisms of the nineteenth century have a single point of origin in common. All of them take form in the world of intellectuals. All focus upon issues of doctrine and regard as important the specification of why people should do what they do, how Israel within their several definitions should see the world and live life. The Judaisms of the twentieth century address questions not of intellect but of public policy. They regard as important not ideology, which they identify with propaganda, let alone theology, which lies beyond their imagination altogether, but collective action. That action works itself out through large-scale institutions of government, politics, economics. In the categories of charisma and routine, individual initiative through intellectual charisma and collective action through bureaucracy, the nineteenth century was the age of Judaisms of intellect, the twentieth, of bureaucracy.

For the Judaisms of the twentieth century, as we shall now see, all take shape in a world that requires the gifts not of intellectuals (though the founders were all persons of substantial intellect and vision) but of organizers, people who could create large-scale institutions and organizations: unions, bureaucracies, even (in Zionism) entire governments. What mattered to nineteenth-century Judaisms demanded the genius of individual minds: writers, scholars, theologians. What made a difference later on would require a different order of abilities altogether: persons not of personal charisma of intellect but of capacity to organize and administer: bureaucrats, lawyers, politicians, businessmen. To such as these, ideas formed not a world-view to make sense of life, but an ideology to make possible persuasion through propaganda. From men and women of individual vocation we shall move on to those who can transform the gifts of charisma into the structures of routine and order.

And the reason for the shift stands near at hand: the urgent issues of the nineteenth century demanded attention to doctrine and individual deed: what should I think? what should I do? The critical concerns of the century beyond focused upon public policy: how shall we survive? where should we go? So the Judaisms of the age testify to the character and quality of the age. Jews could evade the intellectual issues of the nineteenth century. The world forced on their attention the political crises of the twentieth. And that accounts for the difference between the one system and the other.

NOTES

1   I put "post-Christian" in quotation-marks to indicate that I do not regard the adjective as a valid description of the state of affairs, but use it because it signifies that Christianity then met considerable, powerful competition, just as Judaism did. The age was just as much "post-Judaic," and for exactly the same reasons.

2   Britain: because Germany never conquered the country; France, because the Jewish community was brought back to life by Jews from France's North African possessions. In the other countries conquered by Germany in World War II, Jewish communities were refounded after 1945, but Judaism never took root; the Jewish communities in the main are shaped around ethnic, not religious, convictions.

3   I stress that we deal only with the followers of Zionism, Socialism, and Holocaust and Redemption Judaisms. Massive numbers of Jews remained wholly within the Judaism of the dual Torah, which emerged from the twentieth century the single most vital and popular Judaic system of all.

4   Anita Shapira, *Berl: The Biography of a Socialist Zionist, Berl Katznelson 1887–1944* (Cambridge, 1974: Cambridge University Press), p. 343.

Richard L. Rubenstein
"Religion and History: Power, History, and the Covenant at Sinai"

What makes Professor Rubenstein's essay compelling for the study of Judaic systems in the twentieth century is his formulation of religious issues in theological terms and categories. He raises the fundamental question of how in Judaism, meaning the Judaism of the dual Torah, history is to be interpreted, and this leads him immediately to the issue of power. Since, as I have explained, the twentieth-century Judaic systems all tried to cope with the effects of hostile power upon the Jewish people in Europe and the USA, Rubenstein's systematic account of the interplay of power and religion leads us to the very heart of the issue.

What marks the "post-Christian" century is the idea that there can be a power greater than, and unrelated to that of, God, namely, the power of the state. Here Rubenstein forms an account of the idea that there can be a power greater than that of the state, namely the power of God. Rubenstein then pursues that idea, that God transcends the state, which he calls "a source of hope, liberation, and vexation down to our own day." That idea derives from ancient Israel, reaching us through Judaism and Christianity. Rubenstein does well, then, to focus our attention on the conception of divine kingship – counterpart to the waning century's all powerful state, and the competition between the power of the state and the power that transcends all states. Rubenstein shows us, also, how the study of Scripture in its historical context yields important guidelines for reflecting upon the world as we know it.

How shall we understand Judaism, with its God of history, as a system of interpreting history? History itself can be understood as the record of the ways in which men have employed power that have been deemed worthy of memory. Every reflection on history is there-fore a consideration of the nature and the use of power. Nor is the understanding of power irrelevant to the understanding of religion, especially a religion of history, for one of the most important ques-tions in both religion and politics is this: what is the ultimate source of power and how are men and women to relate to that power? Power itself has been defined as "the possibility within a social relationship of imposing one's will, even against opposition."[1] In view of the fact that the state can be understood to be a "human community that successfully claims the monopoly of the legitimate use of force within a given territory," the ultimate source of power must be either the state, which is the human agency with the greatest power, or a suprahuman agency. The suprahuman agency, if such there be, would have to be a god.[2]

The idea that there could be a power greater than and unrelated to that of the state would be most likely to arise in the aftermath of a natural or social catastrophe, in which the state's claim to ultimacy proved dysfunctional to a substantial number of its subjects. In recent times, the failure of the secular government of the Shah in Iran to cope with the social dislocations of rapid modernization and sudden affluence led to the theocratic regime of the Ayatollah Khomeini. In the Near East, the inability of the rulers of the Canaanite city-states to cope with the economic and social needs of their subjects had the effect of facilitating the entry of the Israelites into Canaan and the adhesion of large numbers of the indigenous population to the new community.[3] The religious transformation initiated by ancient Israel was the first in which a human community was organized on the basis of the idea that the ultimate source of power in human affairs is an absolutely unique Divine Being whose potency is greater than and distinct from that of any of the gods of the nations as well as of any divine-human ruler. Once initiated, that idea has had an enduring, vexing, and problematic history. It has contin-ued to be a source of hope, liberation, and vexation down to our own day.

It is, however, important to remember that the religio-political system opposed by ancient Israel has not lacked intelligent and informed defenders to the present day. I refer to the institution of divine kingship. That institution probably has been the most effective means of governing without the use of overt force known to mankind. Perhaps the oldest method of exercising power over human beings involved the threat of force. However, naked fear is an unstable incentive. A state that governs solely by the threat of force must always guard against the possibility of revolt. Moreover, the resources necessary to govern a hostile population are far greater than for a loyal population. Such loyalty is likely to be strongest when members of the community are convinced that the ruler's authority has divine sanction or, better still, when the ruler is regarded as being the living incarnation of a divine being. At its best, divine kingship can assure members of the political community that, whether they be of high or low estate, they can have a secure place in the order of things. The system can offer them the further assurance that the governed can normally expect equitable treatment from their rulers, although, as we shall see, that is not always the case. That assurance was implicit in the Egyptian belief that Pharaoh ruled by *maat* or divinely certified justice.

Nevertheless, the institution of divine kingship has also been a source of misery and even degradation for large numbers of the men and women who have been bound to it. This was certainly the case in the ancient Near East. At the time of Israel's entry into Canaan, the sacralized city-kingdoms of the land were largely governed by foreigners or their descendants who had imposed their dominion on the indigenous population by means of the superiority of their weaponry.[4] One of the king's most important social functions was to serve as the authority responsible for the redistribution of the total wealth of the community. The agricultural surplus of the countryside provided the food for the city. The labor of the agrarian villagers, often exacted with little or no concern for their well-being, was forcibly placed at the disposal of the king and his retainers. Redistribution was frequently little more than naked exploitation exacerbated by the fact that it was practiced by arrogant and alien rulers.[5] The abuses to which the institution of monarchy was prone in the ancient Near East are often depicted in Scripture. In one well-known passage, the prophet Samuel is depicted as warning the people against asking for a king:

> This is the sort of king who will govern you. . . . He will take your sons and make them serve in his chariots and with his cavalry, and will make them run before his chariot. . . . Some . . . will plough his fields and reap his harvest; others again will make weapons of war and equipment for mounted troops. He will take your daughters for perfumers, cooks, and confectioners, and will seize the best of your cornfields, vineyards, and olive-yards, and give them to his lackeys. He will take a tenth of your grain and your vintage to give to his eunuchs and lackeys. Your

slaves, both men and women, and the best of your cattle and your asses he will seize and put to his own use. He will take a tenth of your flocks and you yourselves will become slaves. (1 Sam. 8: 11–17).

Clearly, the claims of the individual, even when just and reasonable, were subordinated to those of the state in the sacred kingdoms of the ancient Near East.

The fundamental political purpose of the institution of sacral kingship is to legitimate the unconditional character of the state's right to govern every sphere of human activity. Theoretically, in a sacralized kingship there can be neither private property nor what is today called "human rights." Strictly speaking, in such a system the ruler can do no wrong. As a divine being or, at least, a divinely sanctioned being, all of his actions are self-legitimating. Whatever privileges the ruler or his agents bestow on the governed derive solely from his cosmically grounded authority.

Obviously, sacral kingdoms are not the only states whose rulers regard their actions as self-legitimating. It can be argued that any form of sovereignty that recognizes no transcendent divine authority is self-legitimating. Moreover, there are undoubtedly many rulers who pay lip-service to the idea of a transcendent divine authority, or even to the "will of the people," but who nevertheless regard sovereignty as self-legitimating. Unfortunately, whether the state be sacral or secular, when it is regarded as the ultimate authority, those men and women who, for any reason, find themselves stateless cease to be human beings in some crucial ways. At the very least, such persons enjoy the protection of no institution that can give them any assurance that they will be treated as human beings. When Aristotle argued that "outside of the polis man is either a beast or an angel," he reflected a common conception that the limits of humanity were coterminous with the limits of one's group.[6]

The Nazi extermination of the Jews is but a contemporary example of one of mankind's most enduring codes of behavior. Knowing that the Jews of Europe belonged to no human community capable of assuring them of any security whatsoever, the Nazis saw no reason to limit the destructiveness they inflicted upon the Jews as well as upon all those whom they regarded as unassimilable to their community and, hence, as they clearly stated, devoid of human status.[7] Nor have the Nazis been alone in their belief in the self-legitimating authority of the state and the total denial of human treatment to those who were perceived to be unassimilable to the body politic. The age-old strategies of enslavement, expulsion, and extermination of the unassimilable stranger have been widely practiced throughout the modern world.

In some important respects there is a similarity between modern doctrines of race as the basis for political unity and the ancient doctrine of the divinity of the king. Both doctrines seek to establish the basis of political and social community in a metaphor of biological kinship. Racism proclaims the unity of common biological origin; the doctrine of divine kingship treats society as an extended family under the leadership of a divine-human parent-figure. However, racism's myth of common origin is often implicit in sacral kingship's view of society.

As we have noted, such societies can work well over long periods of time. Such a system works best where, as in Japan, the emperor is neither a conquering foreigner nor the descendant of conquering foreigners but the leading member of the first family. We have also noted that such societies can work intolerable hardships on outsiders and those at the bottom of the social hierarchy. When conditions become intolerable in any society, the victims may finally be tempted to change their situation through force. Such revolts usually fail. However, Scripture does preserve the memory of a revolt against a sacred kingdom that not only succeeded but became the basis of a decisive transformation in the religious and political life of humanity. I refer, of course, to the Exodus from Egypt.

As is well known, the Egyptian state depended upon a system of corvée labor for many of its most important projects such as the building of the pyramids and temples. As a living god, Pharaoh was regarded as the sole proprietor of all goods and services within the nation. In redistributing the nation's wealth, Pharaoh's agents were thought of as redistributing that which in any event belonged to him. One Egyptian tomb inscription reads: "What is the king of Upper and Lower Egypt? He is a god by whose dealings one lives, the father and mother of all men, alone by himself without equal."[8] As Henri Frankfort has observed, the Egyptians were without any concept of personal freedom. Nevertheless, they did not regard any service they rendered to Pharaoh, whether in the form of goods or labor, as a form of slavery.[9] However, this was not true of those non-Egyptians who had been condemned to corvée labor because they were prisoners of war, hostages, or had experienced a radical degradation in status, such as occurred to the "Hebrews" after the Semitic Hyksos domination of Egypt had been overthrown in the thirteenth century CE.[10] We have terse evidence of this degradation of status in Scripture: "And there arose a new King who knew not Joseph" (Ex. 1: 11). Scripture also records that the Egyptian state dealt with the degraded persons in a manner that has been perennially characteristic of sacred or totalitarian societies when confronted with unwanted persons or groups. They were either enslaved or exterminated. The "Hebrews" were condemned to slavery, and, when their numbers increased beyond the labor requirements of the slavemasters, all male Hebrew infants were ordered put to death at birth (Ex. 1: 16). Apparently, extermination was a method of eliminating a surplus population in ancient as well as modern times.

As the story is told in Scripture, it would appear at first glance that the "Hebrews" enslaved by the Egyptians shared a common religious and ethnic background. This is, of course, the way they are normally regarded within the Judeo-Christian tradition. In reality, Scripture offers hints that the group that escaped with Moses did not share a common inheritance. Referring to the band of Moses' followers in the wilderness, Scripture tells us: "Now there was a mixed company of strangers who had joined the Israelites" (Num. 11: 4). For several centuries before the Exodus, people from Palestine and Syria had entered Egypt, some as prisoners of war, some who were forced to take up residence by the Egyptians after engaging in activities hostile to Egypt in their home communities, others who were merchants. Not all were slaves, but the situation of all resident aliens tended to deteriorate as time went on. It is thought today that each group within the resident aliens retained something of their own identity, particularly insofar as their religious traditions involved some elements of ancestor worship.[11] As we know, Scripture identifies the resident aliens as "Hebrews," but that name probably designated a number of peoples who shared a common condition and social location in Egypt but were of diverse origins.[12] In some respects, the situation of the "Hebrews" was like that of members of a modern multi-ethnic metropolis, in which diverse groups share common problems in the present but remain distinct from each other because of differences in origin, religion, and culture.

When the time came for the escape from Egypt, the "Hebrews" shared a common yearning for liberation and a common hatred of their overlords, but little else. This was enough to unify them so that they could escape. However, as soon as they were beyond the immediate reach of the Egyptians, a compelling basis for unity beyond shared hatred and a desire to escape had to be found, if the band of fugitives and outcasts was to survive the natural and human hazards of the wilderness. Fortunately, the escape provided a further shared experience, the Exodus itself.

An important function of any new religion that originates in a radical break with past tradition is to facilitate the founding of a community for those who share no community.[13] There could be only one basis for communal unity in the ancient Near East where the distinction between group membership and religious identity was unknown. The diverse peoples could only become a single people if they were united by a common God. Moreover, the God had to be a new God whose power was greater than that of the Egyptian God-king. It would have been difficult for any of the peoples among the escapees to assert that its particular ancestral god ought to be the God of the entire band without arousing the mistrust and hostility of the others. *The "Hebrews" shared a common historical experience rather than kinship.* Ancestral gods were an impediment to unity. Only a God who was the author of their shared experience could have unified them. Of course, *after* the new God had unified them, it was natural for the assorted peoples to read back elements of continuity between the new God and their ancestral gods. That process is visible in Scripture.[14]

We know that under Moses the new God and the new unity were found. It also appears that within a relatively short time, the united escapees experienced an extraordinary increase in numbers and energy and that the enlarged group was able to gain control of much of the territory of Palestine and Jordan. The details of the conquest are unimportant for our purposes. What is important is that we understand something of the nature of the new God and his utterly novel relationship to his people.

From the very beginning the followers of this God were convinced that he shared his power with no other being, human or divine. All human power was thought to be subordinate and accountable to his power. Moreover, the new God was thought to exercise his power in a manner that was both rational and ethical. It was rational in that there was nothing gratuitous, arbitrary, or purposeless in its exercise; it was ethical in the sense that it was fundamentally concerned with the well-being of persons rather than with the maintenance of political, social, or even religious institutions. His power was also thought to be ethical and rational in the sense that he gave his followers the assurance that there was a predictable and dependable relationship between their conduct and the way he exercised his power over them.

The structure by means of which the new God offered the followers of Moses a secure relationship resembled a form of treaty that had been used in the ancient Near East in international relations, especially among the Hittites, in order to define the relationship between a suzerain and his vassals. It had, however, never been employed before by a God to define his relationship to a people whom he had adopted as his own. The treaty form was that of a *covenant*.[15] The character of the relationship between the new God and his people was *covenantal*. Unless this fundamental fact is understood, there can be no comprehension of the conception of God to which normative Judaism has been committed from its inception to the present day. Although one cannot speak of Judaism until long after the Exodus, one can with justice assert that the covenant at Sinai was decisive for the Jewish conception of God, the relationship between God and man, and the relationship between man and man.

Modern biblical scholarship has given us a fairly accurate picture of the origins of the covenant form.[16] There were two types of covenant, one between equals, which need not detain us, and the other, the suzerainty type, which was a pact imposed by a powerful lord upon a vassal, stipulating what the vassal must do to receive the lord's protection. These Hittite instruments were basically devices for securing binding agreements in international relations. The Hittite overlords were trying to cope with a problem that continues to plague nations to this day. While there are means of enforcing agreements, once made, within a nation, there is no effective, impartial institution capable of enforcing the keeping of promises between sovereign states if one of the parties should conclude that its interest is no longer served by keeping the pact. In such a case, the injured party has no choice but to accept the breach of faith or to resort to military force to enforce the pact. The purpose of the Hittite covenant was to give international agreements a binding character. This was done by the lord binding the vassal by an oath to meet the obligations stipulated in the agreement. An oath is a conditional self-curse, in which the person appeals to his own gods to punish him should he break the agreement. In the ancient Near East, oaths were initially effective in guaranteeing that a promise would be kept. As we know, they lost their effectiveness later on. We could also say that a covenant was a means of achieving unity of purpose between peoples that were bound to each other neither by ties of kinship nor by common ancestral gods. It was this aspect of the covenant that was to prove so important in its use in biblical religion.

According to George Mendenhall, perhaps the preeminent authority on the subject, the Hittite covenants had an elaborate form which was later used in the biblical covenant.[17] Among the elements that are of interest to us are the following: (a) a preamble identifying the king who was the author of the covenant; (b) a review by the king, speaking in the first person of the past benefits he had bestowed upon the vassal as well as an assertion that these benefits were the basis for the vassal's future obligation to the suzerain (both in the Hittite documents and the biblical covenant, historical events rather than the magical qualities of the lord were the basis of obligation; since history is the record of the ways in which men have used power that are considered worthy of memory, it was the lord's possession of and past use of power that constituted the basis of obligation); (c) a statement of the precise nature of the obligations incumbent upon the vassal. Moreover, in the Hittite treaties the vassal was explicitly excluded from entering into relationship with any other suzerain, just as in the biblical covenant Israel is excluded from having any God other than Yahweh.

An indispensable element of the Hittite past also found in the biblical covenant was the formula of blessings and curses.[18] While a breach of the Hittite covenant could lead to military action against the vassal, the only sanctions explicitly provided for were religious. The covenantal blessings and curses were thought to be the god's response to the vassal's behavior in either keeping or breaking his oath.

Another element of the Hittite pact that resembled the form of biblical covenant was the requirement that the text be deposited in the sanctuary of the vassal, as well as the provision for solemn ceremonies in which the pact was ratified, read in public, and periodically renewed.[19]

It is impossible fully to reconstruct the events surrounding the giving of the covenant at Sinai, but there is no reason to doubt that Moses had a revelatory experience at a sacred desert mountain and that that experience became the basis for the covenant between the new God and the escapees. It is also reasonable to assume that there must have been an enormous sense of wonder and triumph among the Hebrews after their escape. It was natural for them to believe that whoever was responsible for their revelation was a divinity greater than the god-king who sat on Egypt's throne. There may have been some temptation to regard Moses in that light, but Scripture insists that Moses made no such claim on his own behalf. Moses is always depicted as acting on behalf of and in obedience to a power greater than himself. Moses mediates between the new God and his people, but he always does so as a human being. Neither Moses nor any Hebrew experiences a direct, immediate, visible manifestation of the God who had been the author of their liberation.

The novelty of the encounter with the new God can also be expressed sociologically: Before Sinai there had been high gods, nature gods, ancestral gods, and gods of the polis, but there had never been a high God of escaped slaves and declassed fugitives. Moreover, by his election of the outcasts as his people, his "peculiar treasure," he had overturned all existing social hierarchies, in principle if not yet in fact. This was something utterly novel in human history and was to have revolutionary consequences. The Bible does not confirm social hierarchies. As we have noted, in the ancient world, and perhaps also in the modern, to be an outsider to all political structures can involve being deprived of all meaningful human status while possessing the full range of human capabilities and sensibilities. It is precisely such a band of outsiders who entered the covenant at Sinai.

The escapees had witnessed the dark side of Egyptian sacral kingship. They had good reason to reject its ethical and political values. A number of traditions are assigned by Scripture to the covenant at Sinai, but Mendenhall appears to be correct when he asserts that the new religion's values subordinated the power of the sovereign to the ethical concerns of human beings.[20] I would add that human status was no longer a function of membership in a political community in the new religion but derived from the God of the covenant. This was not explicitly stated at Sinai, but it was a corollary of that event, as later religious figures in Israel understood. In Egypt, where the ruler was a divinity, the interests of the state had a claim which transcended any possible claim of its subjects. There was, of course, a strong note of social protest in the new religion of the covenant. Escaped slaves, who had been the object of abusive power, were far less likely to give priority to the state's monopoly of force than were members of the ruling class. Nor is it surprising that throughout history oppressed classes have tended to identify themselves with Israel in Egypt and at Sinai. In place of the kingdom of Pharaoh, there was to be a new kingdom ruled by a very different kind of a God, the God who had brought them forth from Egypt.

Like the Hittite pacts, the Sinai covenant has a prologue, one in which Yahweh, the divine author, identifies himself and states his past benefits to those with whom he is to enter a covenant. "I am Yahweh your God who has brought you out of Egypt out of the land of slavery" (Ex. 20: 2) identifies the author of the covenant and states the basis of obligation. Just as in the Hittite document, the memory of concrete historical events within the human world is the basis of the vassal's obligation. Similarly, just as the vassal is prohibited from fealty to more than one lord, so the Hebrews are excluded from loyalty to any other God. "You shall have no other gods to set against me . . . for I am Yahweh, your God, a jealous God" (Ex. 20: 3–5). Yahweh's insistence on exclusive worship had both political as well as religious import. It united those who accepted it into a community and effectively barred them from giving their loyalty to any of the sacralized kingships of the ancient Near East.

The second set of covenantal obligations dealt not with God but with the relations between man and man. Scholars identify several very old collections in Scripture that offer slightly different accounts of these obligations, but in all these collections the ethical relations between individuals have a priority over both political and cultic values.[21] Moreover, all accounts of the covenantal obligations are based on a new conception of the place of power in human affairs. The functions and the authority that had normally been ascribed to human rulers are depicted in Scripture as the prerogative of God alone.[22]

When, as in ancient Egypt, the ruler is declared to be a god, the state and its institutions are thought of as self-legitimating, a view rejected by Scripture. Where such is the case, whether in ancient sacralized kingdoms or modern secular states, there is no effective limit to the actions that can be committed and legitimated by those who command the political institutions and control the state's monopoly of power. This does not mean that those in command will invariably abuse their power. Nevertheless, when political power is self-legitimating, in principle there is no effective check on those in command. Even in the United States with its constitutional system of checks and balances, in a national emergency the normal checks on the executive branch of government can be suspended. The programs of mass enslavement, extermination, and expulsion that have been initiated by such governments as Nazi Germany, the Soviet Union, the Cambodian Pol Pot regime, Castro's Cuba, and North Vietnam are among the contemporary examples of the extremes to which the exercise of power can go when the authority of the state is regarded as self-legitimating. In the contemporary world, the balance of nuclear terror is the only credible restraint upon sovereign states that recognize no value as overriding their own requirements for security and self-maintenance.

Those who truly accepted the covenant at Sinai as binding upon them, rather than as mere pious rhetoric, were bound unconditionally by values that transcended and sometimes contradicted the state's requirements for self-maintenance. Murder, adultery, theft, false testimony, and coveting are forbidden by the covenant, although such categories of behavior can at times become legitimating means of maintaining or enhancing the power of the state. This is evident in the difference between the kind of behavior a state will tolerate in its citizens in peacetime and the kind of behavior it will not only tolerate but reward when carried out by members of its intelligence agencies. Violent behavior, often carried out in stealth, is legitimated as being in the national interest, a claim that cannot easily or realistically be disputed.

The case of the double agent highlights some of the more complex dilemmas of the assertion of the primacy of the interests of the state. In order to establish his credibility, a double agent may have to act as if he were a traitor and even be responsible for the death of many of his fellow citizens. Sometimes governments may knowingly sustain attacks on their own citizens rather than permit an agent to be uncovered. Thus, when the maintenance of the power of the state is self-legitimating, there can be situations in which there is no predictable relationship between the loyalty and trust of citizens and the actions of their government. In ancient times rituals of human sacrifice were a regular part of the life of almost every community. To this day, the state's insistence on human sacrifice, at least in emergency situations, has not and probably cannot entirely be done away with. There are situations even in peacetime when the state's requirement for self-maintenance may compel its leaders to endanger or imperil the lives of some of its loyal citizens. Undoubtedly, the age-old belief in the ultimacy of the state's interests provided the rationale for such questionable programs as the army's secret introduction of dangerously infectious microorganisms into the ventilating systems of a number of American cities a generation ago, thereby making innocent citizens involuntary guinea pigs in biological warfare experiments. The list could be multiplied. It includes the involuntary administering of harmful doses of LSD to unknowing citizens by intelligence agents who were curious concerning the psychological effects of this drug. As is well known, a number of these experiments resulted in the death of the unknowing subjects. It could be said that the government agents were "playing God" by their abuse of power. There is no doubt that whoever has control over the state's monopoly of force, especially in wartime, does "play God" by virtue of his life-and-death power over others. It is not surprising that ancient man regarded those who possessed such power as gods.

I do not see any viable alternative to the idea that the state's requirements for self-maintenance ultimately override all other claims, if not in peacetime then certainly in times of national emergency. Nevertheless, Israel's ancient covenant with Yahweh was an attempt to create just such an alternative to the state's claim to ultimacy. By positing a God who possessed neither human image nor human incarnation as the power to whom the community owed its fundamental fidelity, the covenant had the effect of rejecting both the doctrine and the institutions that affirmed the ultimacy of the political order. Moreover, by insisting on the primacy of the ethical over the political in the new community's obligations to its God under the covenant, it set forth a principle that imposed unconditional standards on the behavior of men and nations alike. In addition, there was a harsh corollary to the idea that the community's obligations to its God were based upon the fact that he had redeemed them from Egypt and had constituted them a nation. It followed that if ever the new community failed to meet the ethical and religious obligations of the covenant, their God would withdraw his protection from them and they would be destroyed as a nation. In contrast to the sacralized kingdoms of both ancient and modern times that understand their religious traditions as giving assurance that the security and stability of their community is cosmically grounded, Israel's existence as a nation was tentative and conditional on her keeping the covenant.

In the Sinai covenant, we can discern many of the most significant features of Israel's later religious life. By subordinating the political order to the obligations of the covenant, the Sinai covenant laid the foundation of the prophetic protest against the ethical and religious abuses of the period of the monarchy as well as the prophetic idea that men and nations alike stand under the judgment of the God of the covenant. Over and over again, Israel's prophets reiterated their warnings that the very survival of the nation was dependent upon keeping the covenant.[23] Perhaps of greatest long-range significance was the fact that the covenant provided the basis for Israel's extraordinary ability to maintain its religious and communal integrity in the face of repeated military and political catastrophes. Since the political order had been denied ultimacy from the very beginning, it was possible for the community to survive the destruction of the Judean state as well as to interpret its misfortunes as evidence of the uniqueness and majesty of its God.

Nor did this essential community of faith and value based on the covenant come to an end with the close of the biblical period. The rabbis were very much within the tradition of the covenant when they refused to accept the Roman destruction of Jerusalem as involving the end of Israel's communal existence or its distinctive relationship with its God.[24] As much as we may admire the heroism of the men and women at Masada, their response would appear to have been less in keeping with that tradition. Given the biblical-rabbinic understanding of the subordination of the political order to the sovereignty of God, the rabbis were able to educate their community in a mode of life that permitted it to endure for almost two thousand years. Nor has that way of life yet lost its significance in our time. Although ritual was not stressed in the original Sinai covenant, the memory of the historic basis of obligation under the covenant was reinforced daily in the formula that the fulfillment of the commandments was a "remembrance of the going out of Egypt."

The covenant had yet other world-historical consequences, the most important and paradoxical being that its distinctive conception of the ultimate source of power and obligation eventually became the basis for the creation of the modern secular world. At first glance, the idea that the wilderness religious experience of a group of declassed, escaped slaves could produce the modern secular world seems farfetched, yet that conclusion has been increasingly persuasive in the analysis of the modern world since the time of Hegel.

Let us recall that the covenant's insistence that Yahweh alone is the God of Israel constituted a radical desacralization of the political institutions of the ancient Near East. For those who pledged themselves to the new God, both Pharaoh and the gods of Egypt were effectively dethroned. Similarly, the gods of Canaan, as well as their sacralized political and social institutions, were dethroned for those who came to accept the covenant in that land. The long-term effect of the covenant is everywhere the same: whereas sacral kingships see the continuity between the human and the divine orders, the covenant unconditionally distinguishes between them. It took a long time before the full implications of the original desacralization became manifest. Nevertheless, after the covenant had rejected the sacrality of the political institutions of the ancient Near East, it was only a matter of time before *all* human institutions were denied any intrinsic sacrality.[25] The cultural process whereby both the natural and the human worlds came to be regarded as devoid of any inherent sacrality has been called *Entzaüberung der Welt*, the disenchantment of the world. According to Max Weber, where such disenchantment occurs, "there are in principle no mysterious forces that come into play, but rather one can, in principle, master all things by calculation."[26] As we know, it is the aspiration of the modern secular, technological world to "master all things by calculation."

It is sometimes thought that this process of disenchantment is the result of modern intellectual skepticism. In reality, it is highly unlikely that modern secularism could have achieved its mass appeal on the basis of intellectual criticism alone. Only a religious faith that was radically opposed to the forces of magic and to belief in the existence of indwelling spirits could have initiated the profound cultural, psychological, and spiritual revolution that was necessary before entire civilizations could reject the gods and spirits men had revered as sacred from time immemorial. Without faith in the new God, it would have been impossible to dethrone the old gods. Only a God can overturn the gods. Only those who believed in their God's exclusive sovereignty had the emotional and intellectual resources with which to abandon belief in magic, spirits, and sacralized institutions. Thus, secularization is, paradoxically, the unintended consequence of a distinctive kind of religious faith. If one wishes to find the origins of the modern secular world, one must look for its beginnings at Sinai.

Yet, there is irony in such a paradoxical cultural achievement. Once the process of *Entzaüberung der Welt* is initiated, it is difficult to halt until the limit of radical atheism is reached. The same skepticism which the original believers applied to the sacred claims of the monarch of Egypt was eventually applied to the heavenly author of the covenant himself! In place of a world in which all values are ultimately a function of the state's requirements for self-maintenance, we finally arrive at a world in which values no longer have any ground whatsoever. Instead of a world in which only the outlaw, the man or woman who belongs to no political community, is treated with amoral calculation, kept alive and accorded decent treatment only if he or she is perceived to be useful, we arrive at a world in which all relationships are expressions of calculations of utility and no other standard need determine the relationships between man and man, save where the bonds of kinship remain unbroken. Put differently, we arrive at a world in which every man is a potential outlaw to his fellow. Although the covenant originally attempted to solve one kind of abuse of power, it had as its paradoxical and unintended consequence the creation of another set of problems of comparable gravity.

How then shall we evaluate the distinctive Jewish understanding of power and the record of its employment that we call history? Can we say that the entire enterprise was fundamentally mistaken in view of the fact that, against its original intentions, it eventually yielded an amoral, anomic secular world, or shall we perhaps say that the human world is amoral and anomic because it has never truly accepted the ethical obligations of the covenant? I would argue that the Jewish understanding was neither correct nor incorrect but functional in some circumstances and dysfunctional in others. It originally contained cultural and religious values that made liberation and the formation of a new community possible for a group of tenuously united, powerless fugitives who had been without access to the normal levers of power within an established community. Nevertheless, once the community of the covenant was established and in possession of its own territorial base, it found itself confronted with the same dilemmas of power and national interest that faced all the other kingdoms of the ancient Near East. The Israelite kingdoms had to defend themselves, sometimes by making war, sometimes by making alliances with their neighbors. Often, these alliances were ratified by the marriage of an Israelite king and a pagan princess. The covenant's demand for rendering exclusive homage to Yahweh simply could not be maintained by Israel's rulers without dangerously offending their allies and putting at hazard the security of the state. Of course, the prophets insisted that exclusive fidelity to Yahweh constituted the real security of the state, but which of us, had we been a ruler, would have deliberately endangered our nation's security in order to meet the prophetic demand for religious exclusivity? Similarly, the prophets accused the kings of favoring the rich over the poor, an accusation that is still heard in the land. Nevertheless, is it not possible that there are times when those who control large resources are a greater source of strength for the state than those who have no competence in the control of resources? It is not my intention to advocate that the rich be favored over the poor. My purpose is to suggest that there are times when the state must make decisions which do not always conform to our customary ideas of what is fair and equitable between individuals.

It is not surprising that, faced with political and social problems similar to those facing other rulers in the area, the rulers of the Israelite kingdoms began to respond as did those other rulers. Political values, especially the state's fundamental requirement that it maintain its monopoly of force against both internal and external opponents, took precedence over individual ethical values; the religion of landless, escaped slaves was found to be less functional than the agrarian religion of Canaan to men who now possessed and had to defend their own land.

We know how the prophets reacted to this development. We also know that the prophets' response formed the basis for much of the contemporary criticism of the state in countries with a strongly biblical culture such as the United States. What we regard as a natural and perhaps inevitable political and social evolution in ancient Israel was regarded by the prophets as unpardonable idolatry for which Israel deserved the worst kind of punishment. It can, however, be said in defense of Israel's rulers that a very different set of values is necessary to create a community, where none had previously existed, than to maintain that community once it is established. As soon as the problems of maintenance displaced those of creation in ancient Israel, some means had to be found to legitimate the interests of the state. One can dethrone the old gods when one is rejecting the old order. When one seeks a psychologically effective and cost-effective means of maintaining the new order, there will almost always be the strong impulsion to resacralize political institutions or, at the very least, to ascribe primacy to the state.

It can, of course, be argued that Israel's trust in political institutions proved futile, that both the kingdoms of Israel and Judah fell to the assaults of their enemies. Much of the continuing authority of the prophets came from the fact that their prophecies of doom did prove accurate. Nevertheless, it does not follow from the fact that the prophets were correct in predicting disaster that they were also correct in their analysis of its causes. This observation also applies to the contemporary would-be prophets of both the religious right and the religious left who offer their judgments on American politics. Is it reasonable to believe that the kingdoms of Israel and Judah would have been able to withstand the assaults of the Assyrians and the Babylonians if they had scrupulously maintained the personal and religious obligations of the covenant? What destroyed the two small kingdoms was their relative military weakness. Undoubtedly, national morale in ancient Israel would have been higher had the prophets' warnings against the exploitation of the poor been heeded, but even a perfectly just Israelite state could not have withstood the assaults that were directed against it.

After the catastrophe, the prophetic claim about Israel's failure to keep the covenant proved to be both psychologically and sociologically functional. Lacking realistic means to undo their predicament, the defeated at least retained the hope that, were they to repent and meet the obligations of the covenant, God would redeem them, as he had redeemed the Hebrew slaves in ancient Egypt. After 70 CE this hope served as the motive and the basis for the reconstruction of the catastrophically defeated Jewish society. It has continued to serve as a basis for Jewish faith to this day.

If one asks how the drama of human history is understood within Judaism, the fundamental answer has not really changed since Sinai: In Judaism history is ultimately regarded as the ways in which men have either met or failed to meet their obligations to their God who is absolutely sovereign over all things. These obligations are largely ethical rather than political. No human value, even the survival of those institutions that promise communal safety and security such as the state, is of sufficient importance to compromise the imperative to fulfill the divinely certified obligations, for the real safety and security of mankind rest with the God who alone is truly sovereign rather than with any human ruler or institution, all of whom ultimately stand under God's judgment and power.

There is both hope and consolation in this view of history. As we have seen, it is functional under certain circumstances. Nor were the Jews the only people to find hope in this view, which ultimately derives from the blessings and curses of the covenant. After the memory of the redemption of the slaves from Egypt and the subordination of the power of the state to that of the God of the covenant had become a part of humanity's permanent spiritual heritage, this perspective became a rallying point for the disinherited and the disadvantaged, as well as for those who identified themselves with their cause. It gave the disinherited a basis for hope and an ideological weapon in their struggle for liberation. In defeat it also gave them a profound source of consolation.

Unfortunately, while this view of power and history may on occasion enable the powerless to break their bonds and to form a new community, it is highly unlikely that it could ever prove capable of sustaining a community once it has been established, for an established community must inevitably deal with the challenges of power that are manifest and concrete rather than invisible. And, power that is manifest and concrete is human power. When confronted with problems of internal and external security, all governments must be functionally atheistic, no matter how sincere the religious commitments of their rulers or people may be and no matter what religious rituals are used to solemnize important communal efforts. Those in control of the monopoly of force have no choice but to respond appropriately and rationally when their monopoly is challenged, if they are to survive. The Jewish view of history is functional only for those who either do not have to face challenges of manifest power or for those who lack physical force and can only challenge the existing monopoly of force by psychological means.[27] Under such circumstances, the values of the covenant may prove to be a potent psychological weapon.

We do, however, know that the community created by the rabbis remained more or less faithful to the original attitude towards power of the Sinai covenant. It is my belief that this can be partly explained by the fact that the political situation of the Jews of the post-70 CE diaspora resembled that of the original wilderness band in important respects. Until the birth of the State of Israel, the Jews were never accepted as full members of any community that claimed a monopoly of force within its borders. Nor was it possible for the Jews to create such a community. Had they attempted to do so, their effort would have been speedily and violently smashed. Whether one characterizes the Jews of the diaspora as outsiders, exiles, or a pariah people, until the emancipation and in many countries until the present day, they were never given the same protection as were members of the dominant group. The relations between the Jewish outsiders and their overlords were usually motivated by considerations of utility. When their services were needed, they were tolerated. In some cases, they were even accorded privileges. When they were no longer needed, they were expelled and, in modern times, systematically exterminated. Had they lacked a religious basis for community, they would have become an atomized collection of anomic individuals. Covenantal religion, with its subordination of political to religio-ethical values, was indispensable for their survival.

Unfortunately, there is a great difference between recognizing (a) that covenantal religion was functional for Jews during much of their history, (b) that it was also functional for certain other disadvantaged classes, and (c) making the claim, as both Jewish and Christian theologians tend to do, that covenantal religion is the preeminent model for all of humanity at its finest. Not every person or group is an exile, a slave, or an outsider. For those who are more or less at home in their world, alternative religious options are likely to prove more appropriate than that of the God of the covenant, even when, because of family inheritance, one retains membership in a religion that formally affirms the sovereignty of the God of the covenant.[28]

There is, however, a situation in which a large number of people might once again turn to the God of the covenant: Even a cursory glance at biblical and Jewish history shows that faith in the God of the covenant tended to be firmest in times of crisis and catastrophe. Should the worldwide social and economic crisis continue to intensify, modern versions of both sacral kingship *and* faith in the God of the covenant might gain large numbers of new adherents. Those who feel that in a crisis safety and security can only be assured by hunting with one's own pack are likely to find some form of sacral kingship irresistible; those who have reason to distrust even the power structures of their own tribe are likely to find some form of the covenant attractive. Nevertheless, though the options of covenant and sacral kingship are perennial, they are not permanent. Each contains the seeds of its own dissolution.

NOTES

1 Max Weber, *Economy and Society: An Outline of Interpretive Sociology* (New York: 1968), p. 53.
2 Max Weber, "Politics as a Vocation," in H. H. Gerth and C. Wright Mills, eds, *From Max Weber: Essays in Sociology* (New York: 1946), p. 78.
3 See George E. Mendenhall, "The Hebrew Conquest of Palestine," in *The Biblical Archaeologist Reader* (Garden City, NY: 1970), pp. 25–53.
4 See George E. Mendenhall, *The Tenth Generation: The Origins of the Biblical Tradition* (Baltimore: 1973), pp. 122ff.
5 See Mendenhall, *The Tenth Generation*, pp. 23f.
6 Aristotle, *The Politics*, bk. 1, chap. 2, 1253a, 1–4.
7 This was evident in the term *Tiermenschen* ("subhumans") that the Nazis used to designate the Jews. On the subject of assigning a "paranthropoid" identity to those targeted for abusive treatment or extermination, see Gil Eliot, *Twentieth Century Book of the Dead* (New York: 1972), pp. 41, 94, 124.
8 Alan H. Gardiner, "The Autobiography of Rekhmire," in *Zeitschrift für aegyptische Sprache*, 60 (1925), 69, cited by Henri Frankfort, *Ancient Egyptian Religion* (New York: 1948), p. 43.
9 Frankfort, *Egyptian Religion*, pp. 43ff.
10 See Ernst Ludwig Ehrlich, *A Concise History of Israel* (New York: 1965), pp. 10ff.
11 See Gerhard von Rad, *Old Testament Theology* (London: 1973), 1: 8–9, 20.
12 See Moshe Greenberg, *The Hab/Piru*, American Oriental Series, vol. 39 (New Haven: 1955), pp. 55–7.
13 This is stated by Montgomery Watt with reference to the origins of Islam. It also holds true of other traditions as well. See Watt, *Muhammed at Mecca* (Oxford: 1953), pp. 153ff.
14 See, for example, Exodus 3: 13. After God reveals himself to Moses as the God of the Israelites' forefathers, Moses is depicted as asking him, "If I go to the Israelites and tell them, and they ask me his name, what

shall I say?" indicating that the escapees did not know the name of the new God. See also Exodus 6: 2, 3, in which God is depicted as saying to Moses, "I am the Lord, I appeared to Abraham, Isaac, and Jacob as God Almighty. But I did not let myself be known to them by my name YAHWEH."

15 See article "Covenant" in *Encyclopedia Judaica* (Jerusalem: 1971), 5: 1012–22, and George E. Mendenhall, *Law and Covenant in Israel and the Ancient Near East* (Pittsburgh: 1955).

16 See George E. Mendenhall, "Covenant Forms in Israelite Tradition," in *Biblical Archaeologist Reader*, pp. 25–53, and Dennis J. McCarthy, S. J., *Old Testament Covenant* (Richmond, VA: 1972).

17 Mendenhall, "Covenant Forms in Israelite Tradition," pp. 29ff.

18 Ibid., pp. 35f.

19 Ibid.

20 Mendenhall, *The Tenth Generation*, p. 30.

21 See von Rad, *Old Testament Theology*, 1: 187ff., and Mendenhall, *The Tenth Generation*, p. 30.

22 Thus, when God is referred to as a "man of war," it is not the intention of Scripture to glorify war but to ascribe to God an authority previously ascribed to a human ruler. Similarly, when he is depicted as the sole proprietor of the land, this is meant to serve as a contrast to the idea that the monarch was the sole proprietor. See Mendenhall, "The Hebrew Conquest of Palestine," p. 110.

23 The relationship between Israel's fidelity to her obligations under the covenant and her fate are spelled out in many places in Scripture. See, for example, Leviticus 26: 3–45; Amos 4: 6–11; Jeremiah 44: 1–4.

24 See Richard L. Rubenstein, *The Religious Imagination* (Indianapolis: 1968), pp. 127ff.

25 This point is implied in the discussion of the secularization process in Peter Berger, *The Sacred Canopy* (Garden City, NY: 1966), pp. 106ff.

26 Max Weber, "Science as a Vocation," in *From Max Weber*, p. 139.

27 There is an obvious resemblance between the views expressed here and those of Friedrich Nietzsche. See Nietzsche, *On the Genealogy of Morals*, trans. Walter Kaufman and R. J. Hollingdale (New York: 1969), pp. 33ff.

28 It is obviously possible to retain membership in a religious tradition that strongly affirms faith in the covenant while at the same time "bracketing" the demands of that faith when one serves in a position of decision-making power. This was certainly true of both John Foster Dulles and his brother Allen when they served as secretary of state and director of the Central Intelligence Agency, respectively, under President Eisenhower. See Leonard Mosley, *Dulles: A Biography of Eleanor, Allen, and John Foster Dulles and Their Family Network* (New York: 1978).

6

Zionism

The word "Zionism" in modern times came into use in the 1890s, with the sense of a political movement of "Jewish self-emancipation." The word "emancipation" had earlier stood for the Jews' receiving of political rights of citizens in various nations. So "self-emancipation" turned on its head the entire political program of the nineteenth-century Jewry. That shift alerts us to the relationship between Zionism and the earlier political changes of which, at the start of the century, Reform Judaism had made so much. What had happened in the course of the nineteenth century to shift discourse from emancipation to self-emancipation?

Zionism responded to a political crisis, the failure, by the end of the nineteenth century, of promises of political improvement in the Jews' status and condition. Zionism called to the Jews to "emancipate" themselves by facing the fact that gentiles in the main hated Jews. Therefore Zionism aimed at founding a Jewish state where Jews could free themselves of anti-Semitism and determine their own destiny. The Zionist system of Judaism declared that the Jews form a people, one people, and should transform themselves into a political entity and build a Jewish state. Simply defined, therefore, Zionism is the Judaic system that defined its "Israel" as an ethnic and political entity. It spoke of "the Jews" – not holy Israel of Scripture and liturgy, and it held that the Jews form a people, one people, and should create a nation-state of their own. That nation-state should be founded in the Land of Israel (Palestine), the historic homeland of the Jewish people. Its world-view and its way of life followed from its definition of the system's "Israel," as we shall see.

Zionism was the most important Judaism of the now-waning century. As to popularity, among the Judaic systems of the twentieth century, Zionism took second place only to Jewish Socialism and Yiddishism in its attraction to large numbers of Jews. But after World War II, Zionism offered the sole explanation for what had happened and what people then should do: a way of life and a world-view meeting the ineluctable crisis assigned to it by history. Like Jewish Socialism joined with Yiddishism, therefore, Zionism supplied a sizable part of the Jews of Europe and North America with a comprehensive account of themselves and what they should do with their lives. And that account involved deeply mythic-Judaic truths.

How does the Zionist system compare with the Judaism of the dual Torah? If Rabbinic Judaism responded to the positive challenge of Christianity, Zionism formed an answer to a negative fact: the failure of the nations' promises of Jewish emancipation. It came into existence at the end of the nineteenth century, with the founding of the Zionist Organization in 1897, and reached its fulfillment, and dissolution in its original form, with the founding of the State of Israel in May 1948. Zionism is the single most successful Judaic system after the Judaism of the dual Torah. Zionism presented a complete and fully articulated Judaism. In the definition of its "Israel," Jews all over the world now formed a single entity not alone (or at all) in God's view, but in humanity's.

Then came the world-view, which composed of the diverse histories of Jews a single, singular history of the Jewish people (nation), leading from the Land of Israel through exile back to the Land of Israel. Again, this recapitulation of the biblical narrative derived not from a religious but from a nationalist perspective. The way of life of the elitist or activist required participation in meetings, organizing within the local community, attendance at national and international conferences – a focus of life's energy on the movement. Later, as settlement in the Land itself became possible, Zionism defined as the most noble way of living life migration to the Land, and, for the Socialist wing of Zionism, building a collective community (kibbutz).

Zionism therefore is to be understood in "the general background of European and Jewish history since the French Revolution . . . and the spread of modern anti-Semitism."[1] Not only so, but Zionism also arose "within the milieu of European nationalism."[2] But Zionism bears traits all its own, as the Zionist historian Arthur Hertzberg points out in his classic account:

> All of the other nineteenth-century nationalisms based their struggle for political sovereignty on an already existing national land or lan-

guage . . . Zionism alone proposed to acquire both of these usual pre-conditions of national identity by the élan of its nationalist will.[3]

What made Zionism urgent to its followers were, first, disappointment with the persistence of anti-Semitism in the West, and second, the failure to attain political rights in the East. Jews therefore began to conclude that they would have to attain emancipation on their own terms and through their own efforts.

The stress on Zionism as a political movement, however, came specifically from Theodor Herzl, a Viennese journalist who, in response to the recrudescence of anti-Semitism he witnessed in covering the Dreyfus trial in Paris, discovered the Jewish problem and proposed its solution. To be sure, Herzl had earlier given thought to the problem of anti-Semitism, and the public anti-Semitism that accompanied the degradation of Dreyfus marked merely another stage in the development of his ideas. What Herzl contributed, in the beginning, was the notion that the Jews all lived in a single situation, wherever they were located. They should then live in a single country, in their own state (wherever it might be located). Anti-Semitism formed the antithesis of Zionism, and anti-Semites, growing in strength in European politics, would assist the Jews in building their state and thereby, also, solve their "Jewish problem."

The solution entailed the founding of a Jewish state, and that formed a wholly new conception, with its quite particular world-view, and, in the nature of things, its rather concrete and detailed program for the conduct of the life of the Jews. For the Jews were now to become something that they had not been for that "two thousand years" of which Zionism persistently spoke: a political entity. The Judaism of the dual Torah made no provision for a this-worldly politics, and no political tradition had sustained itself during the long period in which that Judaism had absorbed within itself and transformed all other views and modes of life. In founding, in Basel in 1897, the World Zionist Organization, Herzl said that he had founded the Jewish state, and that, in a half century, the world would know it, as indeed the world did.

Three main streams of theory flowed abundantly and side by side in the formative decades. The first, a theory concerning the shared culture of the Jews, represented by Ahad HaAm, laid stress on Zion as a spiritual center, to unite all parts of the Jewish people. Ahad HaAm and his associates laid emphasis on spiritual preparation, ideological and cultural activities, and the long-term intellectual issues of persuading the Jews of the Zionist premises.[4]

Another stream, the political one, from the beginning maintained that the Jews should provide for the emigration of the masses of their nation from Eastern Europe, then entering a protracted state of political disintegration and already long suffering from economic dislocation, to the Land of Israel – or somewhere, anywhere. Herzl in particular placed the requirement for legal recognition of a Jewish state over the location of the state, and, in doing so, he set forth the policy that the practical salvation of the Jews through political means would form the definition of Zionism. Herzl stressed that the Jewish state would come into existence in the forum of international politics.[5] The instruments of state – a political forum, a bank, a mode of national allegiance, a press, a central body and leader – came into being in the aftermath of the first Zionist congress in Basel. Herzl spent the rest of his life – less than a decade – seeking an international charter and recognition of the Jews' state.

A third stream derived from Socialism and expressed a Zionist vision of Socialism or a Socialist vision of Zionism. The Jewish state was to be socialist, as indeed, for its first three decades, it was. Socialist Zionism in its earlier theoretical formulation (before its near-total bureaucratization) emphasized that a proletarian Zionism would define the arena for the class struggle within the Jewish people to be realized. In the reading on Socialism and Yiddishism as a Judaic system, we shall learn more about Socialist Zionism.

We recall the tension between Zionist and religious Jews in the story of Chaim Grade, and the conflict among religious Jews over Zionism. It was cultural Zionism that precipitated the conflict. Ahad HaAm made the explicit claim that Zionism would succeed Judaism, so Hertzberg:

> The function that revealed religion had performed in talmudic and medieval Judaism, that of guaranteeing the survival of the Jews as a separate entity because of their belief in the divinely ordained importance of the Jewish religion and people, it was no longer performing and could not be expected to perform. The crucial task facing Jews in the modern era was to devise new structures to contain the separate individual of the Jews and to keep them loyal to their own tradition. This analysis of the situation implied . . . a view of Jewish history which Ahad HaAm produced as undoubted . . . , that the Jews in all ages were essentially a nation and that all other factors profoundly important to the life of this people, even religion, were mainly instrumental values.[6]

Hertzberg contrasts that statement with one made a thousand years earlier by Saadiah, in the tenth century: "The Jewish people is a people only for the sake of its Torah." That statement of the position of the Judaism of the dual Torah contrasts with the one of Zionism and allows us to set the one against the other, both belonging to the single classification, a Judaism. For, as is clear, each proposed to answer the same type of questions, and the answers provided by each enjoyed that same status of not mere truth but fact, not merely fact but just and right and appropriate fact.

Herzl's thesis, by contrast to Ahad HaAm's, laid stress on the power of anti-Semitism to keep the Jews together, and that was the problem he proposed to solve. So Ahad HaAm's conception serves more adequately than Herzl's to express a world-view within Zionism comparable with the world-view of a Judaism. Hertzberg points out that Ahad HaAm described the Jews' "national spirit as an authoritative guide and standard to which he attributed a majesty comparable to that which the religious had once ascribed to the God of revelation." That conception competed with another, which laid stress on the re-creation of the Jews in a natural and this-worldly setting. In Hertzberg's language, this is to be "a bold and earthy people, whose hands would not be tied by the rules of the rabbis or even the self-doubts of the prophets."[7]

Debates within Zionism focused on the differences between the narrowly political Zionists, who wished to stress work in the diaspora, and the cultural Zionists. By World War I, Zionist progress in European Jewry proved considerable and, with the British conquest of Palestine, a statement, issued on November 2, 1917 (the Balfour Declaration), supplied that charter that Herzl had sought in his lifetime: the British government declared itself to favor a Jewish national home in Palestine, provided that the civil and religious rights of non-Jews in the country were protected. That same declaration won the endorsement of other countries, and Zionism began to move from the realm of the system-formation to the work of nation-building. Its three principal theoretical statements had come to expression.

Let us then return to the analysis of Zionism as a Judaic system. For one thing Zionism enunciated a powerful and attractive doctrine of Israel. It appealed to Jews' sense of their distinctive character as a group, which appealed to this-worldly, not other-worldly considerations. It was now not God who identified the Jews as a single social entity, but anti-Semitism. The anti-Semites made no distinctions among Jews, and therefore Jews saw themselves as unified even while lacking much in common; so many concurred on this-worldly, political grounds, that the Jews indeed form a people, one people.

Given the Jews' diversity, people could more easily concede the supernatural reading of Judaic existence than the national construction given to it. For, scattered across the European countries as well as in the Muslim world, Jews did not speak a single language, follow a single way of life, or adhere in common to a single code of belief and behavior. What made them a people, one people, and further validated their claim and right to a state, a nation, of their own, constituted the central theme of the Zionist world-view. Apart from having in common the status of hated object, Jews all together could identify no facts of perceived society to validate that view. In no way, except for a common fate, did the Jews form a people, one people.

Because of the diversity of the Jews, spread over many countries and speaking many languages, Zionist theory, more than Yiddishist and Socialist, sought roots for its principal ideas in the documents of the received Judaism of the dual Torah. Zionist theory had the task of explaining how the Jews formed a people, one people, and in the study of "Jewish history," read as a single and unitary story, Zionist theory solved that problem. The Jews all came from one place, traveled together, and were going back to that same one place: one people. Zionist theory therefore derived strength from the study of history, much as had Reform Judaism, and in time generated a great renaissance of Judaic studies as the scholarly community of the nascent Jewish state took up the task at hand. The sort of history that emerged took the form of factual and descriptive narrative. But its selection of facts, its recognition of problems requiring explanation, its choice of what mattered and what did not – all of these definitive questions found answers in the larger program of nationalist ideology. So the form was secular and descriptive, the substance ideological.

At the same time, Zionist theory explicitly rejected the precedent formed by that Torah, selecting as its history not the history of the faith, of the Torah, but the history of the nation, Israel construed as a secular entity. Zionism defined episodes as history, linear history, Jewish History, with a capital H. That History appealed to those strung-together events, all of a given classification, to be sure, as vindication for its program of action. Zionism went in search of heroes unlike those of the present, warriors, political figures, and others who might provide a model for the movement's future, and for the projected state beyond. So instead of rabbis or sages, Zionism chose figures such as David or Judah Maccabee or Samson. David the warrior king, Judah Maccabee, who had led the revolt against the Syrian Hellenists, Samson the powerful fighter – these provided the

appropriate heroes for a Zionism that proposed to redefine Jewish
consciousness, to turn storekeepers into soldiers, lawyers into farmers, corner grocers into builders and administrators of great institutions of state and government. Zionism gave pride to beggars and
purpose to perpetual victims. The Judaism of the dual Torah treated
David as a rabbi. The Zionist system of Judaism saw David as a hero
in a more worldly sense: a courageous nation-builder.

In its eagerness to appropriate a usable past, Zionism, and Israeli
nationalism, its successor, dug for roots in the sands of history,
finding in archaeology links to the past, even proofs for the biblical
record to which, in claiming the Land of Israel, Zionism pointed. So
in pre-State times and after the creation of the State of Israel in 1948,
Zionist scholars and institutions devoted great effort to digging up
the ancient monuments of the Land of Israel, finding in archaeologi-
cal work the link to the past that the people, one people, so desperately sought. Archaeology uncovered the Jews' roots in the Land of
Israel and became a principal instrument of national expression,
much as, for contemporary believers in Scripture, archaeology would
prove the truths of the biblical narrative. It was not surprising,
therefore, that in the Israeli War of Independence (1948–9), and in
later times as well, Israeli generals explained to the world that, by
following the biblical record of the nation in times past, they had
found hidden roads, appropriate strategies – in all, the key to victory.

So Zionism framed its world-view by inventing – or selecting – a
past for itself. Its appeal for legitimation invoked the precedent of
history, or, rather, Jewish History, much as did Reform. But Orthodoxy, in its (quite natural) appeal to the past as the record of its valid
conduct in the present, produced an argument of the same sort.
None of the exemplary figures Zionism chose for itself, of course,
served as did their counterpart components in Reform, Orthodox,
and Conservative Judaisms, to link the new movement to the received Torah. Zionism sought a new kind of hero as a model for the
new kind of Jew it proposed to call into being. Like Socialism and
Yiddishism, Zionism in its appeal to history represented a deliberate
act of rejection of the received Torah and construction of a new
system altogether.

But Zionism found far richer and more serviceable than Socialism
and Yiddishism the inherited writings and made more ample use of
them. Its particular stress, as time went on, focused upon the biblical
portrait of Israel's possession of the land of Israel. The Torah (only
in written form, hence, "the Bible," omitting reference to its Christian half!) represented for Zionism, as much as for the Judaism of the

two Torahs, the validation of Israel's claim to the land. But it also contributed a usable past in place of the one now found wanting – that is, the past made up of the dual Torah's sages and their teachings, on the one side, as well as their iron control of the politics of the traditional sector of Israel, the people, on the other.

So we should not find surprising the power of Zionism to appropriate those components of the received writings that it found pertinent and to reshape them into a powerful claim upon continuity, indeed on behalf of the self-evidence of the Zionist position: the Jews form a people, one people, and should have the land back and build a state on it. Above all, Zionism found in the writings of the biblical prophets about the return to Zion ample precedent for its program, linking today's politics to something very like God's will for Israel, the Jewish people, in ancient times. So calling the new Jewish city Tel Aviv invoked the memory of Ezekiel's reference to a Tel Aviv, and that only symbolizes much else. It was a perfectly natural identification of past and present, an appeal not for authority alone to a historical precedent, but, rather, a re-entry into a perfect world of mythic being, an eternal present. Zionism would reconstitute the age of the Return to Zion in the time of Ezra and Nehemiah, so carrying out the prophetic promises. The mode of thought, again, is entirely reminiscent of that of Reform Judaism, which, to be sure, selected a different perfect world of mythic being, a golden age other than the one that to Zionism glistened so brightly.

Alongside the search of Scripture, Zionism articulated a very clear perception of what it wished to find there. And what Zionism did not find, it deposited on its own: celebration of the nation as a secular, not a supernatural category, imposition of the nation and its heroism in place of the heroic works of the supernatural God. A classic shift took the verse of Psalms "who will retell the great deeds of God," and produced "who will retell the great deeds of Israel," and that only typifies the profound revisioning of Israel's history accomplished by Zionism. For Israel in its dual Torah (and not only in that Judaism by any means) formed a supernatural entity, a social unit unlike any other on the face of the earth. All humanity divided into two parts, Israel and the (undifferentiated) nations. The doctrine of Israel in the Judaism given literary expression in Constantine's day, moreover, maintained that the one thing Israel should not do is arrogant deeds. That meant waiting on God to save Israel, assigning to Israel the task of patience, loyalty, humility, obedience, all in preparation for God's intervention. The earliest pronouncements of a Zionist movement, received in the Jewish heartland of Eastern Europe like the tocsin of the coming Messiah, for that same reason impressed the sages of the dual Torah as blasphemy. God will do it – or it will not be done. Considerable time would elapse before the avatars of the dual Torah could make their peace with Zionism, and some of them never did.

The doctrine of Israel joined together with well-considered doctrines, competing with those of Socialism, on how to solve what was then called "the Jewish problem." That same doctrine told Jews what they should do, which, as in the Socialist case, entailed a great deal of organizing and politicking. The world-view, centered on Israel's (potential) nationhood, absorbed much of the idealism of liberal nationalism in the nineteenth century and imparted to it a distinctively Judaic character. So claiming that, in its formative decades, Zionism constituted a Judaism – way of life, world-view, addressed to a social group and lived out by that group – certainly accords with the facts of the matter.

The world-view of Zionism defined the Jews as a people with a single, linear, continuous history. But Zionism made its choices, within that history, of a past it found congenial and useful. Leaping over the long history of the Exile, which Zionism by definition rejected, the Zionist theorists selected Bar Kokhba, with his heroic war against Rome in the second century of the Common Era, as the final precedent before their own time. The Zionist world-view then appealed to a unitary history, Jewish History, no less than did Conservative theologians or Reform scholars.

What about its way of life? When it reached fulfillment, Zionism described the way of life it prescribed in a simple way: living in the land of Israel, and, still, later, building the State of Israel. The world-view of Zionism in contemporary times came to coincide with the policies and programs of the government of the State of Israel. But in the beginning, when Zionism fairly laid claim to compete with Socialism and Yiddishism, on the one side, and the continuator-Judaisms of Reform and Orthodoxy, on the other, matters were different. Then Zionism formed a distinctive way of life, to be lived out in the everyday by adherents of the movement, and Zionism further taught a particular world-view, very much its own, as we have already noted.

Zionism comprised a movement led by intellectuals – not scholars, but also not workers. Its earliest members thought about action, debated with pleasure, and laid their hopes in ideas. Speaking of the Zionist labor movement in what was then Palestine, Anita Shapira characterizes a large sector of the movement:

The labor movement was response to the written word, to education, to dialog . . . Its faith in the power of words was an integral part of its belief that society could be changed by educating mankind and raising their social consciousness.[8]

Zionism therefore found its way of life in organizational activity, much as did the other political and mass movements put forth by Judaisms of the twentieth century. In terms of concrete activity, nothing differentiated the Jewish Socialist from the Zionist in War-saw or New York – except *which* meeting he went to. What Zionists did because they were Zionists was what Socialists did because they were Socialists, labor unionists did to serve their union, Communists to serve their cause, and on and on. The diversity of world-views yielded, in the century at hand, a single way of life, idiomatically expressed, to be sure. We should not miss the power of this kind of activity, its ritual quality, its capacity to express in a rather mundane and undistinguished gesture a very deep commitment.

The Zionist world-view explicitly competed with the religious one. The formidable statement of Jacob Klatzkin (1882–1948) provides the solid basis for comparison:

> In the past there have been two criteria of Judaism: the criterion of religion, according to which Judaism is a system of positive and nega-tive commandments, and the criterion of the spirit, which saw Judaism as a complex of ideas, like monotheism, messianism, absolute justice, etc. According to both these criteria, therefore, Judaism rests on a subjective basis, on the acceptance of a creed . . . a religious denomi-nation . . . or a community of individuals who share in a *Weltan-schauung* . . . In opposition to these two criteria, which make of Judaism a matter of creed, a third has now arisen, the criterion of a consistent nationalism. According to it, Judaism rests on an objective basis: to be a Jew means the acceptance of neither a religious nor an ethical creed. We are neither a denomination nor a school of thought, but members of one family, bearers of a common history . . . The national definition too requires an act of will. It defines our national-ism by two criteria: partnership in the past and the conscious desire to continue such partnership in the future. There are, therefore, two bases for Jewish nationalism – the compulsion of history and a will expressed in that history.[9]

Klatzkin's stress on "a will expressed in history" carries us back to the appeals of Reform and Conservative theologians to facts of history as precedents for faith. The historicism at hand falls into the same

classification of thought. But for the theologians the facts proved
episodic and *ad hoc*, mere precedents. Zionists would find it necessary to reread the whole of the histories of Jews and compose of them
Jewish History, a single and linear system leading inexorably to the
point which, to the Zionist historians, seemed inevitable: the formation of the Jewish state on the other end of time. Klatzkin defined
being a Jew not as something subjective but as something objective:
"on land and language. These are the basic categories of national
being."[10]

That definition, of course, would lead directly to the signal of
calling the Jewish state "the State of Israel," so making a clear
statement of the doctrine formed by Zionism of who is Israel. In
contributing, as Klatzkin said, "the territorial-political definition of
Jewish nationalism," Zionism offered a genuinely fresh world-view:

> Either the Jewish people shall redeem the land and thereby continue to
> live, even if the spiritual content of Judaism changes radically, or we
> shall remain in exile and rot away, even if the spiritual tradition
> continues to exist.[11]

It goes without saying that, like Christianity at its original encounter
with the task of making sense of history, so Zionism posited that a
new era began with its formation: "not only for the purpose of
making an end to the Diaspora but also in order to establish a new
definition of Jewish identity – a secular definition."[12]

In this way Zionism clearly stated the intention of providing a
world-view instead of that of the received Judaism of the dual Torah
and in competition with all efforts of the continuators of that Judaism. So Klatzkin: "Zionism stands opposed to all this. Its real beginning is *The Jewish State* [italics his], and its basic intention, whether
consciously or unconsciously, is to deny any conception of Jewish
identity based on spiritual criteria." Obviously, Klatzkin's was not
the only voice. But in his appeal to history, in his initiative in positing
a linear course of events of a single kind leading to one goal, the
Jewish state, Klatzkin did express that theory of history that would
supply Zionism with a principal plank in its platform. What the
several appeals to the facts of history would mean, of course, is that
the arena of scholarship as to what ("really") happened would define
the boundaries for debate on matters of faith. Consequently the
heightened and intensified discourse of scholars would produce judgments not as to secular facts but as to deeply held truths of faith,
identifying not correct or erroneous versions of things that happened
but truth and heresy, saints and sinners.

The reason that a secular system may be compared to religious ones lies in the consideration of teleology, the purpose and goal of the system. Religious Judaic systems promised salvation, and so did secular ones. That explains why Zionism offered not merely a political program, solving secular problems of anti-Semitism and political disabilities. It gave to its adherents a vision of a new heaven and a new earth, a salvific way of life and world-view, that drew the system closer in overall structure to the more conventionally religious Judaic systems of the nineteenth century. The vision of the new Jerusalem, promised in Isaiah 65: 17–19 and 66: 22, can help us to understand people who have yearned for, and then beheld, the new Jerusalem. Any account of Zionism in the context of the new Judaisms of the modern times will require a grasp of the mental world of the Zionists who lived out the experience of salvation. For when we speak of a transition from self-evidence to self-consciousness to a new age of self-evidence, Zionism rises to the head of the agenda.

The creators of the State of Israel, brilliantly described by Amos Elon,[13] formed a cadre of romantic messianists who realized their dream and attained their goal at the end of time. Elon's account of the founders is pertinent to American Jewry, for the same Jews who created the State of Israel also created the American Jewish community as we now know it. They were the emigrants from the heartland of world Jewry, the East European *shtetls* in Poland, Lithuania, the old Austro-Hungarian empire, White Russia, Romania, and Ukraine. Those emigrants, whether to Palestine or to America, endowed their movement with more than this-worldly, rational meaning. They fled not starvation but hell, and their goal was not a better life, but the Promised Land. Elon has given us a portrait of two generations of exceptional interest. From the perspective of modern Jewish messianism, it is the first – the founders' – that matters.

We deal with generations of figures who fall into the classification of heroes and saints, not ordinary men and women. For the founders lived for a cause. They had little in the way of private lives. Theirs was a public task, a public arena. "Few had hobbies; hardly anyone pursued a sport . . . they pursued and served the idea of Zion Revived. Socialists and Zionists, they were secular rabbis of a new faith of redemption" – so Elon. One cannot improve on Elon's description of these seekers for the new earth and the new heaven:

Resolute and resourceful abroad, at home they often fought one another with a ferocity that seems to characterize the infighting of most revolutions. In their lifetime historical processes normally much longer had shortened sensationally. They had lived their Utopias in their own lives.[14]

What was this Utopia? It was the Jewish state, no less. What reasonable man in nineteenth-century Poland could take seriously such a notion, such an aspiration? The condition of the country was pitiful. Why bother?

The answer was, because it is time to bother. Again Elon: "Zionism profoundly affected the lives of men. It gave people, thus far powerless and disenfranchised, a measure of power to decide their own fate." And it gave them something to do – a sense that their private lives might be spent in a great, public, and meaningful cause. It further lent to the otherwise inconsequential affairs of small people a grand, even transcendental, significance. Zionism means more than messianism; it transformed the worldly and natural to whatever modern, secular man may perceive as the other-worldly and supernatural. Elon writes:

> The crucial experience which lies at the origin of Israel as a modern state was the persecution generated by the failure of emancipation and democracy in Europe. Its myth of mission was the creation of a new and just society. This new society was to be another Eden, a Utopia never before seen on sea or land. The pioneers looked forward to the creation of a "new man." A national renaissance, they felt, was meaningless without a structural renewal of society.[15]

Zionism therefore represents the rejection of modernity, of the confidence of modern man in democracy and – because of Zionism's espousal of a "myth of mission" and a renaissance of society – in secularity. For there is nothing wholly secular about Zionism, and there never was. It is not modern, but, as some say, the first of the post-modern religious movements.

The Zionists, so devoted to that dream, did not take seriously their dependence, in the realization of that dream, on others who spent their lives in the "real" world. Seeing only visions, they did not perceive their time to dream was paid for by more practical people, who also wanted a dream, one to be lived by others, to be sure, and who were willing to pay for the right to a fantasy. Elon portrays Baron Edmond de Rothschild (1848–1934):

> He resented his colonists' European clothes and wanted them to wear the local Arab dress; he insisted they observe meticulously the Jewish

Sabbath, dietary, and other laws of orthodox Jewish religion, which he himself . . . ignored.

Rothschild was the model for American Jewry later on:

> We shall pay a ransom for the absent soul. In exchange, give us pride, purpose, a trace of color and excitement for unheroic lives. We shall pay you to be the new and courageous Jew – to keep the Sabbath on a dangerous hill, to wear *tefillin* in a tank.

Rothschild too was one of the founders; he too lives on. Elon calls the founders "beggars with dreams." But they were honest brokers of dreams. And what they promised they delivered. In time they invested world Jewry with new purpose, gave meaning to its endurance, promised hope in its darkest hour.

Throughout Elon's account one discovers the evidences of a new rite, a new cult, along with the new myth. He stresses, for example, that the changing of names was not mere routine:

> The Zionist mania for renaming was too widespread to be dismissed as a mere bagatelle. The new names they chose were too suggestive to be ignored as elements in the complicated jigsaw that represents the transient sensibility of an epoch. Names are elementary symbols of identity. They are seldom the heart of the matter, but they often shed a sharp light on where the heart can be found . . . A Zionist settler, in changing his name from Rachmilewitz to Onn ("Vigor"), was not only Hebraicizing a foreign sound. He was in fact re-enacting a piece of primitive magic, reminiscent of the initiation rites of certain Australian tribes, in which boys receive new names at puberty and are then considered reborn as men and the reincarnation of ancestors.

Likewise the communities they founded were represented in the minds of some as religious communes:

> David Horowitz . . . compared Bittania to a "monastic order without God." It was no simple matter to be accepted as a member; candidates passed a trial period, a kind of novitiate. Horowitz likened Bittania to a "religious sect . . . with its own charismatic leader and set of symbols, and a ritual of confessions in public reminiscent of efforts by religious mystics to exorcise God and Satan at one and the same time.

No wonder, then, that the impact of Zionism is to be measured not merely in this-worldly matters. In its day, from 1897 to 1948,

Zionism emerged as a powerful movement of salvation and affected women's and men's lives in a more profound way than – if truth be told – Reform, Orthodoxy, and Conservative Judaisms all together.

Zionism changed lives and accomplished its salvific goals. No wonder, then, that it enjoyed the status of self-evident truth to the true believers of the movement – which came, in time, to encompass nearly the whole of the contemporary Jewish world and to affect all the Judaisms of the day. For a brief moment it was the single most successful Judaism since the formation, fifteen hundred years earlier, of the Judaism of the dual Torah. The reason for the success of Zionism derives from that very source to which, to begin with, Zionism appealed: history, Jewish History. In a way no one would have wanted to imagine, what happened to Jews – Jewish History – validated the ideology of Zionism, its world-view, and, furthermore, vindicated its way of life. When the surviving Jews of Europe straggled out of the death camps in 1945, Zionism came forth with an explanation of what had happened and a program to effect salvation for the remnant. Critical to the self-evident truth accorded to Zionism is the historical moment at which Zionism came to realization in the creation of the Jewish state, the State of Israel.

Until the massacre of the Jews of Europe, between 1933 and 1945, and the founding of the State of Israel, three years later, in 1948, Zionism remained very much a minority movement in Jewry. Jewish Socialism and Yiddishism, in the new nations of Eastern Europe, and the New Deal in American Democratic politics, attracted a far larger part of Jewry, and the former, though not the latter, formed a competing Judaic system in particular. Before 1948 the Jewish population of the Land of Israel/Palestine had scarcely reached half a million, a small portion of the Jews of the world. In the USA and in Western Europe Zionist sentiment did not predominate, even though a certain romantic appeal attached to the pioneers in the Land. Down, indeed, to 1967, Zionism constituted one choice among many for Jews throughout the world. Since, at the present time, Jewry nearly unanimously attaches to the State of Israel the status of the Jewish state, affirms that the Jews form a people, one people, concedes all of the principal propositions of Zionism, and places the achievement of the Zionist program as the highest priority for Jewry throughout the world, we may say that, today, but not a great many days before, Zionism forms a system bearing self-evident truth for vast numbers of Jews.

The reason is that the world confirmed the worst prognostications of Zionism and made the Zionist conception of the power of anti-

Semitism seem moderate and understated. Zionism faced reality and
explained it and offered a program, inclusive of a world-view and a
way of life, that worked. The power of the Zionist theory of the Jews'
existence came to expression not only at the end of World War II,
when Zionism offered world Jewry the sole meaningful explanation of
how to endure. It led at least some Zionists to realize as early as 1940
what Hitler's Germany was going to do. At a meeting in December
1940, Berl Katznelson, an architect of Socialist Zionism in the Jewish
community of Palestine before the creation of the State of Israel,
announced that European Jewry was finished:

> The essence of Zionist awareness must be that what existed in Vienna
> will never return, what existed in Berlin will never return, nor in
> Prague, and what we had in Warsaw and Lodz is finished, and we must
> realize this! . . . Why don't we understand that what Hitler has done,
> and this war is a kind of Rubicon, an outer limit, and what existed
> before will never exist again . . . And I declare that the fate of Euro-
> pean Jewry is sealed . . .[16]

Zionism, in the person of Katznelson, even before the systematic
mass murder got underway, grasped that, after World War II, Jews
would not wish to return to Europe, certainly not to those places
in which they had flourished for a thousand years, and Zionism
offered the alternative: the building, outside of Europe, of the Jewish
state.

So Zionism took a position of prophecy and found its prophecy
fulfilled. Its fundamental dogma about the character of the diaspora
as Exile found verification in the destruction of European Jewry. And
Zionism's further claim to point the way forward proved to be Israel's
salvation in the formation of the State of Israel on the other side of
the Holocaust. So Katznelson maintained: "If Zionism wanted to be
the future force of the Jewish people, it must prepare to solve the
Jewish question in all its scope." The secret of the power of Zionism
lay in its power to make sense of the world and to propose a program
to solve the problems of the age. In its context, brief though it turned
out to be, Zionism formed the counterpart, as to power and success
and self-evidence, to the Judaism of the dual Torah of the fourth
through nineteenth centuries.

The power of self-evidence of the Zionist system to overcome the
actual sight at hand comes to expression in the remarkable account of
the great writer Amos Elon, describing the opening days of the first
Zionist congress in Basel in 1897:

The narrow streets of Basel were alive with a strange assortment of people. Students from Kiev, Stockholm, Montpellier, and Berlin, with proud duel slashes across their cheeks. Pious, bearded rabbinical scholars with earlocks mingled with scions of long-assimilated or even baptized families of the West and publishers of obscure little newspapers appearing in Warsaw and Odessa. Neurotic Hebrew poets, who wrote for audiences of a few hundred readers, or spent their lives translating Shakespeare, Goethe, and Homer into Hebrew, came in the hope of reviving their ancient national tongue. There were Romanian and Hungarian businessmen, university professors from Heidelberg and Sofia, a Kiev occulist, doctors, engineers, a small sallow Polish shopkeeper, a yellow-bearded Swede, a bespectacled French intellectual, a stiff Dutch banker, a courtly Viennese lawyer, and many journalists from all over the Jewish world, for whom Zionism was the great and sacred work of their lives . . . All were wearing small blue, seven-cornered shields embossed with twelve red and gold stars and bearing the legend, in German, "The only solution to the Jewish question is the establishment of a Jewish state."[17]

To see these diverse people as "a people, one people" required a vision not of what was, but of what – to be believed – to begin with had to be self-evident. And the power of Zionism was to take that vision and transform it into fact. What gave the whole urgency? The emphasis on the reality of anti-Semitism, so Herzl at Basel:

From time immemorial the world has been misinformed about us. That clannishness for which we have been reproached so often and so bitterly was in the process of disintegration just as we were attacked by Anti-Semitism.[18]

So, as Elon says, Zionism came into being through a "congress [that] was the first authoritative assembly of the Jewish people since their dispersion under the Roman Empire." The power of Zionism as a system of thought and a program of action lay in its capacity to explain events that cried out for explanation.

Anti-Semitism in the early part of the twentieth century, yielding mass murder in the middle – these facts confronted Jewry with a self-evidence of their own. The strength of Zionism lay in its facing these facts of Jewish existence, as effectively and as persuasively as the Judaism of the dual Torah had taken up and sorted out the facts of Christian paramountcy through the fifteen hundred preceding centuries. "History" proved Zionism right. Things that happened made all the difference – actual events, not scholars' idle and self-indulgent speculation on the meanings and endings of events. In the full light of day Zionism presented self-evident truth, the one genuinely successful and enduring Judaism in the age of evanescent self-evidence.

NOTES

1   Walter Laqueur, *A History of Zionism* (New York, 1972: Holt, Rinehart & Winston), p. xiii.
2   Arthur Hertzberg, *The Zionist Idea: A Historical Analysis and Reader* (New York, 1959: Doubleday and Herzl Press), p. 15.
3   Ibid.
4   S. Ettinger, "Hibbat Zion," in "Zionism," *Encyclopaedia Judaica* (Jerusalem, 1971: Keter), 16: 1031–178. Ettinger cited: col. 1041.
5   Arthur Hertzberg, "Ideological Evolution," in "Zionism," *Encyclopaedia Judaica* 16: 1044–5.
6   Ibid., col. 1046.
7   Ibid., col. 1047.
8   Anita Shapira, *Berl: The Biography of a Socialist Zionist, Berl Katznelson 1887–1944* (Cambridge, 1974: Cambridge University Press), p. 137.
9   Cited in Hertzberg, *The Zionist Idea*, p. 317.
10 Ibid., p. 318.
11 Ibid., p. 319.
12 Klatzkin, cited in Hertzberg, p. 319.
13 *The Israelis: Founders and Sons* (New York, 1971: Holt, Rinehart & Winston), p. 39.
14 Ibid., p. 41.
15 Ibid.
16 Shapira, *Berl*, p. 290.
17 Amos Elon, *Herzl* (New York, 1975: Holt, Rinehart & Winston), p. 235.
18 Ibid., p. 239.

David Vital
"Herzl and *The Jews' State*"

The State of Israel began in a book, Herzl's Der Judenstaat, which yields the Jews' state. But, as is often the case, the book stood for much more than its contents conveyed. Here David Vital, the greatest historian of Zionism of our generation, gives a simple account of what, exactly, the book says. The importance of his account for us lies in his factual report of the contents of Zionism in its original and authoritative statement. Vital underscores the basic theory of the social order that underlies the book: "the harmony of human interests, the ultimate compatibility . . . of social forces." It is important for him to insist that when the Jews leave Europe, they will go with good will. He does not propose an escape from hatred but the rational solution of a problem.

That explains why, too, Herzl does not have Utopia in mind. He is talking in practical terms about a real world. Everything we have noted about the power of Zionism to change lives in a radical way is contradicted by the laconic, practical tone of The Jews' State. The various European countries have a problem (in their view at least), which they call "the Jewish problem." Then, Herzl proposes, let Zionism solve the Jewish problem by removing the Jews from those places where they are supposed to present a problem. Anti-Semitism is a problem for the Jews. Zionism solves that problem too (so it is supposed) by taking them away and so ending the great hatred. (Herzl never conceived that in a Europe with few Jews, in countries such as Poland where there are none to speak of, anti-Semitism would remain a powerful social force.) So Herzl put forth a very simple solution to what he conceived to be an equally straightforward problem.

> *The solution is in two parts, first, institutional, second, political.*
> *He wanted to found a public body, a Jewish political entity, to deal*
> *with other public, political entities. So the Jews would form a politics,*
> *a nation, before they got their actual state. He wanted, second, to*
> *organize a Jewish administrative agency, which would undertake the*
> *practical arrangements for moving the Jews out of their places of birth*
> *and into their projected homeland. Both of these bodies took shape in*
> *1897 at Basel, so the book accomplished its immediate, practical*
> *goals. Being a practical man, Herzl also sets forth to the nations at*
> *large what their interests are in the success of Zionism. Whether in the*
> *Land of Israel (Vital's Erez-Israel) or anywhere else, the nations*
> *would find in the new Jewish state a sturdy and reliable member of*
> *the family of nations. Before us is an account of one of the most*
> *successful political visions of the twentieth century – and one of the*
> *most profoundly religious ones, for all its secular garb.*

Der Judenstaat is the length of a novella – some 30,000 words. It is
written in a clear, light style by a man intent on getting it read. Its
author is at pains to be absolutely unambiguous. "The idea which I
have developed in this pamphlet", reads its first sentence, "is a very
old one: it is the restoration of the Jewish State." It is devoid of
pathos. "I do not intend to arouse sympathetic emotions on our
behalf. That would be a foolish, futile, and undignified proceeding."
Its argument is intended to be set (and judged) within the terms of
the forward-looking, practical, scientifically and socially advanced,
optimistic, and liberal current of contemporary thinking. "Whoever
would attempt to convert the Jew into a husbandman [i.e. Baron de
Hirsch] would be making an extraordinary mistake." The peasant's
tools and often his costume are identical with those of his earliest
forefathers. "His plough is unchanged; he carries the seed in his
apron; mows with the . . . scythe and threshes with the . . . flail. But
we know that all this can be done with machinery . . . The peasant is
consequently a type which is in course of extinction . . . It is absurd
and, indeed, impossible to make modern peasants on the old
pattern . . ."

Der Judenstaat assumes the underlying harmony of human interests, the ultimate compatibility and conjunction of social forces, even
those which are, on one level and in the short term, unalterably and
bitterly opposed.

> The [organized and self-initiated] departure of the Jews will involve no
> economic disturbances, no crises, no persecutions; in fact, the coun-

tries they abandon will revive to a new period of prosperity. There will be an inner migration of Christian citizens into the positions evacuated by Jews ... The Jews will leave as honoured friends; and if some of them return, they will receive the same favourable treatment at the hands of civilized nations as is accorded to all foreign visitors.[1]

Der Judenstaat appeals throughout to the reason, the imagination, and the instinctive virtue of its readers. It seeks to anticipate their views and correct them. All in all, it is an orderly and workmanlike piece of writing: the problem, its solution, the method whereby matters are to be advanced, the legitimacy of the proposed means to advance them, the likely character of the result, and finally the answers to probable lines of criticism are all clearly and explicitly laid out.

For Herzl was at pains to persuade his readers that his was a down-to-earth, sensible, *feasible* plan. It was not Utopian. A Utopia may be an ingenious piece of machinery, he says; the problem is always to show how it can be set in motion. But here there was no doubt of the existence, nor of the identity, of a very powerful propelling force: the misery of the Jews. And thus the real questions were how best to employ it, to what machinery it was best harnessed, how that machinery was best constructed. Of course, he wrote, the plan would seem absurd if a single individual attempted to execute it.

> But, if worked by a number of Jews in cooperation, it would appear perfectly rational and its accomplishment would present no difficulties worth mentioning. The idea depends only on the number of its supporters ... It depends on the Jews themselves whether this political pamphlet remains for the present a political romance. If the present generation is too dull to understand it rightly, a future, finer and better generation will arise to understand it. The Jews who wish for a State shall have it; and they will deserve to have it.[2]

The source and context of the Jewish Question, in Herzl's view, are the pressure under which all Jews, in all countries, are subject. The pressure varies in degree and kind, but the phenomenon is a general one. "In our economically upper classes it causes discomfort; in our middle classes continual and grave anxieties; in our lower classes absolute despair." "The nations in whose midst the Jews live are all either covertly or openly anti-Semitic." Why this should be so is not of great interest to Herzl. On the rise and growth of modern anti-Semitism, he is brief and superficial: "Its remote cause is our loss of the power of assimilation during the Middle Ages; its immediate cause is our excessive production of mediocre intellects who cannot find [a social and economic] outlet downwards or upwards."³ It is in this connection that his familiarity with the condition and *mores* of upper middle-class western Jewry exclusively is most marked – and with it his limited, unhistorical, and, in some ways, self-contradictory view of the nature and sources of Jewish nationhood. On the one hand, there is a faint, but constant echo of ancient dignities. It is a "new Jewish State" that he wishes to advance. Yet, on the other hand, "we have honestly endeavoured everywhere to merge ourselves in the social life of surrounding communities"; and, in another passage: "We are one people – our enemies have made us one without our consent." But in fact Herzl's interests lie elsewhere. Origins are less important to him than consequences. "Everything tends to one and the same conclusion, clearly enunciated in that classic Berlin phrase: *Juden raus!*" ("out with the Jews!"). The Jewish Question is therefore an immediate and practical one. "Are we to get out now, and if so, where to? Or, may we yet remain? And how long?" His own answer is that they – or, at any rate, most of them – cannot stay. The pressures are rising. The logic of the Jewish social situation is inexorable. "When we sink, we become a revolutionary proletariat, the subordinate officers of all revolutionary parties; and at the same time, when we rise, there rises too our terrible power of the purse." The Jews cannot wait for "the ultimate perfection of humanity". Assimilation – which he himself does not desire (for "Our national character is too historically famous, and in spite of every degradation too fine, to make its annihilation desirable") – is out of the question, if only because the Jews will not be left in peace long enough to allow them to merge with the surrounding peoples. Nothing is to be gained, however, by petty attempts to transfer a few thousand Jews from one country to another. "They either come to grief at once, or prosper; and then their prosperity creates anti-Semitism." So they must leave, but leave in great numbers and in an orderly and planned and purposeful manner. And they must enter not another people's country, but their own.

> Distress binds us together and, thus united, we suddenly discover our strength. Yes, we are strong enough to form a state and, indeed, a model state. We possess all human and material resources necessary for the purpose . . .
> Let sovereignty be granted us over a portion of the globe large enough to satisfy the rightful requirements of a nation; the rest we shall manage for ourselves.⁴

Herzl's plan, as he himself put it, was "simple in design, but complicated in execution". It was of two parts: assumption of responsibility for Jewish national affairs by a political body to be called the Society of Jews; and management of both the exodus of the Jews and their resettlement by a technical body to be called the Jewish Company. The first was to treat with governments, seek to obtain their consent to an assumption of Jewish sovereignty "over a neutral piece of land", and then administer the territory as a provisional government. The second was to take the form of a Chartered Company, established in London under English law. It was to be endowed with a large working capital and designed to assume responsibility for the liquidation of the migrants' assets in their countries of origin and then provide land, housing, and employment in the new country in exchange. It was to promote industry and commerce – all in an enlightened and progressive spirit exemplified by insistence on a seven-hour working day, severe restriction on women's labour, attractive and healthy housing, good schools "conducted on the most approved modern systems", and whatever else could be devised to contribute to the establishment of a decent life in the new country. It is to the Jewish Company that the longest chapter in *Der Judenstaat* is devoted.

It is characteristic of Herzl's fertile mind and of his strong belief that the Jews' state should be founded on clearly formulated principles of social justice that he goes into considerable detail on some points in his pamphlet. Thus on the "workmen's dwellings" which the Company is to erect:

> They will resemble neither those melancholy workmen's barracks of European towns, nor those miserable rows of shanties which surround factories; they will certainly present a uniform appearance because the Company must build cheaply . . . but the detached houses in little gardens will be united into attractive groups in each locality. The natural configuration of the land will arouse the ingenuity of those of our young architects whose ideas have not yet been cramped by routine . . . The Synagogue will be visible from long distances, for it is only our ancient faith that has kept us together.[5]

Herzl is also at pains to explain just how he envisages the migration of the Jews to their country – the process whereby they will be given a new home "not by dragging them ruthlessly out of their sustaining soil, but rather by transplanting them carefully to better ground". He touches on how they will travel, in what groups, who will lead each group, how the aged will be cared for (". . . we shall not relegate the old to an almshouse. An almshouse is one of the cruellest charities which our stupid good nature invented"), how the sites for towns will be selected, and what he expects will impel middle-class Jews to stir out of their existing relative comfort ("the bright, young, and ambitious professionals will be attracted by the opportunities provided by the Society and the Company; and they will draw the others after them"). . . .

As for the country he had in mind, he had, indeed, thought of Erez-Israel. He noted that it "would have in its favour the facts that it is the unforgotten ancestral seat of our people, that its name would constitute a programme, and that it would powerfully attract the lower masses". But on balance, and although he was opposed neither to one nor to the other on principle, he tended towards South America – or specifically to an empty part of Argentina which he hoped the Republic would be willing to dispense with. The climate of Erez-Israel was not one which most modern Jews were comfortable in, it was not a country in which it would be easy to apply the modern economic techniques he had in mind, and it was too close to Europe for his taste: "In the first quarter-century of our existence we shall have to have peace from Europe and its martial and social entanglements if we are to prosper."[6]

But in *Der Judenstaat* Herzl is at once bolder and more cautious. (It is likely that his return to Vienna, in the summer of 1895, having brought in its wake a reacquaintance with Jewish public opinion, led him to tread more gingerly on the delicate topic of Erez-Israel and reconsider his views.) He speaks, very briefly, of both possibilities. But he speaks at slightly greater length and to more purpose of Erez-Israel. In a passage in which, with characteristic fervour and ingenuity, earlier reservations are put aside, all aspects of the question, as he saw it, the emotive, the tactical, and the regenerative, are tied together, and the outline of his diplomacy in the years to come is firmly laid down.

> Palestine is our ever-memorable historic home. The very name of Palestine would attract our people with a force of marvellous potency. If his Majesty the Sultan were to give us Palestine, we could in return undertake to regulate the finances of Turkey. There we would form a portion of a rampart of Europe against Asia, an outpost of civilization as opposed to barbarism. We should, as a neutral state, remain in contact with all Europe – which would have to guarantee our existence. The sanctuaries of Christendom would be safeguarded by assigning to them an extra-territorial status such as is well known to the law of nations. We should form a guard of honour about these sanctu-

aries, answering for the fulfilment of this duty with our existence. This guard of honour would be the great symbol of the solution of the Jewish Question after eighteen centuries of Jewish suffering.[7]

NOTES

1   *The Jewish State*, trans. Sylvie d'Avigdor (1896), revised trans. Israel Cohen (1934), Introduction.
2   *The Jewish State*, Preface.
3   Ibid., chapter 2.
4   Ibid.
5   *The Jewish State*, chapter 3.
6   *Diaries*, i, pp. 133–5.
7   *The Jewish State*, chapter 2.

7

Jewish Socialism and Yiddishism

Jewish Socialism and Yiddishism formed a distinctive ideology out of aspects of the received system of the dual Torah as defined in Eastern Europe, the Yiddish language, and the social ideals of the prophets and rabbis of old. Jewish Socialism demands attention in the study of the birth of Judaisms beyond the death, for many, of the Judaism given literary substance in the fourth and early fifth century because, as I argued in the opening section, the movement at hand when reshaped to the special interests of Jews – hence, Jewish Socialism – offered to Jews in particular an ideology, a mode of social organization, a way of life and a world-view explaining who is Israel and what the Jews must do: a Judaism. It presented a complete picture of how one should live life – namely, as an active worker for political change and social improvement – how one should see the world – namely, as something to be perfected within the ideals of the biblical prophets and the program of Socialist theorists – and how to so form a new Israel – this one a component in the united working people of the world. This new Israel would take its place within the international working classes, but as a distinct component, just as the Russian or the Polish Socialists recognized their ethnic origins as well.

Hebrew served as the language of the Judaic system Zionism. Yiddish, the language of millions of European Jews until the Holocaust wiped most of them out, was the language of the Judaic system of Socialism that took shape in competition with Zionism. What the two systems have in common is that, while not religious, they both formed distinctively and particularly Judaic systems for forming the social order of (an) "Israel." Each defined its world-view and way of life in dialogue with the received Judaic heritage, and both succeeded in framing for the faithful a vivid life's ideal. Millions of Jews derived from Jewish Socialism not merely economic benefits or political identity of a non-sectarian character, but a life's ideal, a view of the future, a reason for action in the present. This they did together, as a formulation of what it meant to them to be "Israel."

The two Judaic systems were born at the same time. In 1897, the same year in which Herzl founded Zionism, Jews in Poland formed the Jewish Union, the Bund, which embodied Jewish Socialism and gave the movement its institutional expression. The working-class Jews of Poland and Russia, as well as of America, in huge numbers affiliated with the Jewish unions and Socialist political parties (later on: the Democratic Party of Franklin Roosevelt's New Deal).

Before proceeding, let us consider a clear formulation of the world-view, the life-ideal, of the Jewish Socialists. For a statement of the world-view of the radicals – this one in Hebrew, but an example of Socialist poetry, we turn to a poem, "We Believe," published in 1872. Here we find that set of truths held to be self-evident that express the way of explaining the world and the purpose of life that made Jewish Socialism a statement of meaning:

> We believe
> – That misdeeds, injustice, falsehood, and murder will not reign forever, and a bright day will come when the sun will appear.
> – There is hope for mankind; the peoples of the world will not destroy each other for a piece of land, and blood will not be shed for silly prestige.
> – Men will not die of hunger, and wealth not created by its own labor will disappear like smoke.
> – People will be enlightened and will not differentiate between man and man; will no longer say, "Christian, Moslem, Jew," but will call each other 'Brother, friend, comrade."
> – The secrets of nature will be revealed and people will dominate nature instead of nature dominating them.
> – Man will no longer work with the sweat of his brow; the forces of nature will serve him as hands.[1]

The passage in the original may make a more evocative impression than it does in English, where it lies flat on the page.

But there banalities also place on display the ideals of Jewish Socialism, which do emerge with clarity. The world-view of the Jewish Socialists laid emphasis on the building of a better world through science and technology. It elicited commitment and generated hope because of this powerful promise of a better tomorrow. Jewish Socialism promised a bright future, so described a better tomorrow; spoke of an eschatology; addressed the issues of economic justice; took up the Jews' concern for anti-Semitism as part of a larger ideal of universal tolerance; expressed a commitment to science and technology. That, sum and substance, frames the world-view: an amalgam of the Jews' social aspirations and contemporary complaints, a solution to the Jewish problem as part of a solution to the problem of class conflict.

Now the question demands attention: can we call the Jews' particular version of Socialism a Judaism? Not in the case of the many Communists and Socialists who happened to have been born Jews, that is, to have come from Jewish families. For them Socialism had no bearing on their Jewish origins, and they had no special relationships to other Jews. But for those Jews who opted for a Socialist ideal and organized labor unions and other institutions in particular for the betterment of the life of the Jewish masses, Socialism in fact bonded with certain components of the received holy literature to form a distinctively Jewish version of Socialism indeed, one that in the lives of the participants formed their way of "being Jewish." That is why in the distinctively Jewish-ethnic formulation of Socialism, with its chosen language of expression, the Jewish language, Yiddish, we deal with a Judaism. But not all Jews who happened to be Socialists and speak Yiddish participated in the Judaic system we consider here. The ambiguity of the matter requires sorting out.

Many Socialists who happened to derive from Jewish families explicitly rejected that heritage of Jewish origin. In Germany, Poland, and Russia, important Socialist and Communist figures derived from Jewish parents but in no way sought in Socialism or Communism a mode of "being Jewish," or, in our categories, a Judaic system. Quite to the contrary, Rosa Luxemburg, a leading German Socialist, and Leon Trotsky, a major Bolshevik leader in the early stages of the Russian Revolution, and the Jews in the leadership of the Polish Communist Party, though afflicted by anti-Semitism, treated as trivial or distasteful particularly Jewish concerns and said so. Nor do we imagine that because, in some circumstances, Socialism constituted a movement particularly attractive to Jews, Socialism demands attention in the study of the Judaisms of modern and contemporary provenance. Not everything Jews adopt as a way of life and a world-view constitutes a Judaism, and most such things, in the nature of modern life, do not.

True, Jews were attracted to Socialism in Western Europe, partly by the appeal of "building a 'just society' based on the teachings of the prophets, partly by the hope that socialism would overcome anti-

Semitism."[2] Still others turned to Socialism as an instrument for their own exodus from the Jewish group, so Schneier Zalman Levenberg: "There were also Jews who saw in it a way of getting rid of their Jewish heritage and serving the cause of the 'Brotherhood of Man.' Socialism was particularly attractive for Jews anxious to leave the ghetto behind them and who, disappointed with the slow progress of 19th century liberalism, were keen to embrace a new universal faith."[3] None of this has any bearing on our subject, though these themes will take a considerable place in the study of the ideas and politics of Jews in modern Europe and the USA, as well, of course, as the State of Israel.

Ezra Mendelsohn, the master of the subject of Jewish Socialism, describes the matter as follows:

> [Jewish Socialism] refers to specifically Jewish movements and parties which envisaged the creation of a socialist society as an essential aspect of the solution to the Jewish question. This definition, while far from perfect, has the virtue of excluding Jews who happened to be socialist as well as socialist movements in which many Jews were active but which had no specifically Jewish content or aims.[4]

Mendelsohn's definition amply justifies asking whether and how a Jewish Socialism took shape as a Judaic system.

By every criterion, Jewish Socialism serves. Informing its adherents how to conduct their lives, supplying them with a purpose and a meaning to existence, providing them with an explanation for history and a world-view encompassing the entirety of existence, defining for them the meaning of Israel and the place of Israel, the people, in the world, Jewish Socialism qualifies as a Judaism. In ways in which psychoanalysis did not form a Judaism, despite its appeal to Jewish practitioners, the Jewish Socialist system did. Not every Judaism falls into the classification of a religion. Whether or not Jewish Socialism fell into the classification of a religion, it assuredly fitted nicely into the category of a Judaism. As Mendelsohn stresses, in addressing "the Jewish question," Jewish Socialism developed a system that would not only function like a Judaism but would exhibit those indicative traits that, all together, tell us we deal with a Judaism.

It was a Judaism that competed with the Judaism of the dual Torah, just as Zionism did. Chaim Grade's story of the riot in the synagogue leaves no doubt on that score. When through the nineteenth and into the twentieth century, Jews in Eastern Europe ceased to find self-evident the system of the dual Torah, they did not become Reform, Conservative, or Orthodox. Reform answered questions of political definition that those Jews did not face, since no one ever offered them the promise of political "emancipation." Conservative Judaism relied upon Reform for its motive energy. Reacting against what it deemed excess, Conservative Judaism drew its power from the tensions of the center-position. But in Eastern Europe (as in the State of Israel today) it is difficult to locate that center among contending groups of a religious order. Orthodoxy had no message not delivered more eloquently by the life of the villages and the streets imbued with the received system. To explain to Jews within that system that the facts of nature and of supernature were equally facts answered a question of faith in a context of doubt that few within the received system perceived.

And those who did come to doubt in the main sought some system other than the one retained and intellectually enriched by Orthodoxy in its philosophical mode. Those who found the Judaism of the dual Torah self-evidently irrelevant did not then seek a re-visioning of that Torah. The reason is that the problems that occupied their lives scarcely intersected with the issues of that Torah, in any of its versions. What defined those problems? First came a long-term depression, severely aggravated by political stress in the very regions of Jewish settlement; second was the decline of agriculture and the economy that served it; third in line was the growth of population and consequent unemployment. For Jews in particular the chronic problem of the violent anti-Semitism of the state became acute. These, as we have observed, constituted a crisis of a different order from the one addressed by the dual Torah. The age of Christianity was benign and tolerant by comparison.

One of the several interesting systemic alternatives derived from socialism, and it was the Jewish kind that mattered. It mattered because it constituted a kind of "anti-Judaism," a systemic response, of a negative order, to the received system among those choosing to reject that system. Again Mendelsohn:

> Jewish socialism, so understood, could originate only in Eastern Europe, [where there were] . . . thousands of workers, the Yiddish-speaking "masses" so evident in the cities of western and southern Russia. Moreover, by the late nineteenth century a secular Jewish intelligentsia had developed in the Pale, consisting of students and professionals, many of whom were influenced by radical Russian ideologies. That they should be so was quite predictable, given the all-pervasive anti-Semitism which awakened their demands for social justice and made public activity, outside of radical circles, impossible. These Jewish

intellectuals . . . were in revolt against the values and traditions of the ghetto. In many cases socialism, the acceptance of which in itself was a sign of assimilation, led them to discover the Jewish proletariat; this discovery, in turn, led them back to the Jewish people, to whom they preached the new doctrine.[5]

The definition just now given requires that we turn to the other component, Yiddishism: why did a language take on such importance in the formation of a Judaic system?

The Yiddish language formed the vehicle to bring Socialism to the Jewish masses. Hence Jewish Socialism joined to Yiddishism – an ideology of turning a language into the foundation for a way of life – constituted a powerful and important Judaism. Yiddishism was the Judaic movement that identified in the language, Yiddish, a set of cultural values and ideals of personal conduct that, all together, comprise a way of life and a world-view. Its "Israel" of course was constituted by Yiddish-speaking persons. The union of Jewish Socialism and Yiddishism formed the single most popular Judaism of the first half of the twentieth century, enjoying mass appeal to Jews in both Poland and Russia and in America.

In so many words Ruth R. Wisse defines Yiddishism as a system: "*Yiddishkeyt* [that is, the ideology of Yiddish] has come to signify both the culture that is embodied in the Yiddish language and a standard of ethical conduct that preserves the essence of Judaism without the requirements of ritual and law."[6] Since the language is treated as the bearer of ideals and values, the speaking of that language constitutes the principal component of a way of life, and those values, the world-view. The Israel at hand of course comprises Yiddish-speaking Jews.

The connection to Socialism, moreover, proves critical. Jewish Socialists pointed to the Yiddish language, and its supposedly distinctive values of compassion and social idealism, as the cultural vehicle for their movement. They espoused Yiddish as the language of Jewish Socialism. So Yiddishism and Jewish Socialism joined together, even though each Judaism preserved its particular points of stress and concern. As to the special ideology of Yiddishism, again in Wisse's words, we find, ". . . an ideal of behavior in which the whole religious discipline of Jewish life is transmuted into the practice of kindness and decency." We deal then not with yearning for a language but for a social and political ideal.[7] That ideal, moreover, for its holders serves in Wisse's words as "a model for the present and the future." The poem we cited at the outset, out of Jewish Socialism, provides a model for present and future, and we see the congruity – if also the distinction – between Jewish Socialism and Yiddishism.

The appeal to language as an ideology, Wisse points out, has its roots in the end of the nineteenth and beginning of the twentieth century in Eastern Europe. Compensating for the loss of religious credence and the absence of a territorial unity and an autonomous politics, advocates of Yiddish would resort to language to "express . . . cultural autonomy, so that same language would not cement a culturally autonomous community." Wisse observes, in this connection, that the recognition of language as a separate category for Jews runs parallel to the recognition of religion as something subject to discrete definition.[8] This too seems to me a positive indication that the language-nationalism represented by Yiddish forms an encompassing system, not merely a matter of adventitious choice.

The linking of Yiddishism to Socialism requires explanation. For whom did that choice turn into a system? Wisse explains the appeal of Yiddishism to the Socialist:

> A Jew who lived in accordance with the religious tradition could presumably maintain his Jewishness in Spanish as well as English, in German as well as Yiddish, or even in modern Hebrew. A secular Zionist could abandon religious practice and many of the "trappings" of Jewish culture, secure in the belief that statehood would generate a new national identity. The Jewish Left, however, had only its culture to set it apart from the Polish Left and the Russian Left, and that culture, stripped of its religious content, added up to Yiddish – the language, the folklore, the literature.[9]

That accounts for the formation of Yiddishism, now no longer an ideology of language but an ideology of the people.

The Jewish Socialist-Yiddishist Zhitlowsky held, Wisse points out, that "Yiddish had absorbed the Jewish ethics to such a degree that anyone who spoke it was permeated by the Jewish spirit."[10] The difficulty with the ideology at hand, both on its own and when joined to Socialism, hardly escapes notice. Wisse states it very simply:

> Yiddish had developed out of the religious way of life of the Jews, both to express and to protect Jewish separateness. Yiddishists now hoped that a secular way of life, with no other ideological justification for separateness, could be sustained by language alone.[11]

Joined to Socialism and class struggle, treated as the language of oppressed classes, Yiddish found itself bearing a still heavier burden.

Again Wisse: "The transfer of a system of values from religion, where it was appropriately lodged, to language, where it was assuredly not, placed upon Yiddish a new burden of exceptionalism, and one for which there was no national consensus."

The issue of Yiddishism for us frames a different question from the one answered by Wisse. While she explains "the failed politics of Yiddish," for our purpose the ideology built on language forms an excellent example of the move from the Judaism of the dual Torah to other Judaisms altogether. And we cannot deny to Yiddishism, by itself and in union with Socialism, the status of a socio-political ideology.[12] The prophetic tradition made its contribution of proof-texts, but Yiddishism did not emerge from prophetic writings. The values of the Judaism of the dual Torah made their contribution, but Yiddishism joined to Socialism did not take shape to restate these values in a language or in a structure continuous with the one that had gone before. Concern for the poor and oppressed of all nations obviously sustained an established value of the received system, but that concern in Wisse's words was "really socialism with a Jewish face."

The use of the Yiddish language as a vehicle of reaching the Jewish working class and of organizing the labor movement became a matter of ideology. Yiddish found itself transformed from an instrument of communication into a "cultural asset of national and intrinsic value."[13] Clearly, for speaking Yiddish to constitute a statement, then speaking some other language had also to matter, and, among the Jews of Eastern Europe, the choice was Yiddish or Hebrew or the vernacular (Polish, Russian, for example). Yiddish, the language of the working class, took on the status of a symbol of a broader position, that outlined in our rapid look at Jewish Socialism, and speaking Yiddish rather than some other language became an instrument of self-identification.

Because speaking Hebrew stood for the Zionist position, speaking Yiddish constituted a mode of identification with the Jewish Socialist movement. The writers of Yiddish then enunciated an ideology of struggle against the exploitation of the worker, summoning the Jew "to struggle against his exploiters within and without and to sacrifice himself for social, political, and national liberation."[14] If then we ask who participated in that system we identify as Yiddishism, we point first of all to writers and poets. But we have to identify as major players also those to whom they spoke: who spoke the language. Socialists further invoked the idea of class struggle within Jewry, aiming at a liberation of all workers everywhere, so they formed an international movement's Jewish section. Any Judaism has to identify its distinctive type of hero. For Zionism it was the pioneer, the intellectual turned peasant, out clearing the stones and draining the swamps of the then-unoccupied and unwanted parts of Palestine. For Jewish Socialism it was the labor union leader. For Yiddishism it was the poet, the writer. That the writers and poets served as counterparts to the rabbis and saints of the received system found proof in their treatment among the enemies of Yiddishism and Jewish Socialism. The Communists recognized their true enemies: the poets and writers, unacknowledged legislators of civilization. On August 12, 1952, the most important Yiddish authors living in the Soviet Union were put to death by the Communist government of that country, which, for its reasons, to be sure, thereby liquidated proponents of a worldview and a way of life to which it took exception.

The definition of the joined system of Jewish Socialism and Yiddishism gains concreteness when we consider the lives of important heroes of the system(s). These tell us in a vivid way how the Judaic system at hand functioned. What we see in the two figures before us is a trait characteristic of the Judaisms of the twentieth century: the creative power of once-alienated Jews in the forming of Judaic systems. Both of the exemplary heroes of the Judaic system before us began their lives and careers as outsiders and came back to a Judaism, but not to the Judaism of the dual Torah or of its continuators. What they came back to and what they brought with them would define the Judaic systems at hand: they came back to the group, and they brought with them things they had learned elsewhere, much as Moses came back to Israel but was identified, by the Israelites, as an Egyptian.

Born a Jew, Vladimir Medem (1879–1923), after an upbringing in the Orthodox Church and as a Russian, identified himself as a Jew only through Jewish Socialism. He rejoined the Jews in his early twenties and identified, as a Jew and a Marxist, with the Bund. The way of life of the Bund finds exemplification in Medem. He spent his life in the service of the Jewish union, as writer and organizer and public speaker. That way of life encompassed his existence, as much as spending his days in the study of the Talmud would have absorbed his life's energies. He represented the Bund at the second convention, in 1903, of the Russian Social Democratic Party in London,[15] served on the Committee Abroad of the Bund, contributed to Bund newspapers, served on the Bund Central Committee, and on and on. So the way of life of Jewish Socialism, for the elite at least, involved a life of public activity in organizations. Medem held the view that the

Bund should take an interest in Jewish community organization and encourage the teaching of Yiddish and in Yiddish, strongly opposed Zionism while favoring Jewish national-cultural autonomy in the countries of Eastern Europe, and opposed Communism in the Bund.

Medem regained his identification with Jews through Jewish Socialism, and the movement of his life – from one system to the other – strongly points to the comparability, in terms of his existence, between the one and the other. That is not to argue that Jewish Socialism for Medem formed a religion comparable with the (Russian, Christian) Orthodoxy of his youth. The two cannot have differed more radically. One was a religion in the narrow and accepted sense: a system of sacred duties in the service of God, the other was a secular identity, also in a conventional sense. But Medem moved from the one to the other and to the second gave precisely those energies and commitments that he had devoted to the first. So for him one world-view and way of life gave way to another, each addressing the enduring issues of human life and society that he found required sorting out. And in his movement from outside to inside via the media of Jewish Socialism and Yiddishism, he typified the passage of Jews of the twentieth century, indeed, prefigured what would be the norm: traveling the road back. For characteristic of the movement in the nineteenth century was the way out, and in the twentieth (for those who sought the path), the way back. For many already outside, Yiddishism and Jewish Socialism showed the way.

How did Medem express this "Jewishness" that he discovered in Jewish Socialism? For one thing, he learned Yiddish. Speaking that language formed his entry into the Israel he would serve. For another, he identified with the Jews, describing the worship of a synagogue in these terms:

> . . . it was as though I had fallen among torrential waves. Hundreds upon hundreds of worshippers – each one taking his own case to God, each in a loud voice with passionate eagerness. Hundreds of voices ascended to the heavens, each for himself, without concord, without harmony, yet all joining together in one tremendous clamorous sound. No matter how strange to the Western ear, it makes a deep impression and has a great beauty derived from the passion of mass feeling.[16]

The power that brought him to the Jews derived from "constant association with Jews and Jewish life":

> I cannot exactly determine how this "nationalizing" influence of the Jewish labor circles expressed itself. It was the quiet effect of day to day

living. This life became dear and important to me. It was Jewish and it drew me into its environs.[17]

Here we see no clear ideology comparable with the theology that identifies with God's will the way of life so cherished by Medem; no well-defined way of life emerges from (merely) associating with other Jews. Yet for Medem, exemplary of a great many, that is what Jewish Socialism provided: association, together with an articulated appreciation of that association; an ideal of life, in the service of the laboring masses; a teleology of class struggle to which were imputed strong affinities with the prophetic texts found pertinent; a definition of Israel, as apart from the international working classes; an ideal of how to use one's life on earth, and with whom: a Judaism, as self-evidently valid to Medem as was Orthodoxy to Hirsch.

The joining of Yiddishism to Socialism finds its best representative in Chaim Zhitlowsky (1865–1943). Dawidowicz describes him as "the example par excellence of the modern radical Jew drawn to non-Jewish intellectual and revolutionary society, yet reluctant, despite his ambivalence toward the Jewish group, to divorce himself from it."[18] Hostile to Judaism as a supernatural religion, Zhitlowsky provided for Yiddish the ideological position as the foundation for the renewal of Jewish culture, parallel to a renewal of the Jewish people along economic lines: "Jews were to become 'productive' and 'non-parasitic' elements in a socialist economy."[19] So Yiddish would serve as the vehicle of national cultural identity, along with Socialism as the definition of the entity's organization of its productive life. Yiddish was meant to serve as a weapon in the class-war, Dawidowicz points out. Since, in later times, ideologists identified the Jews' participation in socialism, or, in the USA, in liberal politics, as part of their prophetic heritage, it is important to note that that identification, for the thinker at hand, came much after the fact:

Did I assimilate this concept of internationalism from our Jewish prophets? True, the best of them first promulgated the pure internationalist ideal of a fraternizing society . . . But I knew almost nothing of the prophets. We had learned about them in heder, but only incidentally and according to the interpretation of a later Jewry uninterested in such 'trivialities.' . . . Did my internationalism originate in a Jewish religious world view which reigned in our world of Jewish ideas? . . . First, Jewish religion was of no interest to me . . . the idea of chosenness was conspicuous for its glaring chauvinism. Second, national diversity in the Jewish world view was distorted to mean that Jews differed from Gentiles, but all Gentiles were alike. Third, even nationalism, a basic element of internationalism, was not quite a pure element because it was pervaded with religion . . .[20]

Any claim, therefore, that the received system took its natural next steps toward Socialism finds little proof in Zhitlowsky's memoires; he is quite explicit to the contrary. Zhitlowsky found in Socialism a road out of the Jewish condition of being a victim of anti-Semitism: "For me personally, the idea of cosmopolitanism was for a time like healing balm for the pain I had felt ever since it had been explained to me that we Jews lived a parasitic existence."[21] What struck Zhitlowsky was the need for a language and a literature that would explain to Jews the life, ideas, hopes, and aspirations of the Jews.

What Zhitlowsky sought was a socialist theory "that harmoniously united socialist ideals with the problems of Jewish life." Describing a sequence of conversion-experiences, Zhitlowsky explains that, to carry out his moral responsibility to remain faithful to the Jewish people, he would devote his life to a work of "enlightenment and struggle for those universal foundations of human progress which could be advocated even under Russian censorship:"[22]

> The decision to issue the journal in Yiddish did not originate from any conscious Yiddishism. The theoretical works on nationality . . . gave no particular importance to language . . . My reasoning then went something like this: One must talk to a people in its own language. But our people use two languages, Hebrew and Yiddish. In the world in which I grew up, both languages had the same prestige . . . The question facing me was to decide in which language to appeal to Jews, not just the ignorant masses, but the whole people, to train an avant-garde to fight for the ideals of universal progress and for their realization in Jewish life. I decided on Yiddish. This was my calculation: We, the carriers of ideas of universal human progress, had to appeal to the people with our message about quite a new world, the world of modern, progressive, West European culture. Vis a vis this world, the whole Jewish people were like the ignorant masses . . . One had to use the language that everyone understood. That was Yiddish, the vernacular of every Jew . . .[23]

Zhitlowsky's contribution, therefore, was the advocacy of Yiddish as the instrument of Socialism and reform. Others held that the use of Yiddish would form an obstacle to the assimilation of the Jews. Zhitlowsky for his part demanded equal national rights for the Jews, as a distinct national group in the Russian empire.[24] These rights would be effected through their sustaining their own national language. Socialism would transform the Jews into part of the working class. The Yiddish language would express their ideals of productive labor and solidarity with humanity. Socialism did not require cosmopolitanism but allowed nations to develop in a multinational community. So Melech Epstein states:

> Yiddish literature . . . did not originate in a drawing room . . . Yiddish literature was a people's art, a conscious medium for uplifting. It carried an impelling social and moral message to the ordinary man and woman . . .[25]

The Yiddishists found themselves drawn by humanitarian impulses, the Socialists by a more rigorous theoretical vision, but together they formed a powerful phalanx within Jewry. But did they add up to a Judaism? The Jewish Socialists, in the definition of Mendelsohn, assuredly thought so. They clearly formed a consciousness of "uniquely Jewish needs and dilemmas."[26] They did make the effort to draw on inherited writings, "a past culture which could not be totally denied or repressed," and they recognized the need of Jewish workers "to find a Jewish, as well as socialist, identity."[27] Language of this kind points to the formation of a Judaism: a way of life, joined to a world-view, addressed to an Israel. The way of life, we recall, involved union activity and political agitation in causes in no way distinctively Jewish; the world-view was taken over from socialism in its Eastern European redaction; the Israel was the working class of Jewish origin. Yet, as we have seen, Medem and Zhitlowsky found in these components common to all Socialist lives, all Socialist systems of thought, the wherewithal for what they regarded as a distinctive doctrine, which accounted for a life particular to Jews: encompassing, ample, adequate to the purpose.

How then to invoke the categories of our analysis? We begin with the simplest statement, how a devotee of the system would fill out our peculiar questionnaire. Let us make up a questionnaire to administer to our heroic figures. I invent their words in italics, then spell out what they mean for our analysis. *Way of life? Politics.* That is to say, the principal activities of the Jewish Socialist hero encompassed political organization and activity. He wrote to persuade, lectured to organize, spent his life forming of the Jews a political entity to accomplish economic and social goals. *World-view? The issues of international socialism.* The Jewish Socialist hero viewed the world through the perspective of Socialism, seeing the oppression of the working classes and their exploitation by capitalism as the force of evil against which to struggle, identifying activities in support of the working classes as the power of good in the world. History, moreover, found structure and explanation and purpose in this same class struggle. *Judaism? In every fibre of my being.* For in his language, in his social concern, in his every breath the man devoted himself to the welfare of the Israel he identified, the Jewish working classes, speakers of Yiddish, in the sweatshops of Poland, England, and America.

Claiming a continuity in values with the received Judaism of the dual Torah, Yiddishism, both with and without Socialism, to its founders and framers solved important problems. These problems, for those who confronted them, proved urgent and pressing. The way of life – the use of language, the devotion to organizations or to writing or to reading – and the world-view, bound up with a particular evaluation of the Jews and their values (one Wisse calls moral hubris), do coalesce and present a cogent and coherent answer to a large and encompassing question. Self-evident? To those who found the question urgent, the answer scarcely demanded argument and apology. It was beyond all doubt a Judaism. But the urgent questions in no way corresponded to those answered by the received system, and the answers originated in places other than the Torah. So in Yiddishism and Socialism we discern a Judaism out of all relationship with the Judaism of the past, articulately and explicitly alienated from the Judaism of the dual Torah.

Socialism and Yiddishism did not trouble to explain how they related to the received Judaism, because to begin with their framers proposed to break the ties utterly and completely. That is why they undertook their labor of shaping and defining a system of their own. And that is precisely what they accomplished. And yet none can deny that they set forth a Judaic system, precisely as they claimed to do. They specified their Israel, the Yiddish-speaking working classes, they worked out their world-view, the amalgam of Socialist theory and sherds and remnants of appropriate sayings, and, above all, they knew just who Israel was. Some would question characterizing Socialism and Yiddishism as a Judaism. But the framers of the system maintained that we can and should. Wisse's excellent critique of the system confirms that, in its founders' view, the union yielded a new entity, but, unlike the Judaisms of the nineteenth century, a born, *not* a reborn Judaism. It did posit a way of life. It told them the meaning of history and linked the individual to the large movement of time.

Jewish Socialism and Yiddishism did not enjoy staying power. Orthodoxy, Reform, Conservative Judaism, and Zionism did. The Socialist-Yiddishist way of life served only the first generation of Jewish Socialists and Yiddishists, which therefore proved to be a

transitional generation. The Judaic system of social action and linguistic preference did not produce a second generation for itself.
Again Wisse: "It is not simply that the children of the Yiddishists no
longer speak to their children in Yiddish . . . Yiddishism, which was
meant to serve Jewish cohesion, had no . . . self-regenerating powers,
and Yiddishkeyt was but a transitional phase in which a secular
generation enjoyed the fruits of a religious civilization."[28] But for that
first generation the system did answer the same questions as did other
systems. And that is what marks as a Judaism the set of ideas, the
doctrine of how life is to be lived, the definition of the Israel at hand.
How long a system lasts, where it comes from, where it heads – these
form the superficial aspects of description, not the center and heart of
analysis. A system serves for as long as it serves, whom it serves, when
and where it proves serviceable: a butterfly or a boulder, it hardly
matters.

NOTES

1   Quoted by Melech Epstein, *Profiles of Eleven: Profiles of Eleven Men who
    Guided the Destiny of an Immigrant Society and Stimulated Social
    Consciousness among the American People* (Detroit, 1965: Wayne State
    University Press), p. 17.
2   Schneier Zalman Levenberg, "Socialism," *Encyclopaedia Judaica*
    (Jerusalem, 1971: Keter), 15: 24–9.
3   Ibid., col. 25.
4   Ezra Mendelsohn, "Socialism, Jewish," *Encyclopaedia Judaica* 15:
    38–52. Quotation: col. 38.
5   Ibid., col. 38.
6   Ruth R. Wisse, "The Politics of Yiddish," *Commentary* 1985: 80, 1, pp.
    29–35. Quotation on p. 29.
7   Ibid., p. 30.
8   Ibid., p. 31.
9   Ibid., p. 32.
10 Ibid., p. 33.
11 Ibid.
12 Ibid., p. 35.
13 Chone Shmeruk, "Yiddish Literature," *Encyclopaedia Judaica*
    (Jerusalem, 1971: Keter), 16: 798–833. Quotation: col. 811.
14 Ibid.
15 Moshe Mishkinsky, "Vladimir Medem," *Encyclopaedia Judaica* 11:
    1175–6.
16 Lucy S. Dawidowicz, ed., *The Golden Tradition: Jewish Life and Thought
    in Eastern Europe* (New York, 1967: Holt, Rinehart & Winston), p. 432.

17　Ibid., p. 434.

18　Ibid., p. 411.

19　Ibid.

20　Ibid., p. 412.

21　Ibid., p. 415.

22　Ibid., p. 421.

23　Ibid., pp. 421–2.

24　Yerucham Tolkes, "Chaim Zhitlowsky," *Encyclopaedia Judaica* (Jerusalem, 1971: Keter), 16: 1009–11.

25　Melech Epstein, *Jewish Labor in the U.S.A.: An Industrial, Political and Cultural History of the Jewish Labor Movement* (New York, 1969: Ktav), p. 275.

26　Nora Levin, *While Messiah Tarried: Jewish Socialist Movements, 1871–1917* (New York, 1977: Schocken), p. ix.

27　Ibid., p. x.

28　Ibid., p. 35.

Nora Levin
"Socialist Zionism"

Socialism formed a Judaic system in union with not only Yiddishism but also Zionism. And there lasting and important results did come about. For Socialist Zionism brought together the two most powerful Judaic systems of the first half of the twentieth century and claimed to create a Socialist state in the Jewish homeland. This union of Zionism and Socialism is explained by Ber Borochov, its great ideologist, in these terms:

> Jewish immigration is slowly tending to divert itself to a country where petty Jewish capital and labor may be utilized in such forms of production as will serve as a transition from an urban to an agricultural economy and from the production of consumers' goods to more basic forms of industry . . . This land will be the only one available to the Jews . . . It will be a country of low cultural and political development. Big capital will hardly find use for itself there, while Jewish petty and middle capital will find a market for its products . . . The land of spontaneously concentrated Jewish immigration will be Palestine . . . Political territorial autonomy in Palestine is the ultimate aim of Zionism. For proletarian Zionists, this is also a step toward socialism.[1]

The Socialist Zionists predominated in the settlement of the Land of Israel and controlled the political institutions for three quarters of a century. They founded the labor unions, the large-scale industries, the health institutions and organizations. They controlled the national institutions that were taking shape. They created the press, the nascent army – the nation. No wonder that for the first quarter-century after independence, the Socialist Zionists made all the decisions and controlled everything.

They formed a way of life of a quite distinctive order, finding their ideal in collective settlements in farming, and they expressed a world-view entirely their own: the building of an ideal society by Israel, the Jewish nation, on its own land, in agriculture. The Socialist Zionists accepted the Socialist critique of the Jews as a people made up of parasites, not productive workers. They held that the Jews should create a productive society of their own, so that they could enter the arena of the class struggle, which would result in due course in the creation of a classless society. It is a somewhat complicated notion. Socialist Zionism maintained that the Jews had first to constitute an appropriately divided society of classes. This they would accomplish only when they formed their own nation.

They had further to enter productive economies and build an economy of their own. Then the Jews would work out the class struggle in terms appropriate to their nation and produce the classless society. The creation of a Jewish national economy then took on importance as the mode of establishing a healthy class struggle, and, above all, physical labor and the development of rootedness in the soil would accomplish that goal. That thesis then carried within itself the prescription of the way of life that would lead to the founding of collective farms and the building of a Jewish agricultural life in the land of Israel.

Here Nora Levin, the historian of Jewish Socialism in its great age, tells the story of how the founder of the Israel Workers Party, David Ben-Gurion, Zionist and Socialist and first Prime Minister of the State of Israel, came to the Land and what he found there.

Among the places Herzl had visited in the Pale was the small market town of Plonsk in Russian-controlled Poland, about 40 miles from Warsaw. David Gryn (later David Ben-Gurion), a youth at the time, remembered Herzl's visit vividly: "When he appeared in Plonsk, people greeted him as the Messiah. Everyone went around saying 'The Messiah has come,' and we children were much impressed. It was easy for a small boy to see in Herzl the Messiah. He was a tall, finely featured man whose impressive black beard flowed wide down to his chest. One glimpse of him and I was ready to follow him then and there to the land of my ancestors."[2]

His generation, young David believed, was ripe for Zionism. His father's generation had talked and dreamed about "the land of Israel"; some had joined Hovevei Zion. Then Herzl came and galvanized young Jews into thinking that Palestine was achievable. Anti-Semitism in Plonsk was muted, but the town sent a high proportion of Jews to Palestine. In David Gryn's case, two books that he read as a small boy seemed to fuse in his mind: Mapu's *Ahavat Zion* (Love of Zion), vividly describing the life of Jews in biblical times, in Hebrew, and Stowe's *Uncle Tom's Cabin*, in Russian. Although a frail child, and all but crushed by the death of his mother when he was only ten, by the time he reached fourteen he "suddenly emerged from this tunnel to throw myself heart and soul into the Zionist movement."[3]

He and his close friend Shlomo Zemach, who later became a well-known Israeli writer, created a small-scale *ulpan* in Plonsk, called the Ezra Society, to supplement the *heder*. The first pupils, generally from the poorest families, began to teach other children and finally reached the parents. Soon virtually everyone in Plonsk achieved fluency in Hebrew. David planned to study engineering, but in 1904, he decided he had to come to grips with "the land" itself. His friend Zemach, a few years older, left first, writing faithfully every week in great detail but without despair of the harsh realities he found. Labor was a burning issue. Zemach returned to Plonsk for a visit in the summer of 1906 and the two friends eagerly planned to leave together.

Two arrests intervened: David was picked up by a policeman in Warsaw on suspicion of being an anarchist – he wore his hair too long – and later he was thrown in jail while attempting to resolve a quarrel between two rabbis. The local officials accused him of undermining Russian justice, confiscated his papers, and talked ominously of sending him to Siberia,[4] but he was released both times.

While waiting in Odessa for a ship to Jaffa, David and Zemach visited the Russian Zionist leader Menachem Ussishkin. They were astonished to find him annoyed because they were leaving for Palestine without consulting his committee! He warned them that the Turkish government did not want mass immigration. Doctors and agricultural engineers were needed first, Ussishkin insisted. But the youths were not deterred. After a fourteen-day trip on a filthy freighter, fourth-class, they arrived in Jaffa, a poor, run-down port at the time with one main street lined with stalls and shops. From there they walked to Petach Tikvah and tried to get work as day laborers.

Many of the Jewish farmers in Petach Tikvah were sons of the idealistic pioneers of the 1880s, but they preferred Arab workers to newcomers without any farming experience. At Petach Tikvah, David Gryn almost starved. He began wandering from settlement to settlement, taking work when he could get it: carting manure, digging irrigation ditches, moving rocks and boulders. As soon as the rainy season started, he fell ill with malaria, but he hung on grimly, refusing any help from his father as a matter of principle. "When I left Poland," he said, "I believed something I continued to believe, which is that everything we had in Palestine should be created from the beginning. I knew how fundamental was our historical claim to the land. But I also knew that if we were to call it truly ours again, it must be earned with our toil. So living on handouts from my father, no matter how welcome, would not have suited my mission here."[5]

Indeed, as the young Gryn and other Jewish pioneers were waging individual and social struggles, the very institutions and practices they were attacking were themselves going through critical times. Officially, the Zionist movement at the time was turning away from Palestine and considering settlement in Uganda. The Sixth Congress had dispatched an expedition to look into possibilities there. Colonization funds for Palestine had virtually dried up. The Russian Zionists, though part of the congress, had retained a certain amount of autonomy in the Odessa Committee,[6] which had given funds to the Biluim, had established the settlements of Haderah and Rehovot, and provided support for several others. But their funds were also meager. Moreover, Ahad Ha-Am's criticism of "practical" activities and stress on the need for a "spiritual center" brought about an intensification of cultural activities, but could not form the basis of an *aliyah* or settlement movement. Ahad Ha-Am had made several trips to Palestine in 1891 and found the colonization activities "unsystematic and groundless." Colonization languished until the so-called Second *Aliyah* (1904–14) wholly changed the direction of Zionism and Jewish settlement in Palestine.

The impetus for this migration came from the pogroms of 1903 and the failure of the Revolution of 1905 in Russia, but the immigrants were far from homogeneous, politically or otherwise. Some were Marxists, including former Bundists; others were social idealists and romantics who despaired of the Diaspora and regarded Palestine as the last hope for Jews. Some were, of course, ardent Zionists. The first wave of this *aliyah* was a small group from Homel – most from self-defense units – that arrived in Palestine in January 1904. Slightly more than 1,200 came in 1905, and almost 3,500 in 1906, mainly from White Russia, eastern Poland, and Lithuania.[7] These Jews, almost all of whom were young and unmarried, had grown up in a traditional Jewish environment, spoke Yiddish, and knew at least some Hebrew.

Other groups which came from southern Russia were largely assimilated, spoke Russian, and were influenced by socialist ideas and the revolutionary movement. They had come to Zionism in reaction to the pogroms and the failure of the Revolution of 1905. Nourished on socialist ideas, the young men and women of this *aliyah* were, so to speak, resurrected Biluim: proletarian or collectivist in outlook, of middle-class origin, hating the helplessness, misery, and stunted life of Jews imprisoned in Russia. But between the first Biluim and their successors, changed conditions created a new opportunity for testing the Bilu ideas. This was a riper time, but the main difference lay in the single-mindedness, greater numbers, and persistence of the Second *Aliyah* – at least of its enduring segment.

The first group of Poale Zion worker-immigrants arrived in Palestine in 1904. No land was made available to them for settlement; thus, there was absolutely no prospect of creating mass immigration or remolding those who came in the image of a Jewish worker who could till the soil, end the unnatural hired-labor situation, and build a cooperative Jewish society. The process of Jewish national development could not begin until the struggle of the newcomers to obtain work in the colonies of Petach Tikvah, Rishon le-Zion, Rosh Pinah, and elsewhere had run its course, compelling them to start afresh, out of ideological conviction and a commitment to achieve specific national goals.

When the newcomer first came to a colony, he found a European private farming model, with an Arab *fellahin* population existing at the most primitive cultural level and willing to work at extremely low wages because generally the *fellah* already had a house and some land of his own. For the Arab, in sharp contrast with the Jewish worker, outside work in a Jewish settlement was often a secondary occupation.[8] Moreover, the Arab worker, already acclimatized and used to farm work, proved more suitable than the untrained, urbanized Jewish worker. The older settlers themselves, none too well off and depending on support from the Jewish Colonization Association[9] and Baron de Rothschild, when there was a bad harvest, cattle plague, or other crisis, decided that only the Arab worker was suitable for farm work in Palestine. If they had ever had any visions of Jewish *national* revival in the land, they had now lost this hope. The well-intentioned paternalism of the Rothschild system had sapped their initiative and the struggle to stay on the land had led them to make compromises. Worse, they saw their children leaving the land and going to the cities, or returning to Russia.[10]

The high moral tone of the newcomers irritated those who had survived the early struggles to become farmers. It was also guilt-provoking, because the oldtimers had themselves once been idealistic. Strikes, demonstrations, and picketing erupted; there were even riots and arrests by police. The economy of Jewish plantation managers and landlords, in fact, was vulnerable not only because of the extensive use of Arab labor and doubts about its permanence and stability, but also because there was an unbridgeable gap – as in all plantation colonies – between workers and the thin stratum of overseers who lived in an atmosphere of boredom and nostalgia for the life they had left behind. A return to Zion was certainly not possible where there was no organized Jewish community, and the plantation colonies did not provide one. Jewish labor had to fight for its right to work and create decent conditions for both Arab and Jewish workers if the character of the colonies was to change.

This system offered nothing but frustration to the newcomers. Ousted from hired labor, they were also outraged by the stifling and exploitative nature of mean profit-taking. The private farms could give no scope for their intense social and national idealism.

At first the land itself was intoxicating: "I smelled the rich odor of corn," David Gryn wrote. "I heard the braying of donkeys and the rustle of leaves in the orchard. Above were clusters of stars, clear and bright against the deep color of the firmament. My heart overflowed with happiness, as if I had entered the land of a wonderful dream."[11] But reality crushed these first delights. Like so many others, David and Shlomo Zemach trekked wearily from one farm to another. Eventually they found work at 8 piasters a day, a few cents, just enough to buy a meal and rent a bed. The experiences at Petach Tikvah had a profound and lasting effect on the personality and philosophy of the young Gryn. He never lost his deep resentment of the "rich Jewish squatters," a carryover from Diaspora ways.

David and Shlomo toiled in Judea for a year. Hunger was a frequent companion:

> It would stay with me for weeks, sometimes months. During the day I could dismiss it somehow, or at least stop thinking of it. But in the nights, the long racked vigils, the pangs would grow fierce, wringing the heart, darkening the mind, sucking the very marrow from my bones, demanding and torturing, and departing only with the dawn. Then shattered and broken, I would drop off to sleep at last.[12]

The hostility of the colonists toward Jewish workers reached a climax of sorts in the boycott of Jewish workers in Petach Tikvah in 1905, some of whom had held a memorial meeting in honor of the self-defense units that had fallen during the pogroms of 1905. Orthodox colonists were doubly offended because workers of both sexes attended the meeting together. All possible measures had been taken to prevent the commemoration from taking place. Some of the more fanatical men even forbade the colonists to give workers lodging. After this struggle, the workers left Petach Tikvah.

NOTES

1   Cited in Arthur Hertzberg, ed., *The Zionist Idea: A Historical Analysis and Reader* (New York, 1959: Doubleday and Herzl Press), pp. 365–6.
2   *David Ben-Gurion: Memoirs*, comp. Thomas R. Bransten (New York, 1970), p. 34.
3   Ibid., p. 39.
4   Ibid., pp. 42–3.
5   Ibid., p. 52.
6   The Odessa Committee emerged out of an 1887 Katowice conference of Russian Zionists who became the center of the Hovevei Zionist movement. The group was legalized in 1890 under the name The Society for the Support of Jewish Farmers and Artisans in Syria and Palestine. In that year, the committee sent an engineer, Vladimir I. Temkin, to Palestine to purchase more land for colonization, but his mission was unsuccessful.
7   Walter Laqueur, *A History of Zionism* (New York, 1972), p. 279.
8   Walter Preuss, *The Labor Movement in Israel, Past and Present* (Jerusalem, 1965), p. 22.
9   As far back as 1888, the philanthropist Baron de Hirsch had set aside a sum of 50 million francs to carry out plans for improving the condition of Russian Jewry, but the government was not interested. The expulsion of Jews from Moscow inspired Hirsch to found the Jewish Colonization Association (known as ICA) to enable Jews to migrate to Argentina and become farmers there. Meanwhile, Hibbat Zion, which had begun with ambitious dreams of a general exodus, had retreated step by step because of petty worries and pitifully small donations. Rothschild's colonies in Palestine still dominated colonization efforts. In 1899, Rothschild handed over all his Palestine interests to ICA.
10 Chaim Weizmann, *Trial and Error* (New York, 1949), p. 127.
11 Robert St John, *Ben-Gurion* (Garden City, NY, 1959), p. 25.
12 Ibid.

8

American Judaism of Holocaust and Redemption

In mid-1967, on June 9th of that year, a Judaic system burst upon the Jewish communities of the USA and Canada, the one I call the American Judaism of Holocaust and Redemption. It quickly became the dominant Judaic system and attracted nearly universal support among Jews, for whom it answered the urgent question, why should I be Jewish at all? The world-view found its correspondence in a way of life devoted to building Holocaust Museums in the USA and supporting the State of Israel through political action and financial donation. The "Israel" of this Judaism is wholly ethnic, shading over into a political pressure-group in the context of American politics. In concrete terms, therefore, "the Holocaust" refers to the murder by the Germans of six million Jewish children, women, and men in Europe between 1933 and 1945. The Redemption came with the creation of the State of Israel. This Judaic system forms the principal force in the lives of American and Canadian Jews, whether or not they belong to synagogues.

This is not the only Judaic system that flourishes in the USA and Canada. Reform, Conservative, Orthodox Judaism, Zionism, the system of the dual Torah in its received and self-evident formulation – all have made their way. Remnants even of Jewish Socialism and Yiddishism endure. All, by definition, constitute Judaisms in America. But the one distinctively American Judaism is the one that for the last third of the twentieth century has exercised enormous power over the mind and imagination of Jewish Americans. This American Judaism tells Jews who they are, why they should be Jewish Americans, what they should do because of that mode of identification, and, it goes without saying, who the Jewish group is and how that group should relate to the rest of the world and to history.

Answering who, why, and what, it is a fully articulated system of the social order. Whether or not it falls into the classification of religious systems is not clear.

Different from Zionism, which – as we saw in the case of David Ben-Gurion – held that Jews should actually live in the Jewish state, this system serves, in particular, to give Jews living in America a reason and an answer to the urgent question, asked by the descendants of immigrants a hundred years later, why should I be Jewish at all? This Judaism's answer lays particular stress on the complementary experiences of mid-twentieth-century Jewry: the mass murder in death factories of six million of the Jews of Europe, and the creation of the State of Israel three years after the end of the massacre. These events, together seen as providential, as we see, bear the names "Holocaust," for the murders, and "Redemption," for the formation of the State of Israel in the aftermath. The system as a whole presents an encompassing myth, linking one event to the other as an instructive pattern, as I said, and moves Jews to follow a particular set of actions, rather than other sorts, as it tells them why they should be Jewish. "The Holocaust" proved that gentiles should not be trusted, so Jews should stay Jewish. "Redemption," meaning the creation of the State of Israel, proved that Jews could take care of themselves, so they should identify with the far-away state as their reason to be Jewish.

Holocaust-and-Redemption Judaism is the creation of the third and mainly the fourth generations after the great immigration to North America that took place in the late nineteenth and early twentieth centuries. The first generation (1890–1920), completing its migration and settling down in the 1920s, took for granted that its ways would not continue. They did not try to preserve Yiddish. As Wisse has already pointed out, the ideology of Yiddishism proved transient and unappealing to the children of the Yiddish-speaking immigrants in the USA. The Yiddish language within the first generation gave way to English, often in the home, and with it much else that had seemed definitively Jewish in the Central and East European setting. With the notion that Jews (like other immigrants) must become American, the immigrant generation tended to accept, not always benignly to be sure, what it perceived as the de-Judaization of its children. The parents kept the dietary taboos, the children did not. The parents practiced distinctively Jewish occupations, dominating only a few fields and absent in most others. The children spread out, so far as they could in the prevailing climate of anti-Semitism and exclusion.

The second generation (1910–1940) learned the lessons the parents wanted to teach. So the children wanted to be American, therefore not Jewish. Judaism as an inherited religious tradition with rich theological perspectives and a demanding, enduring way of life bore little relevance to the American children of those Europeans who had walked on that path to God and lived by that mode of sanctification. And the immigrants took that fact for granted. The second generation, for its part, accepted more from the founders than it planned. For while explicitly opting for "America" and against "Judaism," it implicitly defined life as a set of contrasts between the Jewish datum of life, on the one side, and everything else, on the other. Being Jewish was what defined existence for the second generation. That fact of life was so pervasive as not to demand articulation, let alone specific and concrete expression.

So the second generation took "being Jewish" for granted; they lived the life of average Americans. But they did it in conditions of near-total segregation: in Jewish ghettos. The upshot was that the second generation would organize bowling leagues and athletic clubs, rather than prayer circles and study groups. But everyone in the bowling league would be Jewish, and they also would be neighbors and friends. The cultural distinctiveness that had characterized the first generation gave way to a Jewishness by association for the second. The associations, whether political or recreational or philanthropic, took for granted that the goal was non-sectarian. Little that proved definitively Jewish would mark the group's collective life. But how non-sectarian could an association become, when all its members lived in pretty much the same neighborhood, pursued the same lines of work, and came from Yiddish-speaking parents? In fact the community life constructed on the basis of associationism characteristic of the second generation constituted as a social fact a deeply Jewish mode – if not a Judaic system. It took for granted exactly what the first generation had handed on, that is, the basic and definitive character of being Jewish – whatever, for the new generation, that might come to mean. The founding generation could not, and rarely tried to, articulate what being Jewish meant. But it imparted exactly the imprint of being Jewish that had become its hope to leave behind. The second generation was American and remained Jewish. More than that the first generation could not imagine.

The third generation (1940–1970) tried to remember what the second generation was glad to forget. It did everything it could to preserve the religion, Judaism. For example, the second generation did little to found camps, youth programs, schools beyond a perfunctory sort. The institutions of the second generation recognized no need to make explicit, through either substantive or symbolic means, their Jewish character. There were few Jewish parochial schools. Jewish community centers regarded themselves as non-"community agencies." Jewish philanthropic agencies maintained a high wall of separation between "church (= synagogue)" and "state (= Jewish community)." The result was that little public Jewish money went into Judaic activities of any kind. A great deal went into fighting anti-Semitism and maintaining non-sectarian hospitals. Proof of these contrasting modes of Judaic life comes readily to hand. Nearly all of the Judaizing programs and activities of the third generation, now received as the norm and permanent, date back only to the decades after World War II. Most of the earliest summer camps of Judaic character come from that period, especially camps under religious auspices (as distinct from Zionist and Hebraist ones).

The third generation changed all that. The several youth movements got under way in the late 1940s. The Jewish Federations and Welfare Funds in the 1960s fought the battle for a policy of investment in distinctively Jewish programs and activities. They undertook to treat as stylish anything markedly Judaic only from the 1970s. These and equivalent facts point to the passage from the second to the third generation as the age of decisive redefinition. The contrast between the children of immigrants and their children tells the story of American Judaism in the first half of the twentieth century. The second generation did not need schools or youth groups in order to explain what being Jewish meant. It could rely on two more effective educational instruments: memory and experience. The second generation remembered things that the third generation could scarcely imagine: genuinely pious parents, for example, mothers and fathers who believed God revealed the Torah to Moses at Mount Sinai. But the second generation also came to maturity in an age in which America turned against the newest Americans, children of the immigrant wave of 1880–1920 – as well as against the oldest Americans, the blacks, who from the mid-1890s suffered the wave of bigotry that would sweep over other Americans a generation afterward. Universities open to Jews before World War I imposed rigid quotas against them afterward. More important, entire industries declared themselves off-limits to Jewish employment. The fact that the climate of bigotry and exclusion affected others just as much as Jews, so that among the excluded minorities were a majority of Americans of the age, changed little for the mentality of excluded Jews. They may have moved to swim among an undifferentiated majority, had the waters been open to them; they were not welcome even on the beaches.

The contrast, then, between the second and the third generation sets up the encounter with a hostile and threatening world, on the one side, against the experience of an essentially neutral and benign one, on the other. The third generation underwent few of the experiences of overt and explicitly exclusionary anti-Semitism that had defined what "being Jewish" meant to the second generation. The third generation had to learn about Jewishness and Judaism in books, because experience in the streets did not teach many lessons. For the second generation, by contrast, to discover what it meant to be a Jew, people had only to open a newspaper. For them, far more profound than the experience of personal exclusion was the impact of the rise of political, organized anti-Semitism as an instrument of national policy in Germany, Poland, and other European countries, with its extension and counterpart in the Western democracies. What this meant was that the exclusion from a country club or an executive suite took on a still more ominous character, as the world at large took up the war against the Jews. Jewish immigration was barred at the very hour that people were fleeing for their lives. In such a setting Jews scarcely needed to find reasons to associate with one another; the world forced them together. They did not lack lessons on how and why to be Jewish, or what being Jewish meant. The world defined and taught those lessons with stern and tragic effect. All of the instrumentalities for explaining and propagating Jewishness, created for the third generation, and, in time, by the third generation, would earlier have proved superfluous.

The third generation held very strong convictions about continuing to be Jews. Most married Jews and hoped their children would. More than half of them joined synagogues and did so because they wanted their children to grow up as Jews. Above all, most of them regarded the fact that they were Jewish as bearing great significance. In all, they were eager to be Jewish – but not too much so. They did not want to be so Jewish that they could not also take their place within the undifferentiated America they assumed lay beyond their social circle. For their children, they precipitated a crisis not merely of identity but of commitment, for the parents did not choose to resolve the dilemma of separateness within an open society, and the children, coming to maturity in the 1960s and 1970s, found that they had to. The underlying problem was to make sense of what the adjective Jewish is supposed to mean when the noun Judaism in its received meanings had been abandoned. It was the system of Holocaust and Redemption that answered that question: who are you? what should you do? what do you make of the other?

Overlapping with the third, the fourth generation (1960–1990) – the one with native-born grandparents, who spoke unaccented American English – responded to three new factors that yielded a Judaic system of a wholly ethnic character, different from the religious systems of the nineteenth century but also the political ones of the earlier part of the twentieth. These factors were, first, the rise of the State of Israel, second, the impact of "the Holocaust," and, third, the re-ethnicization of American life. That return to ethnicity involved a resurgence of ethnic identification among the grandchildren and great-grandchildren of the immigrant generations, on the one side, and among blacks and other excluded groups that long ago had become American by force, on the other. That movement of rediscovery of difference responded to the completion of the work of assimilation to American civilization and its norms. So much for the setting, what about the substance of the Judaism of Holocaust and Redemption?

When we turn to the world-view, we must recall that a Judaism may bear its world-view in the form not of theological propositions but of a myth, a mode of conveying deep truth and abiding meaning in the form of a story. Let me recount the salvific story of Holocaust and Redemption as it is nearly universally perceived by American Jews who reached maturity in the 1960s and 1970s. I refer to the reading of the experience of the community as a whole, that is, how the myth sees things. But the power of the myth, the story at hand, profoundly grips not those about whom the story is told, but those to whom the story bears meaning. So we speak of a long past, but we mean the present. I tell it in the masculine gender, but women have a readily appropriate means of phrasing matters. They of course would rightly add yet other dimensions of exclusion and alienation, from normal education and careers, for example. But here is how the story goes, as a third-generation Jew would tell his part of the story of Holocaust and Redemption:

> Once upon a time, when I was a young man, I felt helpless before the world. I was a Jew, when being Jewish was a bad thing. As a child, I saw my old Jewish parents, speaking a foreign language and alien in countless ways, isolated from America. And I saw America, dimly perceived to be sure, exciting and promising, but hostile to me as a Jew. I could not get into a good college. I could not aspire to medical school. I could not become an architect or an engineer. I could not even work for an electric utility.

When I took my vacation, I could not go just anywhere, but had to ask whether Jews would be welcome, tolerated, embarrassed, or thrown out. Being Jewish was uncomfortable. Yet I could not give it up. My mother and my father had made me what I was. I could hide, but could not wholly deny, not to myself even if to others, that I was a Jew. And I could not afford the price in diminished self-esteem of opportunity denied, aspiration deferred, and insult endured. Above all, I saw myself as weak and pitiful. I could not do anything about being a Jew nor could I do much to improve my lot as a Jew.

Then came Hitler and I saw that what was my private lot was the dismal fate of every Jew. Everywhere Jew hatred was raised from the gutter to the heights. Not from Germany alone, but from people I might meet at work or in the streets I feared that being Jewish was a metaphysical evil. "The Jews" were not accepted, but debated. Friends would claim we were not all bad. Enemies said we were. And we had nothing to say at all.

As I approached maturity, a still more frightening fact confronted me. People guilty of no crime but Jewish birth were forced to flee their homeland, and no one would accept them. Ships filled with ordinary men, women, and children searched the oceans for a safe harbor. And I and they had nothing in common but one fact, and that fact made all else inconsequential. Had I been there, I should have been among them. I too, should not have been saved at the sea.

Then came the war and, in its aftermath, the revelation of the shame and horror of holocaust, the decay and corrosive hopelessness of the DP camps, the contempt of the nations who would neither accept nor help the saved remnants of hell.

At the darkest hour came the dawn. The State of Israel saved the remnant and gave meaning and significance to the inferno. After the dawn, the great light: Jews no longer helpless, weak, unable to decide their own fate, but strong, confident, decisive. And then came the corrupting doubt: if I were there, I should have died in hell. But now has come redemption and I am here, not there. How much security in knowing that if it should happen again I shall not be lost. But how great a debt paid in guilt for being where I am and who I am!

I made up this story, which carries us through the 1950s, to show how this Judaism gives meaning and transcendence to the petty lives of ordinary people. The story recapitulates the most profound traits of myths capable of nearly universal appeal. It forms a Judaic example of the myth of the darkness followed by light, of passage through the netherworld and past the gates of hell, then, purified by suffering and by blood, into the new age. The myth conforms to the supernatural structure of the classic myths of salvific religions from time immemorial.

And well it might, for a salvific myth has to tell the story of sin and redemption, disaster and salvation, the old being and the new, the vanquishing of death and mourning, crying and pain, the passing away of former things. This is the myth – the narrative expression of the world-view – that shapes the mind and imagination of American Jewry within the present model. It supplies the correct interpretation and denotes the true significance of everyday events, and turns workaday people into saints. This is the myth that transforms commonplace affairs into history, makes writing a check into a sacred act. So the generations that lived through disaster and triumph, darkness and light, understand the world in terms of a salvific myth. The generations that have merely heard about the darkness but have daily lived in the light take for granted the very redemption that lies at the heart of the salvific myth.

So much for the Holocaust, transformed from the mundane murders of millions into a tale about cosmic evil, unique and beyond all comparing. We come to the other half, the Redemption, which is symbolized by the use of the word "Israel," the State of Israel, the Jewish state. The Holocaust formed the question; Redemption in the form of the creation of the State of Israel forms the answer. The dramatic events culminating in the Israeli victories in the Six Day War of June 1967 brought that answer home. Before the war began, on June 5th, people throughout the world feared that another Holocaust was at hand; the Arab states were united to destroy the State of Israel, and they said so everywhere. With the end of the war, six days later, the worst fears gave way to a sense of discovery: not another Holocaust but Redemption. That broadly felt emotional tidal wave swept over American and Canadian Jews. Other factors contribute to the status of self-evident truth accorded to the Judaism of Holocaust and Redemption, as we shall see presently.

The "Redemption" part therefore is best understood when we know the answer to a simple question. Why date the birth of the Judaism of Holocaust and Redemption so precisely as the 1967 war? Before that time, the State of Israel did not define the focus of American Jewish consciousness. In the 1940s and 1950s, American Jewry had yet to translate its deep sympathy for the Jewish state into political activity, on the one side, and the shaping element for local cultural activity and sentiment, on the other. So too the memory of the destruction of European Jewry did not right away become "the Holocaust," as a formative event in contemporary Jewish consciousness. In fact the re-ethnicization of the Jews could not have taken the form that it did – a powerful identification with the State of Israel as the answer to the question of "the Holocaust" – without a single, catalytic event.

That event was the 1967 war between the State of Israel and its Arab neighbors. When, on June 5th, after a long period of threat, the dreaded war of "all against one" began, American Jews feared the worst. Six days later they confronted an unimagined outcome, with the State of Israel standing on the Jordan River, the Nile, and the outskirts of Damascus. The trauma of the weeks preceding the war, when the Arabs promised to drive the Jews into the sea and no other power intervened or promised help, renewed for the third generation the nightmare of the second. Once more the streets and newspapers became the school for being Jewish. On that account the Judaism in formation took up a program of urgent questions – and answered them. In the trying weeks before June 5, 1967, American Jewry relived the experience of the second generation and the third.

In the 1930s and 1940s, the age of Hitler's Germany and the murder of the European Jews in death factories, every day's newspaper brought lessons of Jewish history. Everybody knew that were he or she in Europe, death would be the sentence on account of the crime of Jewish birth. And the world was then indifferent. No avenues of escape were opened to the Jews who wanted to flee, and many roads to life were deliberately blocked by anti-Semitic foreign service officials. The contemporary parallel? In 1967 the Arab states threatened to destroy the State of Israel and murder its citizens. The Israelis turned to the world. The world again ignored Jewish suffering, and a new "Holocaust" impended. But now the outcome was quite different. The entire history of the century at hand came under a new light. As we shall see below, a moment of powerful and salvific weight placed into a fresh perspective everything that had happened from the beginning to the present.

The third and fourth generations now had found their memory and hope, as much as Zionism had invented a usable past, Socialism in its Jewish formulation a viable future. It now could confront the murder of the Jews of Europe, along with its parents' and its own experience of exclusion and bigotry. No longer was it necessary to avoid painful, intolerable memories. Now what had happened had to be remembered, because it bore within itself the entire message of the new day in Judaism. That is to say, putting together the murder of nearly six million Jews of Europe with the creation of the State of Israel transformed both events. One became "the Holocaust," the purest statement of evil in all of human history. The other became salvation in the form of "the first appearance of our redemption" (as the language of the Jewish prayer for the State of Israel has it). Accordingly, a moment of stark epiphany captured the entire experience of the age and imparted to it that meaning and order that a religious system has the power to express as self-evident. The self-evident system of American Judaism, then, for the third generation encompassed a salvific myth deeply and personally relevant to the devotees. That myth made sense at a single instant equally of both the world and the self, of what the newspapers had to say, and of what the individual understood in personal life.

Nearly all American Jews therefore came to identify with the State of Israel and regard its welfare as more than a secular good, but a metaphysical necessity: the other chapter of the Holocaust. Nearly all American Jews are not only supporters of the State of Israel. They also regard their own "being Jewish" as inextricably bound up with the meaning they impute to the Jewish state. The American Judaism absorbs and reworks for its own systemic purposes the creation of the State of Israel. American Judaism is not a Zionism. Zionism always insisted, and the State of Israel today maintains, that immigration to the State of Israel forms the highest goal, indeed the necessary condition, for true Zionism. More than five million American Jews, including a great many deeply engaged by the Judaic system at hand, exhibit not the slightest intention of migrating anywhere, though they gladly pay visits. And that is not Zionism. We deal with the world-view of a deeply American Judaism.

What way of life does give substance to the doctrine? And how does a story of a tragedy of incalculable sorrow on one continent, finding a happy ending in the creation of a new nation on a second continent, find so deep meaning for Jews living two oceans away, on yet a third continent? Let us begin once again with a picture of an individual and ask what that person does to carry out in everyday life the expectations of the world-view at hand. The way of life brings into being a culture of organizations, a religion that takes shape only in practical matters of the here and now. Let us meet a saint in the system. Before us stands the president of a federation or a synagogue or a Hadassah chapter. He or she[1] has devoted most of his or her spare time – and much time that could not be spared – to the raising of funds for these and similar good causes for twenty years or more. If a woman, she has given up many afternoons and nights to the business of her organization, has attended conferences of states, of regions, and of "national," has badgered speakers to speak for nothing and merchants to contribute to rummage sales, and all for the good cause. If a man, he has patiently moved through the chairs of the communal structure, on the board of this client agency, president of that one, then onward and upward to lead a "division" of a "campaign," then to head a campaign, to sit on the board. Above all, both men and women have found for their lives transcendent meaning in the raising of funds for Jewish causes.

Mr President, Madam Chairman – both have exhibited not only selflessness but also iron determination. They have enjoyed the good conscience of those for whom the holy end justifies all legitimate secular means. They worked for a salvation of which they were certain, and it was, despite appearances, not of this world. The makers of American Judaism have seen a vision and kept alive its memory. They have dedicated their lives to the realization of their holy vision, just as much as the students of Torah in another place and time gave their lives to the study of Torah – for all, a salvific enterprise, an exercise in the end of time in this heaven realized on earth. They did not see their lives as trivial, their works as unimportant, because their lives were spent on significant things. Not for them the beaches of Florida, the gambling tables of Nevada. Their works were for a sacred goal.

Superficially, these claims seem extravagant. What transcendent importance is to be located in the eleemosynary activities of the mattress makers' division of the local federation of Jewish philanthropies, devoted to raising money for the State of Israel and domestic Jewish purposes as well? Of what salvific consequence the leisure time activities of a pants manufacturer in Hoboken? What great goals are perceived by men who spend their lives filling holes in teeth, litigating negligence claims, or running a store? How has madam chairman attained the end of days, merely by meeting her quota? These are the four questions confronting an interpretation of the Judaism of Holocaust and Redemption.

What do devotees of the Judaic system of American Judaism actually do to deserve classification as people who do things that save the world? Well, for one thing they engage in a life of organizing for the accomplishment of good works. They raise vast sums of money for domestic and overseas support. For one example, in addition to their work of sustaining their community at home and also a myriad of philanthropic activities in Jewish communities abroad and in the State of Israel, they select particular, poor neighborhoods in Israeli towns. These they make their own, through visits and personal concern. Again, since political action forms a vital part of support for the State of Israel, they work hard in political affairs, seeking friends for the Jewish community and the State of Israel. In so doing they undertake selfless commitments that demand much of their energy and time: they are women and men who live for others. That I think the measure of a transcendent goal, a life devoted to improving that part of the human condition for which they feel responsibility. The great goal? Preserving the safe place for Jews to live out their lives – if they need it. In many ways these Jews every day of their lives relive the terror-filled years in which European Jews were wiped out – *and every day they do something about it.* It is as if people spent their lives trying to live out a cosmic myth, and, through rites of expiation and regeneration, accomplished the goal of purification and renewal. Highfalutin language for humble deeds? True. But appropriate words as well.

The participants in American Judaism rightly claim to have helped improve the world. But they themselves claim to be more than merely good and useful people. They see themselves as engaged in serving a cause of salvific valence, whose righteousness confers upon them enviable certainty, a sense of worth beyond doubt or measure. These saints are as certain of their vision of the world – a vision of the work of redemption following the near-victory of evil – as were the saints of the olden days. Enjoying the certainty of a self-validating vision of the world, possessed of the security derived from the right understanding of perceived history, illuminated by an all-encompassing view of Jewish realities, they are the saved. What characterizes group life in modern times is the development of specialists for various tasks, the organization of society for the accomplishment of tasks once performed individually and in an amateur way, the growth of professionalism, the reliance upon large institutions. So, as I said in the prologue, there are no surprises that the way of life of Zionism, Socialism and Yiddishism, and American Judaism should have in common a single type of activity. The way of life of American Judaism, like that of the other Judaisms of the twentieth century, requires joining and supporting organizations.

This account of the urgent question and the self-evidently valid answer to that question that come to expression in the Judaism of Holocaust and Redemption is incomplete. For the circumstances in which that Judaism attained the status of self-evidence for millions of American Jewish faithful have not been fully set forth. The events of May 15 to June 9, 1967, precipitated matters. But three further factors, among the Jews, reinforced one another in turning the Judaism of Holocaust and Redemption into a set of self-evident and descriptive facts, truths beyond all argument. The first was the transformation of the mass murder of European Jews into an event of mythic and world-destroying proportions, the second, the re-ethnicization of American life, and the third, the political upheaval that overtook America during those same years. They are closely intertwined:

THE MYTHICIZATION OF THE HOLOCAUST INTO A METAPHOR FOR ABSOLUTE EVIL   To understand the reworking of a massive human tragedy into Holocaust, we have to turn back, once more, to an earlier period, before the public recognition of the self-evidence of the Judaism of Holocaust and Redemption. From 1945 to about 1965, the Holocaust was subsumed under the "problem of evil." The dominant theological voices of the time did not address themselves to "radical evil" and did not claim that something had happened to change the classical theological perspective of Judaism. The theologians of the day wrote not as if nothing had happened, but as if nothing had happened to impose a new perspective on the whole past of Jewish religious experience. To be sure, the liberal, world-affirming optimism of the old theological left was shaken. But the Holocaust was part, not the whole, of the problem. The evil of humanity in conventional rhetoric came to realization in more than that one way. Indeed, few called to mind the murder of European Jewry, and "the Holocaust" did not yet exist. So, clearly, the transformation of memory into theology has to be explained. In my view, what accounts for the change is the circumstances of American politics and culture, affecting the Jews along with everybody else. And this brings us to what else was happening in America and therefore to Jewish Americans: the renewal of ethnicity, on the one side, the apocalyptic catastrophe of American politics, on the other.

THE UPHEAVAL IN AMERICAN POLITICS   Clearly, something happened between the end of the 1950s and the beginning of the 1970s. This was an experience so fundamental as to import to the massacre of European Jewry a symbolic meaning, self-evident importance, and mythic quality. Jews had been put to death in unimaginably dreadful circumstances. What happened, I think, was a sequence of events, some general, some particular to the Jews: the assassination of President Kennedy, the disheartening war in South-East Asia, and a renewed questioning of the foundations of religious and social polity. "Auschwitz" became a Jewish code-word for all the things everyone was talking about, a kind of Judaic key word for the common cause.

People found a number of problems: the tragic murders of political leaders, the two Kennedys and King in particular, the unwanted war in Vietnam, unrest in the black ghettos – a whole host of national disappointments added up to a malaise. And the Jews' code-word for that malaise was "Auschwitz," which stood for everything troubling everybody, but made it all particular to the Jews. That – and nothing more. The Jewish theologians who claim that from Holocaust events one must draw conclusions essentially different from those reached after the destruction of the Second Temple or other tragic moments posit that "our sorrow is unlike any other, our memories more searing." But they say so in response not to the events of which they speak, but through those events, to a quite different situation – their own.

THE RENEWAL OF ETHNICITY   The third development of the late 1960s and earlier 1970s was the renewal of ethnic identification in American life. The question people had to answer was, who are we in relationship to everybody else? The utility of "the Holocaust" in this context is not difficult to see, once we realize that the TV counterpart to "Holocaust" is "Roots." It follows that, for American Jews, "the Holocaust" is that ethnic identity which is available to a group of people so far removed from culturally and socially distinctive characteristics as to be otherwise wholly "assimilated." "The Holocaust" is the Jews' special thing: it is what sets them apart from others while giving them a claim upon those others. That is why Jews insist on "the uniqueness of the Holocaust." If blacks on campus have soul food, the Jews will have kosher meals – even if they do not keep the dietary laws under ordinary circumstances. Unstated in this simple equation, "Roots" = "Holocaust," is the idea that being Jewish is an ethnic, not primarily a religious, category. For nearly a century American Jews have persuaded themselves and their neighbors that they fall into the religious – and therefore acceptable – and not into the ethnic – and therefore crippling and unwanted – category of being "different." Now that they have no Jewish accent, they are willing to be ethnic. But of what did that ethnicity consist?

Third- and fourth-generation American Jews found in the continuator-Judaisms of the synagogue something conventional and irrelevant. They went in search not of religion but of an ethnic identification, and the synagogue in the end had too much to say about God and God's will revealed in the Torah, not enough to say about bagels and bar mitzvah parties. What was required was either memories few possessed, or the effort to locate a road back in which few found the will to invest. The world of the everyday did not provide access to so subtle and alien a world-view as that of the Judaism of the dual Torah and its conception of humanity and of Israel, let alone to the way of life formed within that world-view.

Another generation would have to pass before the age of reversionary Judaisms, those that form the bridge to the twenty-first century, would arrive.

How then to engage the emotions without the mediation of learning in the Torah? And how to define a way of life that imparted distinction without much material difference? To state matters in a homely way, what distinctively Judaic way of life would allow devotees to eat whatever they wanted anyhow? The answer to both questions – access to the life of feeling and experience, to the way of life that made one distinctive without leaving the person terribly different from everybody else – emerged in the Judaic system of Holocaust and Redemption. This system presented an immediately accessible message, cast in extreme emotions of terror and triumph, its round of endless activity demanding only spare time. In all, the system of American Judaism realized in a poignant way the conflicting demands of Jewish Americans to be intensely Jewish, but only once in a while, and not exacting much of a cost in meaningful difference from others. The remainder of the ethnic tale is now told by Professor Nathan Glazer.

NOTE

1 We deal with a Judaism that makes an ample place for women, so we take account (at last) of that fact. American Judaism is the first Judaic system that consistently accords to women a place of prominence.

Nathan Glazer
"The Year 1967 and
its Meaning"

Rarely can we witness the birth of a star – or of a religious system. But the Judaism of Holocaust and Redemption was born in the three weeks from May 15, 1967 – when Egyptian President Nasser closed the Straits of Tiran to Israeli shipping, abrogating the agreement of 1956 that opened them, and declared his intention to destroy the State of Israel – to June 9, 1967. That was the day that the Six Day War came to a conclusion, with the reunification of Jerusalem, the holy places of which had been closed to Jews for the preceding nineteen years by the Jordanian rulers of the eastern part of the city. From the fear that the Holocaust was about to take place again to the unimagined moment when the Jewish People regained access to the Western Wall of the ancient Temple of Jerusalem, the powerful emotions that swept the world of Judaism shaped the Judaism of Holocaust and Redemption, which would govern for the next quarter-century or more. That Judaism reached its climax in the dedication of the Holocaust Museum on The Mall in Washington, DC, in April 1993.

Here the great sociologist Nathan Glazer places the events of 1967 into the context of the formation of a radical youth-culture in the USA, the development of racial politics, and other critical events of that same period. In his picture, which he here adds to his definitive account of American Judaism as he saw it a decade earlier, he portrays the circumstances in which a Judaism was born.

What happened was the ominous threat to Israel that grew during the spring until the agonizing days of May when the Egyptian and other armies organized against Israel and when it seemed to most observers that inevitably Israel must be overwhelmed by Arab armies lavishly equipped by Communist Russia. Why did this event have such a powerful impact on American Jews? While American Jews supported Israel, their support for many years had not been fervent. The sums they contributed each year remained constant. Young Zionists were hard to find. To the disappointment of Israeli leaders, young American Jews had never shown much interest in going to Israel. More Israelis emigrated to the United States than young American Jews emigrated to Israel. In addition, by 1967 the college youth – and certainly the Jews among them – strongly opposed the Vietnam war, and any American commitment overseas. Many young persons saw every such commitment as imperialistic, and all those countries who accepted such a commitment as puppets or satellites or colonies or imperialist exploiters themselves.

And yet we must record that American Jews, among them even the Jewishly indifferent youth whose energies had for so long been engaged by the cause of the Negroes or the poor or the Vietnamese, suddenly discovered that the fate of Israel, of Jews of different language, culture, and state, meant more to them than these other causes.

It is hard to document a sudden reversal of feeling. Yet everyone who lived through it has attested to it, and perhaps the most persuasive evidence is that given by young Jewish leftists themselves, who wrote and reported and recorded what the terrible danger of extermination through which Israel had lived had meant to them. They were surprised and astonished by their own depth of feeling. A good part of the literature of Jewish youth after 1967 – the literature to be found in many Jewish student newspapers founded after 1969, the pages of *Response*, a magazine founded in that summer of 1967, and elsewhere – refers back to those days of 1967 as a turning point. Writing in the *American Jewish Year Book, 1968*, Rabbi Arthur Hertzberg summed it up:

"The immediate reaction of American Jewry to the crisis was far more intense and widespread than anyone could have foreseen. Many Jews would never have believed that the grave danger to Israel would dominate their thoughts and emotions to the exclusion of all else." And Lucy S. Dawidowicz, in a full and convincing documentation of the response of young Jews in the same issue of the *Year Book*, writes that many "found [that] their ideas of war, which had been shaped by Vietnam, were irrelevant to Israel. Views on pacifism, civil disobedience, resistance to government, and the inherent evil of military might were suddenly questioned."[1] Jewish radicals who were involved in the movement of the New Left, such as Irving Louis

Horowitz and Martin Peretz, documented the great impact the Israeli war had on the Jews in the movement.

But why did the war have such an impact on American Jews, when the Arab–Jewish war of 1956, for example, seemed to have had no particular impact at all? In the middle 1950s, indeed, it appeared that the establishment of the state of Israel had not affected American Jews very much.

There were three reasons for this enormous impact of the 1967 war, and all require some discussion. One was the growing emotional response among American Jews to the Holocaust of 1939–45. A second was the response of black and white radical groups in the United States to the position of Israel. A third was the distinctive role of Russia, the home of the second largest community of Jews in the world, as the chief big-power enemy of Israel. Each of these facts emphasized the overwhelming *aloneness* of the Jews. Each of them emphasized the peculiar *distinctiveness* of the Jews. Each of them justified to Jews, as nothing had for the entire period between 1945 and 1967, and to the young who had not seen themselves as Jews, the right to consider themselves specially threatened and specially worthy of whatever efforts were necessary for survival. Inevitably, such a viewpoint had or could have a religious meaning.

Just as, writing in the mid-fifties, I could see no specific major impact of the state of Israel on the internal life of American Jews, I could see no specific major impact of the Holocaust. After 1967 this was no longer true. During the 1960s American Jews subtly became more sensitized to the enormity of the extermination of the Jews. The Israeli action in kidnapping, trying, and executing Adolf Eichmann in 1961 had some effect in getting Jews to think about the Holocaust. One can hardly avoid psychoanalytic language. These events had been repressed, not only among American Jews but among many of the survivors themselves, hundreds of thousands of whom had settled in the United States. Eichmann's trial made it impossible to repress the events any longer. Hannah Arendt's assessment of the events, which she covered for the *New Yorker* magazine and in her book, *Eichmann in Jerusalem* (New York: Viking Press, 1963), in which modern society in general and Jewish communal leadership specifically seemed to emerge as principal villains in the case, unnerved many Jews and was passionately attacked. Meanwhile Elie Wiesel's direct and unsparing books on the extermination camps, combined with his own commitment to the Jewish fate, also began to lead Jews to confront these overwhelming events.

It can scarcely be suggested that *many* Jews were affected by this reawakening of the impact of the Holocaust before 1967. Indeed, when *Commentary* addressed a series of questions on Jewish belief to a large group of young Jewish religious thinkers and writers in 1966, the Holocaust did not figure among the questions, nor, it must be said, did it figure much among the answers (*The Condition of Jewish Belief*, edited by Milton Himmelfarb [New York: Macmillan, 1966]). Before 1967, young radical Jews were quite capable of using the term "genocide" to describe what was happening to American Negroes or Vietnamese, with no self-consciousness of the fact that their own people had truly been subject, and recently, to a not wholly unsuccessful effort to kill them all. Suddenly, 1967 raised sharply the possibility of real genocide again. Arab spokesmen promised it. The example of Jews being killed while the world stood by was already present in recent history. And in 1967 the world stood by, and Israel was quite clearly alone.

That the United States should talk, that France should caution, that England should follow the American lead, and that Russia was actively supporting the enemies of Israel – all this was bad enough. But young radical Jews were suddenly aware that those with whom they had fought and worked, black militants and New Leftists, were also enemies of Israel. The summer ghetto riots after 1964 had been accompanied by a certain amount of anti-Semitism. Now black militants began to combine domestic anti-Semitism with international anti-Zionism. For various reasons, black militants tended to identify with Islam and with the Arab states. To them 1967 was a "Zionist imperialist war."

Shortly after the 1967 war, one of the largest gatherings of the various groups loosely associated in the New Left met in Chicago in a Convention for a New Politics. As was inevitably the case with such meetings, a large part of the attendance was of Jewish leftists, as was much of the financial backing that made the convention possible. The blacks at the meeting insisted that the convention pass a resolution condemning the "Zionist imperialist" war. This was the breaking point for many Jewish leftists.

Meanwhile, white radical groups on the left, in the course of developing their ideology as to the distinctive role of the United States (often dubbed "Amerika") as the source of all evil in the world, inevitably denounced Israel, too. While those most active in the denunciation of Israel were Jews (as was almost inevitable, in view of the Jewish prominence in left-wing groups in the United States), many other Jews dissociated themselves in anger and disgust.

The internal developments in the black and white left had one other effect in shaping the Jewish response to Israel. Black self-assertion, now being copied by other groups in the United States, for many Jews legitimated Jewish self-assertion. It was not easy for any group of Americans simply to insist that their homelands or the countries with which they were associated should be defended by the United States independently of the interests of the United States. Some Jews had always been troubled by the problem of dual loyalty. But the legitimation of the assertion of the validity of distinctive group interests, which was one result of the black revolution, made it easier for Jews, too, directly to support the interests of Israel, and for young Jews on the campuses to support Jewish interests. The black example should not be underestimated in explaining why young Jews turned inward and became active supporters of what they now conceived of as Jewish interests, rather than embarrassed rejecters of the validity of such interests.

Finally, the international role of the left also served to awaken young Jews to the special danger to Israel. Communist Russia – generally seen in the New Left as bureaucratic and without revolutionary vigor – provided arms to the Arabs. But Communist China, admired in the New Left, provided arms and support for the most extreme of the Arab guerrilla groups, the one most active in claiming credit for such outrageous acts as the killing of Jewish schoolchildren. And Communist Cuba, most widely admired in the New Left, also supported the Arabs. Thus young Jews who were more or less influenced by the New Left had to confront directly the conflict between any Jewish feeling they possessed and the uniform hostility of the Communists in all countries to the Israelis. In this confrontation, many discovered in themselves more Jewish feeling than they had suspected.

We must note too the special impact on young Jews of the situation of Jews in Russia and Eastern Europe. In the wake of 1967, a new wave of anti-Semitism (called anti-Zionism) swept Poland, where the pitiful remnants of what had been one of the largest Jewish communities in the world were forced out of their jobs and into emigration. In the wake of the 1967 war, Russia's anti-Zionist propaganda campaign reached new extremes of violence and irrationality, as the Israelis were regularly denounced for "Hitlerite" acts. Young Jews became aware of the three million Jews who lived in Russia and were far more deprived of rights than the Negroes whose cause the young American Jews had so long supported. The organized Jewish community had for some years been trying to develop public pressure over the problem of the Jews of Russia, who were deprived of the right to practice their religion and culture freely, who could not associate with Jews outside Russia, could not express their sympathy with Israel, and could not emigrate. After 1967 young Jews took up the issue. Unfortunately some of them began to apply the militant tactics that had been made popular by young blacks and New Leftists, disrupting concerts of visiting Russian artists, harassing Russian representatives, on occasion even planting bombs and attempting hijackings. In particular a "Jewish Defense League," organized in the poorer, Orthodox, working-class sections of New York and other large cities, engaged in the more obnoxious tactics. But for the most part the young Jews concerned with Soviet Jewry eschewed such tactics.

NOTE

1 *American Jewish Year Book*, 1968, pp. 69 and 210.

Epilogue

9

What Do We Learn about Religion from Judaism in Modern Times?

The study of religion is a generalizing science. We therefore conclude by asking what is at stake in the information we have surveyed: exactly what do we learn about religion from Judaism? In the present context, the question may be formulated in these terms: how is it possible that one period – the nineteenth century – produced a range of Judaic systems of depth and enormous breadth which attracted mass support and persuaded many of the meaning of their lives, while the next – the twentieth – did not? Why – as a rapid review will show us – the nineteenth century proved productive and the twentieth sterile form the reverse and obverse sides of one coin. What Judaism has to teach us about religion is, when, why, and under what conditions religious systems emerge. The same explanation must account for the failure to form religious systems when and where we do not find them. A theory of the matter then is to be tested in the study of other religions in the same time and place. Which European and American religions proved productive of new systems, and which did not? And what makes the difference?

To begin with, therefore, let us look backward and see how things sort themselves out. From after the beginning of Reform Judaism at the start of the nineteenth century to the later twentieth century, on the surface, we identify three periods of enormous system-building. At each of these the manufacture of Judaic systems came into sharp focus: 1850 to 1860 for the systems of Orthodoxy and the Positive Historical School, 1890 to 1900 for Jewish Socialism and Zionism, and 1967 to 1973 for the system of American Judaism. In those brief periods – decades at most – the important books were written, the influential organizations set up. And that observation yields a different calculation. If we begin at the start of the nineteenth century and end at 1900, then all of the Judaic systems but one took shape in those hundred years: Reform, then, some decades later, in the middle of the century, Orthodoxy and the Historical School, then, again some decades later, at the end of the century, Zionism and Jewish Socialism.[1]

During that period all but one of the Judaisms we have surveyed, and massive and popular ones we did not consider, had reached articulated statement, each with a clear picture of its required deeds and doctrines and definition of the Israel it wished to address. What all these nineteenth-century Judaic systems have in common, and what distinguishes them from the American Judaism of Holocaust and Redemption, is that all appeal to ideas and drew upon the documents of the Judaism of the dual Torah, Reform, Orthodoxy, and Conservative Judaism in a rich way – Zionism in quest for proof-texts, Jewish Socialism and Yiddishism in search for components of a folk culture (the Yiddish language is extraordinarily rich in Talmudic allusions, for example). Only the twentieth-century Judaism abandoned all interest in the canon of the Judaism of the dual Torah. That utterly secular Judaic system addressed emotions and attitudes, substituting stories for propositions subject to rigorous, logical analysis, sentimentality replacing intellectual substance. That is the upshot of the first eight chapters of this book. What difference does it make, and what is at stake in this sustained examination?

What we see is how the framing of systems of the social order on the part of religious conceptions of humankind ceases. The three integrationist Judaic systems of the nineteenth century show the power of the received system to respond to a new set of questions with responses out of the established repertoire. The urgent question of the nineteenth century – integrationism versus segregationism – provoked system-building. The life or death question of the twentieth did not. To be or not to be – that question rules out sustained intellectual reflection; it focuses the attention on altogether other issues than those that system-builders, religious or secular, address.

An age of mass murder forces religions into silence about the social order, a silence broken only by the individual cries of the martyrs. For who can worry about framing a theory of the social order when life is at stake? We see that fact in a striking way in the case of Judaic systems. The same five of the Judaisms that took shape in response to issues that predominated in the nineteenth century put forth solid intellectual formulations of world-views. The twentieth-century one, the American Judaism of Holocaust and Redemption, proved lacking a very formidable intellectual quotient. That is why, to present its world-view, I had to resort to story-telling. What we learn is that under certain conditions, a given family of religious systems – for example, Christianity or Judaism – will beget more systems, and, under other conditions, it will not.

The case of Judaism produces that simple hypothesis: for religion to flourish, the sheltering world beyond must affirm life, ask life's questions. In an age in which death prevails, the kind of thinking religion does best, which concerns the formation of a vital society, does not pertain. Other sets of religious systems, now and in times past, will allow us to form experiments to test and to try to explain why now, not then; why here, not there; why under this condition, not under that. Simply to point to the first century, for Christianity, with its remarkable range of Christianities, expressed in portraits of Jesus, doctrines of the Church and other theological and formative issues, even types of writing; to the century of the Hegira, for Islam, with its formulation of theology through the genealogy of the Prophet; to the sixteenth century, for the age of the Reformation, with the fissiparous effect of reform yielding reformation after reformation, right and left and even at the Western center, in Rome itself; and to the nineteenth century, for Judaism in Germany in particular, makes the point perfectly clear. And, to refine the question, we ask, why for Judaism the nineteenth century but not the twentieth? And our answer is simple: in an age of hope, Judaic systems contemplated new beginnings. In an age of despair, none found much worth while to say concerning the formation of the social order.

And that brings us back to formulate the question: why did the nineteenth century witness a great efflorescence of Judaic system-building, a rich repertoire of Judaic theories of the social order – the how, why, and what of lives lived together – while the twentieth did not? We may eliminate answers deriving from the mere accidents of political change; given the important shifts in the political circumstances of Israel, the Jewish people, we should have anticipated exercises in symbolic redefinition to accommodate the social change at hand. The advent of a tremendous personality, such as Moses, Jesus, or Mohammed, marks an explosive age of system-formation: orthodoxies, heresies, alike. Nearer at hand, the name of Martin Luther makes the same point. He not only founded his own religion, he also provoked the formation of other Christianities round about, not to mention the reformation of Roman Catholic Christianity.

The question gains in weight when we consider what we do not find in the twentieth century. The stimulus for system-building surely should have come in the middle of the twentieth century from the creation of the Jewish state, an enormous event. But, outside of the State of Israel, nothing of broad social influence and considerable intellectual density emerged except the American Judaism of Holocaust and Redemption. The creation of the first Jewish state in two thousand years within the State of Israel itself yielded a flag and a rather domestic politics, but not a world-view and a way of life. When we compare the broad theories of the social order set forth by the founders of the American republic, Madison and Hamilton, enunciated, for example, in the *Federalist Papers*, when we consider the intellectual structure for practical politics put forth by their contemporaries, Washington and Jefferson, for instance, the intellectual poverty of the State of Israel within the framework of Judaic system-building becomes striking indeed. State-building did not yield large visions and re-visioning of everyday life and how it should be lived.

No Judaic systems influential beyond the borders of the State of Israel have emerged there, only rehearsals and re-presentations of the European ones we have considered here: segregationist and integrationist Orthodoxy, for religion; an ideology of blood and peoplehood, for Zionism; a Socialist experiment that failed. From the viewpoint of the study of Judaism as a world religion, phenomena of more than local consequence do not derive from the State of Israel. The new state best provides the opportunity to recapitulate Judaisms formed elsewhere. Given the enormous impact of the transformation of the Jews' social entity from a non-political to a politically empowered one, the failure of intellect underscores the fact at hand: the twentieth century was not an age of system-building in Judaism (however broadly constructed).

American Jewry presents the same picture. Enormous, defining events provoked little sustained reflection that came to the surface in the statement of theories of the Judaic social order. Wars and dislocations, migration and relocation – these in the past stimulated those large-scale reconsiderations that generated and sustained system-building in Jews' societies. The political changes affecting Jews in America, who became Jewish Americans in ways in which Jews did not become Jewish Germans or Jewish Frenchmen or Englishmen or women, yielded no encompassing system of broad, popular impact.[2] The Judaic systems of the nineteenth century have endured in America. That means millions of people moved from one world to another, changed in language, occupation, clothing, patterns of family life, use of leisure time, food habits, and virtually every other significant social and cultural indicator – and produced nothing more than a set of recapitulations of systems serviceable under utterly different circumstances. The failure of Israeli Jewry to generate system-building finds its match in the still more startling unproductivity of American Jewry.

Nothing much therefore has happened in either of the two massive communities of Israel in the twentieth century. The segregationist circumstance of the State of Israel, the integrationist situation of diaspora Jewry – neither seems to have made much difference when we consider the formation of theories of the social order that shaped the shared community life of Jews. Israeli nationalism as a Jewish version of third-world nationalism. American Judaism as a Jewish version of an American cultural malaise on account of a lost war, the one in Vietnam. The Judaism of Holocaust and Redemption leaves unaffected the conduct of private life, home and family. So the larger dimensions of human existence of Jewish Americans are unaffected by the single most influential Judaism of North America. On the surface, Jews explain to themselves what separates them from gentiles; but, in their way of life and their world-view, the distinction makes no difference. An ethnic religion at the same time distinguishes the ethnic group from all others and also trivializes the difference.

Now that we have identified the point of differentiation as one of time and circumstance – the nineteenth as against the twentieth centuries – we ask ourselves what we learn about the human condition in the circumstance of those two distinct ages, the one ending in July 1914, with an assassination in Sarajevo, the other in December 1989, with the demolition of the Berlin Wall and the collapse of the last international totalitarianism of the several that flourished in the seventy-five years of the twentieth century. We focus upon the Jews' situation, then, once more, generalizing. I see three pertinent factors to explain why no Judaic systems have come forth since the end of the nineteenth century. I do not claim that these factors are sufficient. But I think they are necessary to answer the question before us.

The Holocaust

First of all comes the demographic factor. Approximately six million Jews perished; entire communities were wiped out, a whole language was lost in its native territories of Eastern and Central Europe. The demographic factor divides into two parts. First, the most productive sector of world Jewry perished. Second, the conditions that put forth the great systemic creations vanished with the six million who died. Stated as naked truth, not only too many (one is too many!), but the wrong Jews died. What I mean is that Judaic systems in all their variety emerged in Central and Eastern Europe, not in Western Europe or America or in what was then Palestine and is now the State of Israel, and, within Europe, they came from Central and Eastern European Jewry. We may account for the *systemopoeia* – the system-making – of Central and Eastern European Jews in two ways. First, the Jews in the East, in particular, formed a vast population, with enormous learning and diverse interests. Second, the systems of the nineteenth and twentieth centuries arose out of a vast population lived in self-aware circumstances, not scattered and individual but composed and bonded. The Jews who perished formed enormous and self-conscious communities of vast intellectual riches.

To them, being Jewish constituted a collective enterprise, not an individual predilection. In the West the prevailing attitude of mind identifies religion with belief, which is personal, to the near-exclusion of behavior, which is a fact of public life; and religion tends to identify itself with faith. It follows that religion is understood as a personal state of mind or an individual's personal and private attitude. Systems of belief, theological or philosophical, will flourish. Systems meant to design the social order of a community, explaining the who, what, and how of their life together, are not going to find a broad hearing. So the Judaic systems that took shape beyond 1900 and in the USA exhibit that same Protestant-Western and deeply American bias not for society but for self, not culture and community but conscience and character. Under such circumstances *systemopoeia* hardly flourishes, for systems speak of the social order to living communities and create worlds of meaning, answer pressing public questions, and produce broadly self-evident answers.

The demographic fact then speaks for itself. Massive communities perished; isolated individuals survived – by definition, and in mind as well. Whether one can specify a particular demographic (and not merely intellectual) base necessary for the foundation of a given Judaic system I do not know. The Jews all together are not very numerous and can never compete with the Chinese in numbers. Yet everyone who has traced the history of Judaic systems in modern and contemporary times has found in the mass populations of Central and Eastern Europe the point of origin of nearly all systems. That fact then highlights our original observation, that the period of the preparation for and then the mass murder of European Jewry, from the later 1930s to the mid-1940s, marked the end of Judaic *systemopoeia*.

We cannot, then, underestimate the impact of the destruction of European Jewry upon the intellectual life of Judaism, its capacity for imagination and speculation, its power to contemplate how people should form a group and live in one way rather than some other.

Accordingly, one of the as yet untallied costs of the murder of six million Jews in Europe therefore encompasses the matter of system-building. The destruction of European Jewry in Eastern and Central Europe brought to an end for a very long time the great age of Judaic system-construction and explains the paralysis of imagination and will that has left the Jews to forage in the detritus of an earlier age: rehearsing other peoples' answers to other peoples' questions. Indeed, I maintain that until Judaic system-builders come to grips with the full extent of the effects of the "Holocaust" upon the intellectual life of Judaism in the diaspora,[3] they will do little more than recapitulate a world now done with: systems that answer questions urgent to other people somewhere else.

Yet the demographic explanation by itself cannot suffice. For today's Jewish populations produce massive communities throughout the diaspora, three hundred thousand here, half a million there. If Judaism died in the Holocaust countries, Jews did survive. When we consider, moreover, the strikingly unproductive character of large populations of Jews, the inert and passive character of ideology (such as it is) in the Jewries of France, Britain, South Africa, Australia and New Zealand, Scandinavia, Brazil and Argentina and Mexico, and the former Soviet Union, for instance, in which, so far as the world knows, no Judaic systems have come forth – no world-views joined to definitions of a way of life capable of sustaining an Israel, a society – the picture becomes clear. The fact may be stated in few words: even where there are populations capable of generating and sustaining distinctive Judaic systems, none is in sight. So we have to point to yet another factor, which, as a matter of fact, proves correlative with the first, the loss of European Jewry.

The Demise of Intellect

What we noticed about the Judaic systems of the twentieth century – their utter indifference to the received writings of the Judaism of the dual Torah – calls our attention to the second explanation for the end of *systemopoeia*. It is the as yet unappreciated factor of sheer ignorance, the profound pathos of Jews' illiteracy in all books but the book of the streets and marketplaces of the day. The second generation beyond immigration to the USA received in the streets and the public press its education in Jewish existence. The third generation in a more benign age turned to the same sources and came away with nothing negative, but little positive. And by the fourth generation, the Jews in North America had attained complete illiteracy.

The Judaism that now predominates in the diaspora, the Judaism of Holocaust and Redemption, to be sure provides ready access to emotional or political encounters, readily available to all – by definition. But it offers none to that confrontation of taste and judgment, intellect and reflection, that takes place in worlds in which words matter. People presently resort mainly to the immediately accessible experiences of emotions beyond expression and of politics indifferent to reflection.

How was it otherwise in the nineteenth century? Books preserve human experience and make it accessible later on. We recall that the systems of the nineteenth and twentieth centuries made constant reference to the Judaism of the dual Torah, at first intimate, later on merely by way of allusion and rejection. The nineteenth-century systems drew depth and breadth of vision from the received Judaism of the dual Torah, out of which they produced – by their own word – variations and continuations. So the received system and its continuators realized not only the world of perceived experience at hand. They also made accessible the alien but interesting human potentialities of other ages, other encounters altogether with the potentialities of life in society. The repertoire of human experience in the Judaism of the dual Torah presents as human options the opposite of the banal, the one-dimensional, the immediate. Jews received and used the heritage of human experience captured, as in amber, in the words of the dual Torah. So they did not have to make things up fresh every morning or rely only on that small sector of the range of human experience immediately accessible and near at hand.

The appeal to contemporary experience, whether in emotions or in politics, draws upon not so rich a treasury of reflection and response to the human condition. And the utter failure of imagination, the poverty of contemporary system-building where it takes place at all, shows the result. Israeli nationalism and American Judaism of Holocaust and Redemption – the two most influential systems that move Jews to action in the world today – scarcely concern themselves with the Judaic world made accessible in books. They find themselves left only with what is near at hand. They work with the raw materials made available by contemporary experience – emotions on the one side, politics on the other. Access to realms beyond requires learning in literature, the only resource for human experience beyond the immediate. But the Judaic system of the twentieth century does not resort to the reading of books as a principal act of the way of life, in the way in which the Judaism of the dual Torah and its continuators did and do. The consequence is a strikingly abbreviated agenda of issues, a remarkably one-dimensional program of urgent questions.

American Jewry forms a community of Jews without books, one with virtually no school system for fully half of its children. And most of the other half receive an education of slight consequence. So Jewish Americans have neither studied Torah nor in light of the written-down human experience of Jews through the ages have they closely reflected on their own lives in a free society. They work out their lives as not the last Jews on earth, but the first and only Jews who ever lived. That is not to say that they propose to reinvent the wheel; rather, they have never heard of it. They therefore have opted for neither the worst of one world nor the best of another. They have focused such imaginative energies as they generated upon "the Holocaust," and they have centered their eschatological fantasies on "the beginning of our redemption" in the State of Israel. But they had not gone through the one nor chosen to participate in the other. Not having lived through the mass murder of European Jewry, American Jews restated the problem of evil in unanswerable form and then transformed that problem into an obsession. Not choosing to settle in the State of Israel, moreover, American Jews further defined redemption, the resolution of the problem of evil, in terms remote from their world. That is what I mean by failure of intellect.

The Triumph of Large-Scale Organization

Third and distinct from the other two is the bureaucratization of Jewry in consequence of the tasks it rightly has identified as urgent. To meet the practical problems of organization and politics that Jews find self-evidently urgent, they have had to adopt a way of life of building and maintaining and working through very large institutions. That requires money and opens a monopoly on power to the rich to the exclusion of everybody else.

The contemporary class structure of Jewry places in positions of influence Jews who put slight value on matters of intellect and learning to begin with, and that same system accords no sustained hearing to Jews who strive to reflect. The tasks are other, and they call forth other gifts than those of heart and mind. The exemplary experiences of those who exercise influence derives from politics, through law, from economic activity, through business, from institutional careers, through government, industry and administration and the like. As the gifts of establishing routine take precedence over the endowments of charisma of an intellectual order, the experiences people know and understand – politics, emotions of ready access – serve, also, for the raw materials of Judaic system-building. Experiences that, in a Judaic context, people scarcely know, do not.

What I have said applies not only to the Jews. It is merely another instance of the consequence of the ineluctable tasks of the twentieth century: to build large-scale organizations to solve large-scale problems. Organizations, in the nature of things, require specialization. The difference between the classes that produce systemic change today and those who created systems in the nineteenth and earlier twentieth centuries then proves striking. What brought it about if not the great war conducted against the Jews, beginning not in 1993 but with the organization of political anti-Semitism joined to economic exclusion, from the 1880s onward? Both Zionism and Jewish Socialism set about building large-scale institutions – a shadow-government for a nation in the process of formation, in Zionism, and enormous unions, in Jewish Socialism. So in a profound sense the type of structure now characteristic of Jewry represents one of the uncounted costs of fighting for life in the war against the Jews conducted by anti-Semitism, whether Nazi or Communist or Fascist or nationalist – the definitive fact of the twentieth century.

Intellectuals create systems. Administrators do not so, when they need ideas, they call for propaganda and hire publicists and journalists. To conduct a battle in the nineteenth century, you fired salvos of books. To fight a war in the twentieth century, you set out to organize a mass movement, manipulated from the top. When we remember that all of the Judaic systems of the nineteenth and early twentieth centuries derive from intellectuals, we realize what has changed. Herzl was a journalist, for instance, and those who organized Jewish Socialism and brought Yiddishism all wrote books. The founders of the system of Reform Judaism were mainly scholars, rabbis, writers, dreamers and other intellectuals. It is not because they were lawyers that the framers of the Positive Historical School produced the historicist system that they made. The emphases of Hirsch and other creators of Orthodoxy lay on doctrine, and all of them wrote important books and articles of a reflective and even philosophical character. So much for Reform, Orthodox, Conservative, Socialist-Yiddishist, and Zionist systems: the work of intellectuals, one and all.

These three factors, demographic, cultural, institutional and bureaucratic, scarcely exhaust the potential explanation for the long span of time in which, it would appear, Jews have brought forth few Judaic systems, relying instead on those formed in a prior and different age and circumstance. But I do think all of them will figure in any rigorous account of what has happened, and not happened, in the present century. And they point directly or indirectly to the extraordinary price yet to be exacted from Jewry on account of the murder of six million Jews in Europe. The demographic loss requires no comment, and the passage of time from the age in which the Judaism of the dual Torah predominated has already impressed us. Those causes are direct and immediate.

Mass Murder and the Culture of Organizations

But one has also to justify the correlation between mass murder and an exemplary leadership of lawyers and businessmen and politicians and generals. The answer is simple. Because of the crisis presented by the German war against the Jews and the Soviet war against Judaism, the Jews had to do what they could to constitute themselves into a political entity, capable of mass action. So the leadership of the sort that came to the fore in the twentieth century responded to the requirement of that century, and thus the correlation between Holocaust and bureaucracy: that was what was needed. Administrators, not intellectuals, bureaucrats, not charismatic thinkers formed the cadre of the hour. In an age in which, to survive at all, Jews had to address the issues of politics and economics, build a state (in the State of Israel) and a massive and effective set of organizations capable of collective political action (in the USA), not sages but *politicians* in the deepest sense of the word – namely, those able to do the work of the polity – alone could do what had to be done. And they did come forward. They did their task, as well as one might have hoped. The time therefore demanded gifts other than those prized by intellectuals. And the correlation between mass murder and a culture of organizations proves exact: the war against the Jews called forth, from the Jews, people capable of building institutions to protect the collectivity of Israel, so far as anyone could be saved. Consequently much was saved. But much was lost.

Celebrating the victory of survival, we should not lose sight of the cost. Determining the full cost of the murder of upwards of six million Jews of Europe will require a long time. The end of the remarkable age of Judaic *systemopoeia* may prove a more serious charge against the future, a more calamitous cost of the destruction of European Jewry, than anyone has yet realized. More suffocated than Jews in gas chambers. The banality of survival forms a counterpoint to the banality of evil represented by the factories built to manufacture dead Jews in an age of the common and routine.

The Corporate Model and What is to be Learned about Religion from Judaism in Modern Times

Judaism provides an interesting case of how in the twentieth century the corporate model has taken over the life of religion. We do not have therefore to wonder whence come the nullities that have taken the place of the system-builders. The answer, ready at hand, brings us to the end of the story of the death and birth of Judaism. The twentieth century presented to Jews the necessity to create large bureaucracies to deal with large problems. It is no accident that system-building came to an end in the encounter with an age of large Jewish organizations: armies and governments, in the State of Israel, and enormous instruments of fund-raising and politics, in America.

Building, by specialists of large organizations, excluded individual engagement with the goals of the organization, limiting individuals to providing the means by which experts or elites accomplished the goals. To explain this point is simple. In the Judaism of the dual Torah, every individual is required to say his or her prayers or to observe holy days or carry out religious obligations. But in Zionism in its day, a few went off to build the Jewish state in what was then Palestine, and everybody else stayed home and sent money. Systems of organization, meaning specialization for all, left the doing of the distinctive work of the system to only a few. The specialized work of organizations excluded the money from a role in the general scheme of the system. In so stating, of course, I draw upon the image of the iron cage created by the great social theorist Max Weber. Weber alludes to the "iron cage" in the following famous passage: "The care for external goods should only lie on the shoulders of the saint like a light cloak, which can be thrown aside at any moment, but fate decreed that the cloak should become an iron cage." What he says about economic action applies equally to the sort of large-scale systemic, existential behavior to which we refer when we speak of a Judaism:

> Where the fulfillment of the calling cannot directly be related to the highest spiritual and cultural values . . . the individual generally abandons the attempt to justify it at all . . . No one knows who will live in this cage in the future . . . For of the last stage of this cultural development, it might well be truly said: "Specialists without spirit, sensualists without heart; this nullity imagines that it has attained a level of civilization never before achieved."[4]

The point of intersection with organizations in the twentieth century I locate at the reference to "specialists without spirit." When we note the division of labor that has rendered a mockery of the category of a way of life joined to a world-view, we understand why we cannot define a distinctive way of life associated with a given world-view.

When we consider the world-view of a Judaic system in the nineteenth century we allude to an encompassing theory that explains a life of actions in a given and very particular pattern. When we speak of the world-view of a Judaic system of the twentieth century, we refer to the explanation of why people, in a given, distinctive circumstance, should do pretty much what everyone is doing somewhere, under some equivalent circumstance: an army is an army anywhere, but study of Torah is unique to Israel. Anyone can join a union, and why invoke a Judaic world-view to explain why to join a Jewish union? I know only that Judaic world-views did offer such an explanation and made a great difference to those to whom that explanation answered an urgent question. What has changed? Once more I find the answer in the history of Western civilization. The processes that shaped the Judaic systems of modern and contemporary times form part of the larger movement of humanity – a distinctive and therefore exemplary part, to be sure.

Learning about religion from Judaism requires a further step in the argument: about whom else do we learn here? The real question is, about whom else do we not learn? For we deal with an age in which the condition of Israel, the holy people, stood for the condition of nearly the whole of humanity: no one's life was worth much, whoever lives now survives from an age of death. If I had at the end to point to other religions that have had to address circumstances as critical as those that confronted Judaism in modern times, I should point to Christianity in Armenia and Ukraine, one population massacred by the Turks, the other by the Communists; Buddhism in Cambodia and Tibet, one population massacred by its own government, the other by the occupying power; Islam in Bosnia, where hundreds of thousands of believers perished and the social order tottered – and these only by way of example.

More examples: Germany, France, Britain, Russia, and Austria-Hungary in World War I suffered extraordinary casualties; the USSR in World War II conceded at the end that it had lost more than twenty million people, approximately 10 per cent of its population; in the Israeli war of independence, 1 per cent of the entire Jewish population, and 10 per cent of the males of fighting age, died. And the age of total war leaves a legacy not only of miles of marked graves and a continent of unmarked ones but of the ruins of cities, monuments of a thousand years of sustained civilization. Today the rubble has disappeared, new buildings replace old ones. But from the Arctic Circle at Rovaniemi, in Finland, burned by the retreating German armies even after the end of World War II in May 1945, to the ruined and rebuilt Coventry and London in the West, Volgograd in the East, and countless villages in Italy in the South, people remember. Where in Europe can we walk about and not encounter memorials to those who fell in the war? And if we consider Japan and China, the Philippines and Papua New Guinea and other Pacific battlegrounds, the pattern is repeated.

These and other memories therefore tell the story of the century of total war. Then what we learn about religion in that same age is two contradictory facts. On the one side, the difficulty of identifying major religious systems of the social order, realized on a large scale by well-defined groups, tells us that the twentieth century was not an age of religious regeneration. It was not comparable, for example, with the seventh, with the advent of Islam, or the sixteenth, with its Reformation, or the nineteenth, with its remarkably courageous effort to negotiate the difference between religions, science, learning, and culture. On the other hand, the twentieth century also was an age of religious renewal. At the end of the nineteenth century people claimed religion formed a vestige, claimed the wave of the future would sweep away the religious past of Europe and its diaspora. Communism, Socialism (except Christian Socialism), philosophical and scientific atheism, political secularism, psychology in its several applied forms – all concurred that religion no longer possessed a future. God is dead.

But God did not die in the twentieth century. Nor did religion. Christianity was not extirpated by Soviet Communism, nor Judaism by Nazism, nor Buddhism by Chinese Communism, nor Islam by imperialistic missions in the name of Christianity, to take three obvious examples among many. And no religion, faced with the challenge of militant secularism, ends the century in weaker condition than at the outset, or with diminished capacities. And that is because religion – and in my view, religion alone – proved the sole enduring medium for the defense of humanity in the age of total war.

Let me specify what I think in the examples of Judaism and Christianity has made all the difference. The critical Judaic component of the Christian civilization of the West spoke of God and God's will for humanity, what it meant to live in God's image, after God's likeness. So said the Judaism of the dual Torah, so said Christianity in its worship of God made flesh. The power of God's will and exact words in the Quran of Islam surely is congruent as well. So that message of humanity in God's image, of a people seeking to conform to God's will, found resonance in the Christian world as well: both components of the world, the Christian dough, the Judaic yeast, bore a single message about humanity.

The first century beyond the time in which Christianity defined the structures of society and civilization in the West, that is, the twentieth century, spoke of class and nation, not one humanity in the image of one God. Calling for heroes, it demanded sacrifice not for God but for the state. When asked what it meant to live with irreconcilable difference, the century responded with total war on civilians in their homes, made foxholes. Asked for a theory of the other, the century responded by invoking metaphors from the world of insects to speak of men, women, and children: "extermination," for example. Asked to celebrate the image of humanity, the twentieth century created an improbable likeness of humanity: mountains of corpses, the dead of the Somme of World War I and of Auschwitz of World War II and all the other victims of the state that had taken the place of church and synagogue.

The first century found its enduring memory in one man on a hill, on a cross, the twentieth, six million making up a Golgotha – a hill of skulls – of their own. These monuments to a century's vision of humanity form a tower at the end of the century, even up to the third of the population of the Khmer killed by their own government, five million Ukrainians by theirs, the half of the world's Armenians by what, alas, was theirs – and the Jews, and the Jews, and the Jews.

No wonder then that the Judaisms of the age struggled heroically to frame a Judaic system appropriate to the issues of the age – and no wonder that they failed. Who would want to have succeeded to frame a world-view congruent to such an age, a way of life to be lived in an age of death? And no wonder – if I close by stating my own opinion – that the Judaisms of the age proved transient and evanescent. For

I like to think that no Judaic system could ever have found an enduring fit with an age such as the one that now draws to a close. The twentieth-century Judaisms had struggled to speak to their Israel of hope and of life in the valley of the darkest shadows. But for reasons of circumstance they failed because they had to fail, and their failure forms their true vindication.

For the Jews, who drink a toast by saying "to life," are a people that never could find themselves truly at home in the twentieth century, the century of mass murder and cheap death and governments built upon the corpses of their own subjects. That, in the aspect of eternity, may prove the highest tribute God in the end will choose to pay to those whom God among humanity first loved.

NOTES

1 To keep matters accessible, moreover, I did not describe and analyze a variety of other influential Judaic systems of the nineteenth century. For example, we have not taken up segregationist Orthodoxy and its formations. But in that sector as well, further Judaic systems took shape and achieved enormous influence. They gained great popularity among the Jews to whom they turned. A review of Grade's wonderful vignette of the battle in the synagogue tells us there were well-formed social groups we have not addressed in these pages, for example, anti-Zionist and pro-Zionist Orthodox Judaisms, Hasidism (mystical) and the Musar (ethical) systems formed somewhat earlier than or in the nineteenth century, and the like. By contrast, on its own, the twentieth century marked the advent of a single substantial and popular Judaism, the American Judaism of Holocaust and Redemption. The twentieth century in fact for nearly seventy-five years produced no important and massively popular Judaic systems, until that of Holocaust and Redemption.

2 Since a religious system begins in the social entity that it describes and defines, I ignore Reconstructionism, which has yet to form a distinctive social entity of consequence, comparable with Reform, Integrationist-Orthodox, segregationist Orthodox, and Conservative Judaisms. It remained a single-digit Judaism; its corpus of ideas is large but not dense, and it is expressed in language that is wooden and clumsy, hardly a mark of a passionate response to an urgent question.

3 I underscore that Judaism in the State of Israel presents a completely different problem and is not under discussion in this book at all.

4 Max Weber, *The Protestant Ethic and the Spirit of Capitalism*, trans. Talcott Parsons, with a foreword by R. H. Tawney (New York, 1930: Charles Scribner's Sons), p. 182.

Index